PAGANISM
TODAY

PAGANISM TODAY

EDITED BY

Charlotte Hardman
and Graham Harvey

Thorsons
An Imprint of HarperCollins*Publishers*

Thorsons
An Imprint of HarperCollins*Publishers*
77–85 Fulham Palace Road,
Hammersmith, London W6 8JB
1160 Battery Sreet
San Francisco, California 94111–1213

Published by Thorsons 1995
3 5 7 9 10 8 6 4

Charlotte Hardman and Graham Harvey assert
the moral right to be identified as the authors of this work

A catalogue record for this book
is available from the British Library

ISBN 0 7225 3233 4

Printed and bound in Great Britain by
Creative Print and Design (Wales), Ebbw Vale

CONTENTS

Notes on Contributors

Marion Bowman is Lecturer in the Study of Religions at Bath College of Higher Education, where she organises the annual Contemporary and New Age Religions Conference. She was formerly Honorary Secretary of The Folklore Society. Her research interests include the spiritual aspects of the current Celtic revival, popular religion, New Religious Movements, religious pluralism, pilgrimage and healing.

Vivianne Crowley is Senior Lecturer in the Psychology of Religion at King's College, University of London, Adjunct Professor at the Union Institute, Cincinnati, Ohio, a Pagan priestess and author of *Wicca: the Old Religion in the New Age* and *Phoenix from the Flame: Pagan Spirituality in the Western World* (Aquarian). She is Interfaith Co-ordinator of the Pagan Federation and UK Co-ordinator of Pagan chaplaincy services for prisons.

Leila Dudley Edwards is a folklorist currently researching her PhD on the traditions and modern practices of Halloween at the Centre for English Cultural Tradition and Language at the University of Sheffield. She became interested in contemporary Paganism whilst doing research on traditional moonlore in Scotland and Appalachia when at the School of Scottish Studies in Edinburgh.

Susan Greenwood first became involved in Paganism in 1984. This led her to carry out research exploring women's spirituality and magic and she is now completing a PhD in this topic at Goldsmith's College, University of London, where she also teaches anthropology.

Charlotte Hardman is Lecturer in Religion and Contemporary Society at the University of Newcastle Upon Tyne. She first became interested in Paganism whilst working at INFORM (Information Network Focus on Religious Movements). Her research interests include contemporary Paganism and neo-Shamanism.

Adrian Harris' environmental campaigning began in the early 1980s while studying philosophy and literature at Essex University. His interest in philosophy and the environment led to Paganism and thence to the formation of Dragon Environmental Group, a Pagan organisation combining environmental work with eco-magic. He was initiated into Wicca in 1991. He has recently completed an MA and continues to research into Ecology and the Sacred.

Graham Harvey was a research fellow at the University of Newcastle upon Tyne, and is now lecturer at King Alfred's College, Winchester. He has been researching into Paganism in contemporary Britain for over four years and also has interests in Judaism.

Ronald Hutton is a reader in British History at the University of Bristol. His previous publications include *The Pagan Religions of the Ancient British Isles* and *The Rise and Fall of Merry England*. He is currently working upon a history of various forms of modern Paganism.

Shan Jayran is a working Priestess of the Craft and has run her own temple (House of the Goddess) for ten years. She was one of the pioneers of the new open Paganism, with its vigorous shamanic creativity. She created a national contact network (PaganLink), made training openly available to the public in small groups (Circlework), held open meetings and rituals, and in 1987 held the first completely Pagan national festival open to the general public.

Prudence Jones is a Pagan writer and spokesperson who has been active in the Pagan movement for over twenty years. From 1979–91 she was President of the Pagan Federation, and from 1985–90 ran the Pagan Anti-Defamation League with Nigel Pennick. Her publications include *Voices From the Circle* (Aquarian, 1990, with Caitlin Matthews) and *A History of Pagan Europe* (Routledge, 1995, with Nigel Pennick).

Gordon MacLellan works in environmental education and interpretation where he sees the greatest challenge facing modern conservation as engaging the hearts and spirits of people in long-term commitment to the world we live within. 'A pagan life, and especially a shamanic one, is a life of celebration and joy in life and in other living peoples. That sense of celebration is at the heart of all I do and is the inspiration that keeps me going and that I hope infuses the work I do with others.'

Lynne Morgan has been a Psychotherapist and Group Work Trainer in Leeds for the last nine years and now in London. She has worked mainly with women individually and in facilitating workshops and courses on subjects which include Assertiveness, The Sexual Cycle, and Women's Mysteries. She has been involved in Women's Spirituality since the early 1980s and in Paganism for the last six years.

Kenneth Rees is a sociologist and adult educationalist whose fieldwork on Wicca and neo-paganism began in the 1970s. Since the early 1980s he has lectured in mythology, shamanism and witchcraft at numerous London colleges including the City University and City Literary Institute. This role has enabled him to continue his research into pagans.

Philip Shallcrass is a writer, artist, musician and lecturer who has studied and practised Druidry for more than twenty years. He is

Chief Druid of the British Druid Order and editor of *The Druid's Voice*, the Journal of the Council of British Druid Orders. He is also a Wiccan High Priest.

Amy Simes has recently completed a PhD in Theology at the University of Nottingham. Her thesis, entitled 'Contemporary Paganism in the East Midlands', has combined anthropological fieldwork with sociological and anthropological theory in order to provide a broad view of Pagan phenomena as currently practised in four East Midlands counties. Her current work focuses upon the secularisation debate and neo-shamanism.

Richard Sutcliffe is a PhD research scholar currently engaged in research connected with the Department of Anthropology at the University of Sydney, Australia, and University College, London. He is currently conducting fieldwork in the Pagan and Magickal subculture in Britain with particular emphasis on the role of mythopoeic imagination in magick.

Michael York is a post-doctoral researcher currently working at the Academy for Cultural and Educational Studies in London. He has been researching into the New Age and neo-Pagan movements and is author of *The Emerging Network: A Sociology of the New Age and Neo-Pagan Movement* (Rowman and Littlefield, 1995).

Charlotte Hardman

INTRODUCTION

Paganism or neo-Paganism is fast developing as the new religion of the twenty-first century, a religion based on Nature worship and ancient indigenous traditions. The contributions for this volume were brought together to fill a gap in the literature on Paganism. Although there is a growing literature on Druidry, Wicca, Shamanism, and Goddess Spirituality, there are few looking at Paganism in general.[1]

An increasingly serious attitude towards Paganism as an alternative religion is reflected in the media and in mainstream institutions. In December 1994 Leeds University students chose a Wiccan witch to be their chaplain and in the same month the 1000 or so members of the Milton Keynes Wicca group were given land on which to hold open-air ceremonies. Pagans are being asked to participate in Interfaith Dialogue, the Pagan Federation has an Interfaith Co-ordinator (at present Vivianne Crowley) and there is a Pagan Prison Chaplain.[2] There is both official and academic recognition that Paganism is a serious religion. Moreover, as Vicki Ward states in *The Independent* newspaper, 'After 300 years of persecution and 200 years of near invisibility, it is all the rage again.'[3]

The number of Pagans in Britain and the United States is growing fast. Only estimated figures can be given since there are varying degrees to which people can be involved–from 'consumers', who show sufficient interest to buy a book or a magazine, to 'practitioners'. The number given by Margot Adler for active, self-identified Pagans in the United States is 50,000 to 100,000. Tanya Luhrmann's estimate for the UK in 1989 of several thousand seems low and many have suggested a more realistic figure is 30–50,000.[4]

In spite of this increasing popularity Paganism remains a much misunderstood new religion. Most people's prejudices are based on misrepresentation by the media and opposition from Christians who often, without knowing much about it, see it as New Age or occult and hence evil. Paganism has become for many a loaded word along with the pejorative use of the word 'pagan' meaning 'uncivilized', 'heathen' or 'irreligious because unchristian', rather than its literal meaning of 'rural' (*pagus*, Latin for 'from the countryside'). According to *The Oxford English Dictionary* 'pagan' in late middle English comes from the Latin *paganus* meaning 'civilian' as opposed to 'soldier', meaning those who were not Christian since the Christians called themselves the enrolled soldiers of Christ. In Christian language it came to mean 'heathen' as opposed to Christian or Jew indicating that 'the ancient idolatry lingered on in the rural villages and hamlets after Christianity had been generally accepted in the towns and cities of the Roman Empire'(OED). The recent negative connotations with 'pagan' thus have to do both with a history in which anyone who did not follow the Christian religion was looked down upon as godless and with a recent situation in which the tabloid media can increase sales of their newspapers and magazines by repeating inflated stories about witches, goddess worship and magic rituals. To some people the very words 'pagan' or 'witch' conjure up Satan, a Christian concept. In Adler's 1985 questionnaire, 'The Most Important Thing You Want To Tell People' she reports that more than half wanted to say

> *We are not evil. We do not worship the Devil. We don't harm or seduce people. We are not dangerous. We are ordinary people like you. We have families, jobs, hopes and dreams. We are not a cult. We are not weird. This religion is not a joke...*[5]

The interest in Paganism today in the UK and the USA may be interpreted as a response to an increased dissatisfaction with the way the world is going ecologically, spiritually and materially; people are disillusioned by mainstream religion and the realisation that materialism leaves an internal emptiness. They see they can change the world by changing themselves and following one of the spiritual paths that form what is essentially a kind of Nature Religion. The Pagan Federation itself defines neo-Paganism as

> *A group of modern Earth religions. Practices are derived from pre-Christian Paganism, often with input from their on contemporary theologians*[6]

In this introduction I want to look briefly at modern Paganism and at the main developing features of this movement brought out by the contributors to this volume.

The main spiritual paths of Paganism to be found in the UK and the United States are Wicca, Druidry, Shamanism, Goddess Spirituality, Sacred Ecology, Heathenism and various Magical Groups and all these are represented in the second part of this volume. Some core beliefs are shared by all these groups. Firstly, Pagans believe that no one belief system is correct and that each person should have the freedom to come themselves to the path of their choice. Article 18 of the Universal Declaration of Human Rights is often quoted:

> *Everyone has the right to freedom of thought, conscience and religion; this right includes freedom to change his religion or belief, and freedom, either alone or in community with others and in public or in private, to manifest his religion or belief in teaching, practice, worship and observance.*

For all Pagans there is no place for either dogma or proselytising. The Pagan Federation Statement of the following three principles reflects the basic beliefs of many Pagans:

> **Love for and Kinship with Nature:** rather than the more customary attitude of aggression and domination over Nature; reverence for the life force and its ever-renewing cycles of life and death.
> **The Pagan Ethic:** 'Do what thou wilt, but harm none'. This is a positive morality, not a list of thou-shalt-nots. Each individual is responsible for discovering his or her own true nature and developing it fully, in harmony with the outer world.
> **The Concept of Goddess and God** as expressions of the Divine reality; an active participation in the cosmic dance of Goddess and God, female and male, rather than the suppression of either the female or the male principle.[7]

Those Pagans expressing some dissent from these principles are mainly Heathens who are more explicitly polytheistic and some magicians who are more concerned with Self understanding and less with deities. For most Pagans, however, many paths may lead to the same destination and most share a belief in the oneness of ultimate reality, the interrelatedness of everything, and the worship of many Gods and Goddesses, not one male monotheistic God; most Pagans consider 'right living' as being an important aspect of being Pagan and that life is a two-way exchange. Many Pagans believe in the 'threefold effect', that whatever they do, whether for good or for bad, will be returned to them threefold. All Pagans then also respect the cycles of Nature whilst most celebrate the festivals of Imbolc, Spring Equinox, Beltain, Midsummer Solstice, Lughnasadh or Lammas, Autumn

Equinox, Samhain, and Winter Solstice.

If we examine Paganism today, we can see the growth of certain main features; that, for example, for most Pagans the magic of Nature is reflected in harmony and balance and hence the importance of worshipping the God and the Goddess. Feminism has always been a significant feature of Paganism but now, in the 1990s, Pagans are even more conscious about their feminism. All Pagan groups stress the Goddesses as well as the Gods. The Fellowship of Isis is dedicated exclusively to the worship of the Goddess and both sexes are ordained to be priests and priestesses to the Goddess. Some Dianic groups exclude men. Wicca, the Craft and Goddess Spirituality groups in particular proclaim the importance of female symbols of divinity and the effect such symbols have on the emotional and psychological health of modern women. This approach is exemplified in the paper by Lynne Morgan, a psychological counsellor and practising member of a Goddess Spirituality group. The Goddess Movement has had a forceful impact on Paganism as a whole; not only has it claimed for women the right to their own spirituality unmediated by men, giving them back self-worth and a power derived from inside themselves, to be recognised in aspects of their lives such as menstruation or childbirth, but it has also forced Pagans to review the way they look at the world and live their lives. Women and their bodies are to be respected alongside Nature. Nature and women are to be appreciated and not exploited and the divine is manifest in both Nature and women.[8]

> *The Goddess is around us and within us. She is immanent and transcendent...the Goddess represents the divine embodied in nature, in human beings, in the flesh.*[9]

Pagans have begun to talk more explicitly about polytheism. Wicca has always stressed bitheism, the wonder of all things as being manifest in the God and Goddess. The Alexandrian and the Gardnerian traditions both see the One in the Many. In Druidry the emphasis has always been on the polarity of the masculine and the feminine and in the past Druids have talked about this polarity appearing in humans, plants, animals and perhaps in deity, though they talked about the One and would have been less willing to talk about the many deities of the Celtic world. Since the 1970s, however, Druids, for example, have become as polytheistic as other Pagan groups, talking of the Oneness as being manifest in the polarities of masculine and feminine deities. Wiccans talk about The God and The Goddess; Druids talk about the Oneness; all Pagans now talk about the many deities, about the many or One who contains the many, who is immanent within the world and within everyone and everything in Nature; about the oneness behind it all, the balance of male and female within the oneness and a 'balanced wholeness' in which the polarities of masculine and feminine have become more manifest. Odinists in particular are stressing the polytheism of their revived tradition and in demonstration of this, in 1995, the Odinic Rite sent out a magazine, stating that Paganism has to become more polytheistic, provoking Pagans to respond to this whole issue.

In the last ten years, therefore, there has been a shift in the way that Pagan Gods and Goddesses are viewed; from being seen primarily as archetypes, somewhat abstract beings, they are now more typically polytheistic beings, real beings who share the world with us. This has accompanied a stress on things Celtic, as is brought out in Marion Bowman's paper, and the view of the Celtic Gods and Goddesses as anthropomorphic beings who eat, fight, quarrel, and copulate just like the living. In addition, Pagans have become more activist and this is exemplified in this volume in Adrian Harris's paper on Deep Ecology and that of Gordon MacLellan on Shamanism in which MacLellan emphasises the importance of contemporary shamans involving themselves in their community. He suggests that shamans only have 'power' when they belong to a community and questions how many modern shamans are actively involved in any community. The impact of Shamanism on Paganism began in the 1960s and 1970s with hippies doing 'their own individual thing'. This fitted into the Gardnerian emphasis on rituals to face themselves and on experience. Shamanism works with a direct experience of spirits and MacLellan emphasises the importance of learning to 'be' and not to 'know', learning not to analyse objectively but to understand from within. The shamanic worldview, seeing the interrelatedness of everything and emphasising the experiencing of the spiritual world, fitted in with the seeds of the shamanic worldview already contained in the developing Pagan tradition. This more recent emphasis on Shamanism and the shamanic cosmic view, discussed by Gordon MacLellan, goes along with the newly emphasised polytheism. The earthiness of shamanism fits the more anthropomorphic view of the Gods and Goddesses and emphasises the degree to which the spirit world is here beside us; spirit imbues everything, and is not separate from the earth we walk on; we can learn to contact that spirit world at will. Many Pagans today are happy to say that the deities are with us; we can see this in Shan, Pagan priestess and founder of the House of the Goddess in London, in her paper in which she leads the reader through the basic stages of a Pagan ritual, pointing out some of the ideologies that have influenced modern Paganism. Most Pagans have now come to the polytheistic view that the Goddesses and Gods share the world with us.

Pagans today are typically individualistic practitioners and their worship is largely a private affair, though in the United States there are Church organisations. Amy Simes suggests in her contribution that from her observations of Pagans since 1992 she can discern three types of Pagan groups and two types of Pagans, those known as 'solitaries' who prefer to work alone and what she calls 'groupies' who prefer working with groups. She examines the differences between these types of group and person, how the groups change, how people shift from 'solitary' to 'groupie' and how members cope with changes in group structures. She also notes that over the years many Pagan groups have been emerging, growing and dispersing; the growth of contemporary Pagan organisations is both rapid and volatile. 'Hedgewitches', Rae Beth's term for individual practitioners of the Craft,[10] have not only continued to increase in number but a recent significant change has occurred in the formation of a network for these solo practitioners, founded by Geoff White. Pagan groups are usually explicitly non-centralised and non-hierarchical. We can see an exception in the Odinist groups, described by Graham Harvey in his chapter on the north European Pagan tradition. These Odinist groups prefer more organisation than other Pagan groups.

As we can see, the state of Paganism in the UK has been changing in the last ten years or so and in several key areas. Ecologically, although Paganism has always had behind it a romantic view of the land and has always been 'green' philosophically, it has now also become more clearly an activist movement in this area, working more on the front line and becoming more coherent about the link between theory and action than it ever has been before. A few Pagans do not want this progression into activist ecology as well as into fights for animal rights, but they remain a minority and many Pagans are involved in such activities as collecting money for buying woods and planting trees. Druids, for example, are supporting the Buddhist group, Samye Ling's project for planting trees on Holy Island off the Isle of Aran. Certain Odinist groups are also tree planting (the Land Guardian scheme of the Odinshof). Adrian Harris, founder of the Dragon Environmental group (an eco-magical group), describes in his chapter on Sacred Ecology how the group goes beyond other Environmental groups, such as the Social ecologists or Deep Ecologists, by incorporating magical practice into environmental protest. Paganism can be a solution to the environmental crisis by putting people back in touch with their own bodies, with their own direct experiences of their physical selves, the Earth and the physical universe. Respect for Nature, being 'green', is no longer just part of the philosophy; the eco-magic of Pagan ritual can be activated towards environmental, social and spiritual change.

Combining philosophy and activism is one of the key ways in which Paganism is demonstrating its developing maturity as a religion. Pagans are looking to bring together as a coherent whole the ideas in their philosophy which relate to the outside world ecologically, and economically and politically.

Pagan rites reflect this new maturity. In recent years Pagans have been working with more rites than just those for the eight seasonal feasts. They have introduced, for example, rites of passage for births, deaths and marriages[11] and, under the influence of the Goddess Movement, other rites for menarche and menopause have been developing, along with rites for 'aligning oneself with the season, with the elements, relinquishing baggage that had become inappropriate such as conflict, depression, under-valuing oneself, etc and affirming one's hopes and identity'[12] and others for coping, in an individually affirmative way, with crisis situations. For example, rites are being held for victims of abuse or specifically for rape counselling. The purpose of the crisis rites are to encourage victims of abuse to face what has happened to them; the ritual concentrates on cleansing the individual and making them whole again. There is no dogma in the rite and, in a typically Pagan fashion, the individual must decide how they want to use the rite and what they want to say–whether they are going to express their anger or feelings of forgiveness.

The two most public and numerically predominant groups in Paganism today are Wicca and Druidry. Philip Shallcrass, in this volume, shows how Druids, often perceived as rational and patriarchal, in contrast to the feminism and intuitive character of Wicca, have changed to the extent that the vestiges of patriarchy so important in the eighteenth-century revival groups are only to be found in one contemporary Druid group. Druids and Wiccans have much in common; some Druid Orders having grown from beginnings as Wiccan covens continue to incorporate Wiccan elements in their rituals, emphasising the Goddess, for example. Pagan groups as a whole are becoming increasingly eclectic in the traditions they use–and Druids like Wiccans have increasingly included shamanic practices of drumming, journeying and contacting the spirit world. The emphasis in Druidry today is on direct experience and on developing a framework in which to develop and know the self and in particular to reconnect to the land. Druidry is a mystery tradition like other aspects of Paganism, and Wicca in particular. Druidry and Wicca are similar, though Druidry can be more Celtic. Philip Shallcrass describes the diverse practices that can be included under the name of contemporary Druidry, which has no set theology, and explores the differences between Druidry and Wicca. Druids revere the sun and perform rites in the day; Wiccans revere the moon and prefer the night. Though some Druids celebrate in public, more do so in the privacy of their homes and gardens. Druids emphasise esoteric lore, the development of self-understanding through reconnecting with the land or through poetry and music. Wiccans focus on self-development and the Goddess. For many Pagans and particularly for many Druids, the Celts have come to be regarded as repositories of an authentic native spirituality and ancient wisdom, otherwise lost from mainstream British life. For some Pagans, being Celtic, as Marion Bowman shows in her chapter on images of the Celts, has become almost a 'thing of spirit not of heritage'. Her chapter explores the renewed interest in and honouring of Celts and the different models of Celts and being Celtic.

Vivianne Crowley in her chapter on Wicca as a modern-day Mystery religion brings out the dual function of Paganism, one exoteric and the other esoteric. The latter is concerned with the inner Self and its development through initiation ceremonies, in which the approach to the Self is made through an external expression of the inner psychological process. The former, exoteric aspect of modern Paganism has to do more with the needs of society and providing meaningful ceremonies and rites of passage for members of that society, providing religious education for their children and ministry to those who need it, whether in hospital, hospice or prison. Her book *Phoenix From The Flame* shows how this 'exoteric aspect' has developed in modern Paganism. Her paper here explores the religious rituals of Wicca, the threefold system of initiation in particular, in terms of their psychology, symbolism and impact on those who participate in them. The role of the Goddess is particularly significant in Wicca and the Craft.

One of the initial aims of the conference[13] which formed the basis for this collection was to encourage debate between practising Pagans and academics working on aspects of Paganism. There has been a history of relationship between practising Pagans and academics, particularly anthropologists and historians. Eilberg-Schwartz[14] has taken this relationship further than most, arguing that we can see the roots of neo-paganism in the Enlightenment, a position that is controversial since neo-Pagans are highly critical of the Enlightenment and its emphasis on Reason and the modern notions of scientific rationality. Eilberg-Schwartz argues, 'Neopagans are firmly rooted in the Enlightenment tradition that seeks to deny the differences between various antitypes and ourselves'.[15] Eighteenth-century philosophers, responsible for the emergence of this modern period, made appeal to Pagan antiquity as part of their critique of Christianity and Judaism; the religion of nature was set up as an antithesis to Western religious traditions. Moreover, by celebrating diversity, by giving credibility to 'the savage', by attacking Revelation which set itself in opposition to other 'superstitious' religious and cultural traditions, which undermined autonomy and self-worth by encouraging people to accept what was received on authority alone, the works of Rousseau, Voltaire and the literature of the Enlightenment created the environment in which Pagans could believe in the Earth for itself. They could challenge exclusivist claims, not to truth as Revelation claimed, but to the Earth as a resource. They could criticise the stress on rationality, exploiting the Earth because of Reason–that it was a resource to be used–and could argue for bringing back the sacredness of the Earth, for seeing her as a Goddess, they could argue that to exploit her was rape of the Goddess Earth. Neo-Pagans have argued that overemphasis on reason has led to many of the problems in society today; the language of Religion and religious experience has to be restored. This view comes from the tradition developing from the critique of religion and the notion of Revelation in the Enlightenment.

Less controversial is the relationship between Pagans and the anthropologist Margaret Murray, whose book *The Witch Cult in Western Europe: a Study in Anthropology*, first published in 1921, documented the theory current in Europe at the time that the mass of the population in Europe remained Pagan under a Christian ruling class until the sixteenth- and seventeenth-century Witch Hunt which finally destroyed the pre-Christian religion. Her book heavily influenced the revival of Paganism in Britain after the repeal of the Witchcraft Act in 1951 and was also generally accepted by many academics until the 1970s when it was heavily attacked by two historians, Keith Thomas and Norman Cohn.[16]

The extent to which present-day Paganism can be linked to a tradition in the past remains a controversial issue.[17] Though the arguments against Margaret Murray's theory by Thomas and Cohn and other historians working on local studies have demonstrated that the witches of the Great Witch Hunt were not practitioners of an Old Religion, many Pagans continue to see neo-Paganism as a revival of the Old Religion. The works of the two anthropologists Sir Edward Tylor and Sir James Frazer greatly encourage the notion that religious forms have survived in uncorrupted traditions from early times to present days. Frazer's *The Golden Bough*, from an anthropological point of view, offers a vast array of European and tribal folklore and ancient ways, completely ignoring contexts and discrepancies as he attempts to demonstrate that the Christian myth of the resurrected god is simply one example of a universal Pagan myth. Ronald Hutton's paper tackles this controversial area of survival and gives a clear picture of the only continuities existing between ancient and modern Paganism; high ritual magic, 'hedge witchcraft', folk ritual and lastly the European love affair with the literature and art of Pagan Greece and Rome. Hutton looks at who and what was involved in these four areas and how they have combined into the single movement of modern Paganism. In a recent book Ronald Hutton concludes that we know very little about pagan religions of the ancient British Isles, religions more diverse than any historians had anticipated. He suggests they completely died out a long time ago, and that most of what historians thought they knew they are now finding out is not true. Nevertheless, as he himself says, 'establishing that we really do know very little...provides a greater freedom to those who wish to make their own interpretations of it...will give sceptics peace of mind, and yet leave others free to dream'.[18]

As a final comment Graham Harvey and I would like to thank all the contributors to this volume who inspired both the conference and this book.

Notes

1 For reading on Paganism in general see Margot Adler, *Drawing Down the Moon: Witches, Druids, Goddess Worshippers and other Pagans in America Today*, Beacon Press, Boston, 1986 ed; Prudence Jones and Caitlin Matthews (eds), *Voices from the Circle: The Heritage of Western Paganism*, Aquarian, 1990; Vivianne Crowley, *Phoenix From the Flame: Pagan Spirituality in the Western World*, Aquarian, 1994; Prudence Jones and Nigel Pennick, *A History of Pagan Europe*, Routledge, 1995.

2 The need for a Pagan Prison Chaplain in the UK is not because there are numerous Pagan prisoners! The Home Office originally asked the Pagan Federation to help with some training in the prison service because they anticipated an increased number of Pagan prisoners when the

government bill was passed making trespass a criminal offence.

3 *The Independent*, 16 December 1994.

4 Margot Adler, *Drawing Down the Moon*, p455, Beacon, Boston, 1986, and Tanya Luhrmann, *Persuasions of the Witch's Craft*, Blackwell, 1989.

5 Margot Adler, *Drawing Down the Moon*, p453.

6 The Pagan Federation, *The Pagan Federation Information Pack*, p12, Pagan Federation, London, 2nd ed 1992.

7 The Pagan Federation, *The Pagan Federation Information Pack*, p14.

8 See Asphodel Long, 'The Goddess Movement in Britain Today' in *Feminist Theology* 5 (January 1994), pp11–39, for a description of the feminist movement, its developments and impact on Paganism.

9 Starhawk, *Dreaming the Dark: Magic, Sex and Politics*, p8–9, Beacon Press, Boston, 1982.

10 Rae Beth, *Hedgewitch*, Robert Hale, London, 1990.

11 See Vivianne Crowley, *Phoenix From the Flame*, Chapter 8.

12 Asphodel Long, 'The Goddess Movement in Britain Today', *Feminist Theology* 5, p25.

13 The conference, 'Paganism in Contemporary Britain', was held in the Religious Studies Department, University of Newcastle Upon Tyne, from 12–14 September 1994. The gathering was the first full-scale conference concerned solely with Paganism in Britain.

14 Howard Eilberg-Schwartz, 'Witches of the West: Neopaganism and Goddess Worship as Enlightenment Religions' in *Journal of Feminist Studies in Religion*, Vol 5, No 1, (Spring 1989), USA.

15 Howard Eilberg-Schwartz, p85.

16 Keith Thomas, *Religion and the Decline of Magic*, pp514–19, Penguin, Harmondsworth, 1971, and Norman Cohn, *Europe's Inner Demons*, pp102–25, Heinemann, London, 1975.

17 See Ronald Hutton, *The Pagan Religions of the Ancient British Isles*, Chapter 8, Blackwell, 1991, and Prudence Jones and Nigel Pennick, *A History of Pagan Europe*, Chapter 11.

18 Ronald Hutton, *The Pagan Religions of the Ancient British Isles*, pxii.

I

PAGANISM AND HISTORICAL PERSPECTIVES

Ronald Hutton

THE ROOTS OF MODERN PAGANISM

To speak of 'Modern Paganism' is of course to invite debate in itself, for the expression covers a multitude of faiths and practices, with only a limited (though important) amount in common. To an historian, the divisions and distinctions are of considerable moment, only some of the traditions having a long enough continuous existence in Britain to warrant investigation. Those which concentrate upon Scandinavian or Germanic deities, for example, use ancient images and ways of working but are clearly a recent revival of them based upon surviving texts. Likewise, groups working under the umbrella term of Shamanism are self-consciously a creation of the past two decades, drawing upon tribal models, often from native America, fused with ancient European imagery. Druidry, by contrast, has a well-documented history which is continuous from the late-eighteenth century. There was, however, nothing specifically pagan about any of it until the 1980s, when some overtly pagan orders were founded. Nineteenth and early-twentieth century Druidry was perfectly compatible with Christianity and indeed overlapped considerably with it, focusing upon a single creator god, identified with the sun and working through wise men.

All this puts Wicca, or Modern Pagan Witchcraft, very much in a category of its own, being from the start of its public existence (over forty years ago) both an unequivocally pagan religion and one which claimed very long roots. Where the latter actually run is now the subject of considerable debate. Until the 1970s, the matter was not seriously problematic, as the Wiccan claim fitted into an academic semi-orthodoxy; that the people persecuted as witches in Europe's Great Witch Hunt were members of a surviving pagan religion. Wicca could quite plausibly be stated to be that religion, having survived in secret into the twentieth century. In the 1970s, however, this idea about the Witch Hunt collapsed inside academe, helping to instigate a search for the genuine origins of Wicca.

Much of that search has to date concentrated upon the lineages of particular Wiccan groups or traditions, and has tried to trace them back, initiation by initiation. The results so far have been interesting, but not at all conclusive, for all the documents or reliable memories seem to run out in the years around 1940, leaving a welter of modern claims about old, family-based or coven-based practices.[1] Historians are in no position to deny these but neither, in default of evidence, can they accept them. I prefer, instead of working backwards, to research forwards; to try to reconstruct the context of nineteenth- and twentieth-century culture out of which Modern Paganism either arose or resurfaced. What follows is an interim report upon that work, which is still very much in progress. In the course of my study of ancient paganism in Britain, I identified four direct lines of connection between that complex of beliefs and the present: high ritual magic, 'hedge' witchcraft, the general love affair of the Christian centuries with the art and literature of the ancient world, and folk rites. It is time to look again at all four, bearing in mind the new question of the origins of Modern Paganism.

High ritual magic consists of the summoning and control of supernatural forces by the use of invocations and sacred equipment. Some of the latter is solid, such as consecrated knives, wands, swords or flails, and some of it spatial, such as the sacred geometry of circles, quarters, cardinal points, pentagrams and triangles. This sort of magic can first be certainly identified in Hellenistic Egypt, from which it was taken and developed in Arab Spain, often by Jewish practitioners, and passed on to the late-medieval Christian world, where it was developed further in the early modern period. The main alteration thereafter was that whereas until the seventeenth century it was largely the preserve of the solitary practitioner, the 'magus', after then it was increasingly associated with magical societies, such as the Rosicrucians, the Freemasons, the New Knights Templar, the Order of the Golden Dawn, the Fraternity of the Inner Light, and the Ordo Templi Orientis.

Until the mid-nineteenth century, ceremonial magicians worked with the names of spirits or demons, often in Hebrew. After that, ancient pagan deities, especially those of Egypt or Mesopotamia, were increasingly added to invocations. In part this was simply a return to the source of the tradition which had, after all, actually come from Egypt, and could be refreshed by the study of Hellenistic texts by Victorian magicians. It was also, however, the result of archaeology, as the scholars of the century translated hieroglyphic and cuneiform script and increasing quantities of paintings, inscriptions, statues and papyri were recovered by excavation. The result is that by the early-twentieth century, it is very hard to distinguish some magical groups from pagan witchcraft; the only key difference that is immediately apparent is the lack of the name 'witch'.[2] It could, however, also be argued that the pagan element in ritual magic had remained incidental. The careers of the two best-known, best-documented and ostensibly most pagan practitioners, may illustrate this. One is Dion Fortune, whose magic became more or less Christian according to the phases of her life and seems to have ended up as a hybrid of religions.[3] The other is Aleister Crowley, who amalgamated pagan deities, Hebrew demons and redeveloped Christian ritual to produce a personal set of rites and beliefs linked by what may be termed therapeutic blasphemy.[4] In these cases, as in all documented ceremonial magic of this period, the central impulse was not essentially religious; it was not to worship or honour supernatural beings so much as to gain personal power from them.

What needs to be emphasised now is how deeply ritual magical practices had penetrated ordinary British society in the nineteenth century. Freemasonry (though now generally lacking a genuine occult content) was found even in small country towns, and had quite a high public profile; at Melrose in the Scottish Lowlands, for example, the local lodge paraded through the streets carrying torches every Midsummer's Eve. All its branches preserved rituals of initiation and celebration which had a quasi-magical character, and Masons referred to their traditions collectively as 'the Craft'. Then there were Friendly Societies or Benefit Clubs, rudimentary insurance societies to provide members with sick pay, unemployment benefits and a decent funeral. These sprang up in both town and country in the early-nineteenth century, flourished until its end, and incorporated ceremonies loosely modelled upon those of Freemasons. They could be very dramatic; one initiation rite of the Oddfellows, for example, involved leading the newcomer blindfolded into a circle of members and tearing off the blindfold to reveal that a sword was pointed at his chest. He then had to take the oath of secrecy and fidelity to the society. It is worth bearing in mind through all this that what he was actually supposed to be doing was buying an insurance policy! Membership of these groups was often linked to a particular trade or 'craft', and meanwhile the old-style trade guilds or 'crafts' still survived in many towns. Some adopted the trappings of the quasi-ceremonial societies; in Shrewsbury in 1840, a trade guild bought up a job-lot of Masonic regalia for its meetings in order to add dignity and excitement to them.[5]

Such groups continued to proliferate into the early twentieth century. Some were drinking clubs in which the rites were largely humorous, such as the Royal Antediluvian Order of Buffaloes.[6] Others were much more serious. One of the most important was the Order of Woodcraft Chivalry, a socialist and pacifist alternative to the Boy Scouts and Girl Guides, inspired largely by the writings of the American, Ernest Thompson Seton. It met in woodlands, especially the New Forest, and conducted ceremonies within a sacred circle, consecrated by people standing at the quarters in the order east then south then west then north. Its leaders were called the Witan, Anglo-Saxon for 'wise'; and so its practices were 'the craft of the wise'. In 1938, the Order went into schism, and split into a number of different groups, meeting at different places in the New Forest in subsequent years and developing their own rituals of which more later.[7] It seems to be clear, therefore, that Victorian and Edwardian society was filled with groups which practised secret rites and demanded initiation, most of them linked to the word 'craft'. The terms 'Hereditary Craft' or 'Traditional Craft' consequently represent such a wide category as to be almost meaningless to an historian.

The second important link between old and modern Paganism is what can conveniently be called 'hedge witchcraft', the popular magic of the local wise woman and cunning man. It is clear that these people were not merely respected because they had a knowledge of herbs, cures and spells, for virtually everybody in traditional British society knew some of these. They were regarded, rather, as possessing some personal magical powers in addition. A huge amount of information upon these people was gathered in the late-nineteenth century by middle- and upper-class folklorists, to whom they represented the very essence of a romantic, rural world which the collectors were trying to rediscover. The data is so rich that a large book could probably be written upon that from Somerset and Essex alone.

Two things are plain from even a cursory investigation of it. The first is that these local practitioners formed part of a spectrum with 'high' ritual magic, rather than representing a self-contained world. Most cunning men were known to have owned books, and when these are itemised in the occasional court case, they turn out to be manuals, or grimoires, of old-fashioned ceremonial magic. The second rapid discovery is that these individuals were not very important in the development of modern Paganism. For one thing, they were almost always solitary workers; they are increasingly significant as role models now that the individual practice of witchcraft is coming into ever greater vogue, but they have little relation to the essentially communal character of mid-twentieth century paganism. For another thing, there is no evidence that they worshipped pagan deities. The closest approach that I have found to such worship is in the tale of a Herefordshire witch who, when asked to swear by God, carefully swore only by 'her' god. Unfortunately for its use as an example, the story makes plain that the god concerned is the Devil, whom the woman is thus forced to acknowledge as her master, and the whole anecdote is a cautionary one, rather than an account of an actual incident reported by a witness.[8]

Nevertheless, the low-level folk magic is significant for our purposes because of its overlap with occult societies. The most widespread and remarkable of the latter was the Horse Whisperers, also known as Toadmen or the Horseman's Word. They practised folk magic concerned with the management of horses, but were organised in a society and had an initiation ceremony. In north-east Scotland, at least, this was rumoured to involve the confrontation of the novice by a personification of the Devil. The all-important 'word' itself turns out to be a Latin term of conjuration familiar in traditional grimoires.[9] Such meetings could look, to outsiders at the time and later, very like witches' covens.

The third strand of connection, the love affair with the pagan ancient world, has remained strong throughout the Christian centuries. The latest study of early medieval monastic literature, by Ludo Millis, concludes that the monks were so overawed by the Greek and Roman classics that this stifled their creativity.[10] When the most original twelfth-century scholar, Pierre Abelard, dedicated himself to a life of learning (by definition, within the Church), he described himself as 'kneeling at the feet of Minerva'. This addiction to classical imagery and quotation was, of course, massively reinforced by the Renaissance. In nineteenth-century England there were three distinct attitudes (in this case the fashionable term 'discourse' is absolutely appropriate) to the pagan past. The first characterised pagans as enemies of Christianity and civilisation, who bowed down to idols, made blood sacrifices, tortured saints to death or threw them to lions, and enjoyed sexual orgies. Such a discourse could be readily absorbed from the most widely read of all books, the Bible, and hitched to one of progress by equating paganism with barbarism. It was widely employed to describe and condemn the religions of tribal peoples and of old Asiatic cultures with which Europeans were colliding in the expansion of trade and Empire.[11] It also represented the view of ancient civilisation taken by the popular novels of Bulwer Lytton and Marie Corelli, and later became the dominant one in Hollywood historical epic.

It co-existed, however, with a tremendous admiration for the achievements of ancient Greece and Rome, and a tendency to identify with them, inculcated further in the educated by the predominance of Greek and Latin classics in the school and university curricula. The quintessential Victorian muscular Christian, Charles Kingsley, could tell his juvenile readers approvingly that they would find the Greeks all round them in the language of 'well-written books', the buildings of 'great towns' and the decorations of 'well-furnished rooms'. On that most characteristic monument of the age, the Albert Memorial, Homer sits enthroned, with Shakespeare at his feet. The Tory, William Huskisson, could be said to have been the first politician to die in a truly modern way, run down by a railway train in 1830; yet his memorial statue in Pimlico portrayed him wearing a Roman toga. As the British were Protestants, and traditionally allergic to religious statuary, there were far more pagan deities than Christian saints decorating their parks and public buildings.

If the Greeks stood for thought and exploration, the Romans represented imperial destiny. Both were patterns not only of beauty and wisdom, but of moral force; as Richard Jenkyns has put it, 'if something was Hellenic, then it was almost bound to be pure'. In this second discourse, the ancient world was only deficient in its religion, not because the latter was barbarous, but because it was immature, better fitted for entertainment and secular edification than as a vehicle of divine revelation. This discourse also drew upon the Bible, but not on the Old Testament (upon which the first had relied) so much as upon the New; in this the Jews could be discerned to be the villains, while the pagan Roman Pontius Pilate featured as a bemused and well-meaning gentleman.[12]

There was, however, a third set of attitudes, which glorified ancient paganism itself. To John Keats, the latter was a culture of innocent joy and close identification with the beauties of nature. In the second half of the century, the intimate association with the natural world was retained, but the joy was no longer so innocent; to poets such as Rossetti, Swinburne and Wilde, paganism had been a carefree celebration of sexuality as part of its uninhibited 'naturalness'. This discourse was fast developing into a counter-cultural attack upon Christianity and conventional morality. Muted but persistent echoes of it are found in the novels of Thomas Hardy, in which the word 'pagan' is used repeatedly for many different purposes and in different contexts, but always with the same shiver of the alluring, the abandoned, and the amoral.

Underlying the last two discourses, moreover, was a tremendous qualitative change in nineteenth-century English attitudes. Its source may be expressed in a simple statistic: in 1810, twenty per cent of the English had lived in towns while, by 1910, the proportion had risen to eighty per cent. England had become the first urbanised and industrialised nation, the balance between town and country tipping (neatly) in the 1850s. After then it seemed a real possibility that the whole land would turn into one vast, smoking conurbation. From the 1870s, therefore, an almost hysterical celebration of rural England began, gaining strength into the early-twentieth century; a phenomenon well studied recently by Alice Chandler, Alun Howkins and Jan Marsh.[13]

What concerns us most here is the way in which (like all Victorian civilisation) it drew upon ancient images. One of the most important was the figure of the Greek god of nature, Pan. It must be emphasised that Pan was actually a minor Greek deity; Ken Dowden, author of the best recent introduction to Greek mythology, has termed him 'the Citroen 2CV of Greek gods'.[14] To the classical ancient world, as to the succeeding centuries until the nineteenth, the favourite deities had been those of civilisation. Now, however, the wild, horned and goat-footed god came into his own, featuring as the patron of Kenneth Grahame's *The Wind in the Willows*, being hailed by Oscar Wilde, and appearing in the works of a host of lesser writers. Others preferred to adopt another ancient Greek image, that of Gaia, the presiding female spirit of the globe itself, so that references to Mother Earth and Mother Nature began to multiply, reverently, in the literature of the age. By 1900, the poetic vision of the English, when contemplating the rural world, was dominated as never before by the great goddess and the horned god.[15]

The same development had a marked impact upon attitudes to the fourth direct link between pagan past and pagan present: folk custom and rituals. Scholars had believed ever since the Renaissance that many of these derived from the old religions, and current research can establish that in a few cases at least this is perfectly correct. In the sixteenth and seventeenth centuries, antiquaries tended to assume that they came down from Roman festivals, while in the eighteenth and early nineteenth it became more fashionable to attribute them to the Druids. In the late-nineteenth century this long-established assumption was given a new importance by the work of (above all) Sir Edward Tylor, Sir Lawrence Gomme, and Sir James Frazer.

These writers were inspired by the new theory of biological evolution and the discovery of the fossil record of the past, which suggested to them the possibility that surviving folk customs could be fossils of old religions, embedded in later society. If this were so, they reasoned, then a close comparative study of these survivals might enable specialists to reconstruct these religions.[16]

It should be stressed that Tylor and Frazer were both motivated by a distaste, rather than an admiration, for all religious beliefs and practices. They especially despised those like paganism and Roman Catholicism which relied heavily upon ritual. Their ultimate aim was to discredit all religion, including Christianity, as part of a progress towards a wiser and more rational society. Nor was their theory of survivals ever fully accepted by the scholarly community. At the opening of the twentieth century, the Folk-Lore Society held a full-scale debate upon it by devoting most of an issue of its periodical, *Folk-Lore*, to reviews of Frazer's key work, *The Golden Bough*. One historian and expert in comparative religion after another examined Frazer's methodology and pointed out serious faults in it. The notable exception was Sir Lawrence Gomme's wife, Alice, a pioneer of the collection of children's lore, who said that she was not an expert in the material of *The Golden Bough*, and knew little about it, but that Frazer's arguments just sounded right to her.

This established the pattern of the future; historians lost interest in the Folk-Lore Society and it became almost wholly the preserve of people like Lady Gomme, enthusiastic collectors of folk customs who uncritically accepted Frazer's view of them as pagan survivals. They simply fitted the data which they observed into his interpretative framework. This pattern also harmonised perfectly with the new nostalgia for the English countryside and the idealisation of the natural world. If the theory of survivals was correct, then apparently old rural customs literally were solemn and sacred rites; by linking them to an old fertility religion of greenery and nature spirits, Frazer had told the public exactly what it most wanted to hear. His work helped to perfect a vision of a timeless, sealed off, rural world, full of ancient secrets.[17]

But how did all this get linked to witchcraft? The answer lies in a political debate over the origins of the Great Witch Hunt, the roots of which, in turn, run far back into the eighteenth century. During that century it became generally accepted by the educated elites of Europe that magic did not exist. If this was so, then logically the Witch Hunt had been a terrible mistake, and could be used by the liberals of the Enlightenment to castigate and mock the traditional order in Church and state. This situation invited a reaction, and one appeared during the period of intensely conservative government often characterised as the Age of Metternich. Two scholars serving authoritarian German rulers, Karl Jarcke and Franz Josef Mone, suggested that the witches persecuted during the early modern period had in fact been practitioners of a surviving pagan religion; a view which, if it were true, made the persecution rational and even justifiable.[18] A reply to it was demanded in turn from the liberal camp and was provided resoundingly by one of the nineteenth century's great radical historians, the Frenchman Jules Michelet. Michelet was a bitter enemy of the Catholic Church and the feudal aristocracy, an unqualified admirer of the French Revolution, and an author of vivid and immensely popular books. He knew literally nothing of the Middle Ages except romances and fairy tales, and virtually all his information upon the Witch Hunt was taken from anti-clerical pamphlets. This did not inhibit him at all. In 1862, he published *La Sorciere*, a bestseller which portrayed the pagan witch religion postulated by Jarcke and Mone as having been the repository of liberty all through the tyranny and obscurantism of the Middle Ages. In his dream of it, it was feminist, led by a priestess. It was nature-loving and also joyous, democratic, and peaceful. Michelet, indeed, went far further than even the most uninhibited modern pagan writer, to claim that the Renaissance had been caused by the natural wisdom of the witch religion working its way upward to artists and writers. After the commercial success of *La Sorciere*, it is easy to believe that Wicca was a religion waiting to be re-enacted.

Perhaps it was, indeed, re-enacted soon afterwards. There is, however, no firm evidence of this, and it is not difficult to see why not. French culture of the time did not include the same reverence of the countryside and respect for rural people that the English were acquiring. Nor does France seem to have had the same tradition of popular quasi-magical societies. Although the British cultural elite certainly read *La Sorciere*, and admired it, they could do so only because they spoke French; it was not available in English until 1904. By then an English readership also had Charles Godfrey Leland's *Aradia*, published in 1899. Inspired directly by Michelet, it purported to provide the gospel of the Italian branch of his witch religion. Leland likewise made his political purpose clear; to argue against a newly-fashionable nostalgia for the Middle Ages which offended his own radical ideas. His text was yet more feminist than Michelet's, for it made the main deity of the religion a goddess. The theory was finally given academic respectability in 1921 by the

English archaeologist Margaret Murray, who was acquainted with the work of both Michelet and Leland and was, moreover, a member of the Folk-Lore Society and an admirer of Sir James Frazer. Her work on witch trial records (proved much later to have been selective, inaccurate and misleading) united Frazer's old rural fertility religion with modern folk customs and Michelet's witch cult, upon an apparently sound basis of evidence. Murray's own attitude was strictly rationalist, based upon a dislike of all religion and superstition. Nevertheless, as time wore on her antipathy towards Christianity became more overt and her sympathy for ancient paganism correspondingly more pronounced. If her first book on the subject, in 1921, had won the respect of academe, her second, *The God of the Witches*, published in 1933, made a much greater impact upon the public. It portrayed the witch religion as having been the universal one of ancient northern Europe, carefree and natural.

It is hardly surprising, therefore, that it is in England towards the end of the 1930s that the first apparently reliable evidence can be traced of groups who embodied this religion. They range from a set of Cambridge students, to a gathering of middle-class intellectuals, including individuals with a colonial background, to a convention of ordinary, if very literate, lower-middle-class people.[19] This chapter can end, however, with a quick glance at the man who was to be the first publicist, and perhaps the co-founder, of Wicca, Gerald Gardner. Even a relatively swift examination of his social world between his arrival in England in 1936 and his first 'Wiccan' publication in 1949, reveals that he was a Freemason, a Rosicrucian, a spiritualist, a friend and probable member of the Ordo Templi Orientis, a member of the governing council of a Druid order, a very active member of the Folk-Lore Society and fervent admirer of Margaret Murray, and a member of one of the divisions of the Order of Woodcraft Chivalry. Representatives of all or most of these were active in the New Forest area in the time around 1940, when Gardner later claimed to have been initiated into Wicca.[20] It is no wonder that when one reads his books or (more to the point) reads his papers in Toronto and his surviving manuscripts of Wiccan rituals, one likewise finds elements from all or most of them as well as direct borrowings from authors such as Crowley and Leland and grimoires such as the Key of Solomon.

The story suggested here is no more than an outline, and still leaves mysterious the matter of how exactly particular modern Pagan groups and traditions came into existence. There is room for a very large quantity of further research, and much of it will, undoubtedly, be carried out by academics as part of the burgeoning scholarly interest in new and revived religions, of which Newcastle University's conference, 'Paganism in Contemporary Britain' was in itself a striking manifestation. Modern pagans themselves have, however, a clear opportunity to preempt an academic investigation which may prove to be insufficiently sensitive or sympathetic for the liking of some, by conducting research into their own traditions.[21] If the data which they provide is susceptible to proof by scholarly analysis, then they will earn the respect and gratitude of professionals and possess much of the initiative in the study of their own history. What this chapter has suggested is that the task is likely to be long, complex and fascinating. It proposes that modern Paganism was neither the descendant of a continuous sectarian witch cult, nor born fully-fledged from the imagination of one man in the 1940s. It is, on the contrary, a particular, and extreme, incarnation of some of the broadest and deepest cultural impulses of the nineteenth and twentieth century British world.

Notes

As this essay is an interim report upon research in progress, many of the references are given in general terms, to illustrate the fields being covered, and will be provided in detail when the project is completed.

1 Compare, for example, Aidan Kelly, *Crafting the Art of Magic* (1991); Doreen Valiente, *The Rebirth of Witchcraft* (1989), and WE Liddell and Michael Howard, *The Pickingill Papers* (1994).

2 For overviews, see Francis X. King, *Ritual Magic in England* (1970); Kenneth Grant, *The Magical Revival* (1972); James Webb, *The Occult Establishment* (1982), and *The Occult Underground* (1988); Francis X. King and Isabel Sutherland, *The Rebirth of Magic* (1982). For rituals, see Israel Regardie, *The Golden Dawn* (4 vols., 1937–40), and *The Secret Rituals of the O.T.O.*, ed. Francis King (1973).

3 The best guide to Fortune's thought is in her own writings, the best known probably being *The Sea Priestess* and *Moon Magic*. The biography is by Alan Richardson, *Priestess* (1987).

4 Again, his many publications are the best guide to his thought. A good starting-point could be *Magick* or *Magick Without Tears*. For commentaries of varying quality, see John Symonds, *The Great Beast* (1954) and *The Magic of Aleister Crowley* (1958); C.R. Cammell, *Aleister Crowley* (1969); Kenneth Grant, *Aleister Crowley and the Hidden God* (1973); Francis X. King, *The Magical World of Aleister Crowley* (1977).

5 Among what is, again, a very large literature, basic reading could be William Preston, *Illustrations of Free Masonry* (1788); George Oliver, *Signs and Symbols of Freemasonry* (1856); A.E. Mason, *The Accepted Ceremonies of Craft Freemasonry* (1874); P.H.J.H. Gosden, *The Friendly Societies in England 1815–1875* (1961), and *Self-Help: voluntary associations in nineteenth-century Britain* (1973); Margaret Fuller, *West Country Friendly Societies* (1964); Mark C. Carnes, *Secret Ritual and Manhood in Victorian America* (1989); and H. Polling, *A History of British Trade Unionism* (1956) (the Shrewsbury reference is on p40). The 'folkloric' rituals are in *British Calendar Customs: Scotland* (Folk-Lore Society, 1937–41).

6 Into which Robert Graves was initiated in 1914: Graves, *Goodbye to All That* (1929), p105–6.

7 The Order's history can be traced through its periodical, *Pine Cone*. I am grateful to Messrs Glynn Faithfull and Bran Labworth for clarifying additional points.

8 There are hundreds of such studies, compiled between 1800 and 1980 and usually arranged by county when in book form, or else published in *The Folk-Lore Journal* and then in *Folk-Lore*. The best way of conducting a detailed local study seems to be to begin with these and then to work systematically through newspapers and Quarter Sessions records, using parish registers and Poor Law entries to trace especially interesting individuals. The anecdote is from Ella Mary Leather, *The Folk-Lore of Herefordshire* (1912).

9 Compare, for example, George Ewart Evans, *The Horse in the Furrow* (1960), pp239–71; Ronald Blythe, *Akenfield* (1969), p54; J.M. McPherson, *Primitive Beliefs in the North-East of Scotland* (1929), p290–1; Ian Carter, *Farmlife in Northeast Scotland 1890–1914* (1979), pp154–6. There is a large correspondence on the subject in national and local newspapers.

10 Ludo J. Millis, *Angelic Monks and Earthly Men* (1993), pp92–100.

11 There is a rich harvest of such works easily found by following up the footnotes to J.G. Frazer, *The Golden Bough* (1890).

12 For an assortment of images like these, see Richard Jenkyns, *The Victorians and the Greeks* (1981), and *Dignity and Decadence* (1991).

13 Alice Chandler, *A Dream of Order: The Medieval Ideal in Nineteenth-Century English Literature* (1971); Jan Marsh, *Back to the Land: The Pastoral Impulse in England, from 1880 to 1914* (1982); Alun Howkins, 'The Discovery of Rural England', in Robert Collis and Philip Dodd (eds.), *Englishness: Politics and Culture 1880–1920* (1986), pp62–88.

14 Ken Dowden, *The Uses of Greek Mythology* (1992), p126.

15 There are surveys in Helen H. Law, *Bibliography of Greek Myth in English Poetry* (1955), and Patricia Merivale, *Pan the Goat-God: His Myth in Modern Times* (1969).

16 J.W. Burrow, *Evolution and Society* (1966); Robert Ackerman, *J.G. Frazer: His Life and Work* (1987); Gillian Bennett, 'Geologists and Folklorists', *Folklore* 105 (1994), pp25–37.

17 Georgina Boyes, 'Cultural Survivals Theory and Traditional Customs', *Folk Life* 26 (1987–8), pp5–10; Gillian Bennett, 'Folklore Studies and the English Rural Myth', *Rural History* 4 (1993), pp77–91; Theresa Buckland and Juliette Wood (eds.), *Aspects of British Calendar Customs* (1993).

18 Karl Ernst Jarcke, 'Ein Hexenprozess', in *Annalen der Deutchen und Auslandischen Criminal-Rechts-Pflege* 1 (1828), p450; Franz Josef Mone, 'Uber das Hexenwesen', in *Anzeiger fur Kunde der Teutschen Vorzeit* 8 (1839), pp271–5, pp444–5.

19 This would include Gardner's original circle, the 'Pentacle Club' at Cambridge, and the Chanctonbury group, all based upon the testimony, written or spoken, of former members.

20 Some of this information is in his biography by Jack Bracelin. The manuscript diary of Aleister Crowley confirms Gardner's membership of the O.T.O., and the minutes of the Ancient Druid Order place him upon its council. His activity in the Folk-Lore Society can be traced through its periodical, *Folk-Lore* (after 1960, *Folklore*) between 1938 and 1963, and Bran Labworth testifies to his connection with the Woodcraft Chivalry.

21 This is the subject of work in progress by Aidan Kelly, Ceisiwr Serith, and Gareth Medway.

Kenneth Rees

THE TANGLED SKEIN:

the Role of Myth in Paganism

Introduction

I propose to use in this chapter a tripartite model of the term 'myth' arguing that it may operate in terms of three distinct functions or levels of meaning which may, on occasions, work simultaneously and in inter-related ways:

a. substantively, i.e. actual narrative structures as instanced by specific bodies of myth across the world, e.g. Hebrew, Greek, Teutonic and so on and including allied texts such as fairy lore, legend or saga.
b. in myth's perhaps most commonly used mode today as meaning something simply untrue or a fiction.
c. as an overall controlling image incorporating beliefs, attitudes and values which direct ways of behaving and derive from a range of sources–cultural, familial, institutional and the like–and which inform both a society and the individuals within it.

This last usage is well in line with the role given to myth in traditional cultures as documented, for instance, by Joseph Campbell, Mircea Eliade or Claude Levi-Strauss and goes beyond any Barthesian over-identification of myth as solely ideology. The model as a whole is offered as an analytical tool for exploring the multiple meanings encoded in pagan and personal mythologising. The crucial themes of this chapter are the dynamic interaction between personal and collective myth and how the creative use of myth structures legitimates and gives content to the project of paganism today.

Two other terms I will refer to throughout the text are 'tradition' and 'reconstruction'. By the former I mean the corpus of belief, knowledge, symbols and behaviour which is embodied in a particular outlook or world view and congealed through time within a localised culture. In the context of native spiritualities we thus find

Amerindian traditions, the Bon Po tradition, the Shinto tradition and so on. More abstractly, the notion of tradition implies a sense of having a living continuity with the past, the feeling of ownership that goes along with ideas and values from the past.

By 'reconstruction' I mean the modelling or building of new traditions out of elements drawn from one or more such native cultures as they existed (or were deemed to exist) at a particular time and place. One of these elements is substantive myth both in its portrayal of divine gods, goddesses and other characters and in its rendition of widely distributed themes across the globe such as the journey to the underworld, death and rebirth scenarios, the wisdom of the clown and so on. Modern paganism consists, to a high degree, of just such reconstructed traditions.

Part 1: Personal Mythologising Through the Pagan Labyrinth

Personal Myth

The concept of personal myth is especially tied to usage c) in the myth model proposed above. Not a concept in common use in Britain as yet, neither in academe, in New Age circles or even within the alternative psychotherapies, it has a currency in the United States and two valuable introductions to the idea are contained in the works of Stephen Larsen[1] and David Feinstein and Stanley Krippner[2] respectively.

A seeker's personal mythology has numerous roots within family, gender identity, social class background, ethnic and overall cultural milieu. Personal myths are never fully conscious but exist on pre-conscious levels also. To quote Feinstein and Krippner (p24):

> *...personal myths explain one's world to oneself, guide personal development, provide social direction and address spiritual longings. They organise one's sense of reality and guide one's actions.*

Such a concept can therefore also include emotive as well as purely rational factors that inform how people negotiate their way through the post-modern web of life. The idea implies a formative tension between the growth of individual identity and wider cultural forms and processes. In many cases personal myths may become so thoroughly internalised as to effectively constitute the personality. Self-reflection and many other devices may be necessary before they are brought to awareness or 'seen through' in Larsen's terminology.[3]

In this chapter I am concerned with the possible sociological function an understanding of an individual's myth and a group's collective myth can play in the task of unmasking and demystification. Due to my original fieldwork in England in the 1970s and consequent teaching of college-based courses in paganism, mythology and witchcraft from 1982 onwards, together with ongoing research, I have perhaps had a unique opportunity to observe the passage of those seekers pursuing a deepening engagement with paganism, the operation of their personal myths over time and subsequent interactions with the traditions they found within the field if and when they chose to engage with them.

Such classes often appeared to be the first formal structure in respect to paganism that people had encountered on their journey. My role was perceived by many students–rightly or wrongly–as that of a gatekeeper or bridge, existing to assist their future direction and entry into hidden worlds. Typically I could have sustained regular contact with such seekers for up to thirty weeks each academic year in both formal (classroom) and less formal (e.g. public house or practical workshop) situations. In some cases the later destinations of those who have been through these classes have become known to me, quite a few apparently now occupying responsible positions within the magical subculture.

In passing it is worth noting that the nature of an individual's personal myth is such that it might not necessarily be significantly revealed by methodologies of a wholly empiricist nature, i.e. interviews and questionnaires. In my own experience in-depth qualitative research and prolonged observation, tracking and monitoring yield the best insights into individual (and collective) myth. The possibilities of deception or distortion of response, deliberate or unintended, are ever present and need to be guarded against, most of all in any short-lived study.

Personal Myth and Identity

Thus one's personal myth will inform an individual's expectations on the point of entry to a defined segment of the magical subculture and often long beforehand. Such expectations are typically an amalgam of images and stereotypes derived from the mass media, one's friends and acquaintances, in some cases popular books read on the subject plus, on occasion, distinct fantasy projections and wish-fulfilments, e.g. the past as desired in the case of the ancient Druids, the present as hoped for in regard to the presumed sabbatical orgies of modern witchcraft, the future ideal for an earth undefiled in respect to eco-paganism and so on. Obviously the specific configuration will vary with the seeker concerned.

I submit that there is a continuing interaction between those personal myths that a seeker brings to his or her search and the more composite myths–often firmed up to have the character of an ideology–that inform the various subcultural segments of paganism. These ideologies can shape and support identity formation and change in many ways depending on eventual 'consumer choice' (but see below). Some seekers may choose the myth they like the best–perhaps because it appears to have the most compatibility with their initial expectations–but later grow out of it and/or discover that 'the emperor/empress has no clothes', in which case the original myth could well be thoroughly demystified for the individual concerned (in this case by disenchantment). They may however have to seek for another myth elsewhere or even develop one for themselves which has the right balance of solidity and mystique to attract recruits.

Where early disillusion does not occur the accruments of a changing identity may become readily apparent through an assimilation of the appropriate regalia (both internally and externally) of the segment which one is inducted into. A resocialisation process occurs into the thoughts, the rituals, the ethos of the specific grouping–an adoption of the visualisation practices, application of specialised symbolic systems within specified interpretative frameworks and the like.

A new set of peers emerges re-enforcing a new myth. It is clear that people are not merely taking on new beliefs here. Even total retailoring of lifestyle is possible in theory if not always in practice. Seekers, in fact, will usually stop at the level they feel comfortable with–where there is a degree of synchrony between their own informing myths and the outlook of the segment which they have become lodged in. From this time forth (or until they become disillusioned/find a new myth on offer) they will variously speak from within the mythos of their preferred segment (or segments) and reproduce it in their turn to newcomers–*they speak from within the myth*. Or, to put it differently, following fuller integration into a particular tradition the individual's personal myth, for all practical purposes, becomes synonymous with that grouping's collective outlook whether the tradition be organised hierarchically (e.g. having an initiatory structure) or democratically (e.g. practical consensus decision making).

The magical subculture can thus be seen as a maze or, if preferred, as a labyrinth or patchwork quilt over which individuals attempt to steer themselves following the dictates of their personal myths. Some seekers may self-reflectively articulate their journeying in terms of the hero's quest for the Grail. For the Grail offers a redemption of identity at the end of one's search. In the meantime all one can do is to navigate the uncharted seas with varying degrees of discernment. It should be noted that substantively Arthurian myth does help inform more than one of the segments available. Others may seek the womb of mother earth and they can be predictably found in those segments–again multiple–that put their emphasis on the Goddess.

Environmentally-conscious pagans (100 per cent we might hope for and expect to find) professing a green spirituality will gravitate to, for instance, the eco-pagan network known as Dragon, this organisation being a particularly fine example for stressing the *myths of holism, totality and interdependence* summed up by the substantive symbol of Gaia. Such a myth of holism functions both as an aspiration for the future (the greening of the earth anew) and as an ideological principle breeding a brand of radical politics and civil disobedience in the present.

Some women may be drawn to goddess figures as empowering role models for today and help form the basis of a feminist witchcraft rooted in the significant stories of Classical culture and beyond (see Part 2). The *myth of the noble savage* has been applied to early Celtic society and contemporary Amerindian tribes alike. The ethos of much modern Druidry has the capacity to trigger off responses in that direction for those moved by such views today.

The attractions of quasi-secret society membership, those special and different from the rest with additional magical powers to boot, supports the *myth of the Chosen Few* and segments within paganism exist to meet the needs of those seduced by such elitist conceptions. All of the elements cited above are common strands encountered time and time again throughout the subculture. At any point one or more of them may act as a hook, an allure latching into the special predispositions of the quester built on his or her personal mythic concerns.

I therefore feel that contemporary paganism does articulate distinct conceptions of the self, typically either in a tightly bounded esoteric social context like a lodge or a temple, or as a member of a much looser federal or associational network. Often a combination of both is possible given that memberships are usually not mutually exclusive and a high degree of movement and fluidity can exist overall between sectors.

Such identities are often temporary in respect to the relationship an individual may have to any one segment or even to the subculture as a whole. This can easily be deduced even by just casually observing the age-band structures of attendees at conferences on the pagan circuit throughout twelve months. The age banding is typically from the middle-aged downwards. When identities are not so transient then seekers may have found a permanent second womb which, supposedly, meets a simple majority of their needs.[4] For those who appear to have forged such remade identities (sometimes via formal initiatory procedures) the experience is often described by such expressions as a 'coming home', 'where I've always longed to be' and even (inevitably?) 'enlightenment'.

Interestingly, those entering the subculture at young, impressionable ages (arguably, the majority) are likely to be *both* the 'occult flirts', dipping into this, dipping into that with a merely skeletal commitment *and* those who are most likely to remain if their identity gets solidified through the mutual processes of quest and provision by the occult establishment. Orrin E. Klapp's work[5] is still very valuable reading here.

In the case of temporary or provisional identity we often have window shopping phenomena where individuals look at the goods from a certain, safe distance and then decide whether or not to get any closer. Whether they will actually buy the goods is a different matter again. Temporary and permanent identities alike in this area, it should be remembered, are typically constructed in relation to tradition, albeit very recent traditions in truth–neo-Egyptian, the new Golden Dawn, Wicca and so on. And it is these very traditions that provide and are supported by foundation myths and the like.

Rationality and Fluidity

Personal mythologising, therefore, in contemporary neo-paganism is socially sanctioned through the medium of overlapping groups, often of considerable literacy, promotional flyers, books and events all fitting broadly into the particular path espoused. But because myth is a symbolic language and always operates on more than one level at a time it is important to take into account the subliminal and preconscious levels at work as well as the conscious.

Thus, I think we are never witnessing completely voluntary, rational choices here. The process of choice is both more subtle and more complex. By using the notion of personal myth we avoid the error of positing an over rationalised model of the seeker freely choosing between alternatives whether it be for instrumental benefit or affective fulfilment. Seekers do not go into religious movements as *tabulae rasa* or possess the ability to wield unfettered, calculatory free choice. This is where the consumer/marketplace model breaks down. People have their controlling myths. It is the personal myths of the seekers operating in conjunction with the variably manifest mythos of the groups in question which effect a choice for the person–or not.

The use of the concept of personal myth helps us to understand why individuals initially enter paganism, the orientations they may take once involved, and their eventual destination–whether their identity voyaging be just a temporary fad or fashion or something more substantial. Both the personal mythologising process and the consequent firmed-up outcomes arise out of a fluid configuration of effective and rational meanings held at various levels of awareness by the seeker and the sought alike.

Part 2: Substance and Romance

Substantive Mythologies

Perhaps out of the three layers of meaning I have isolated as making up a properly-constituted, critical and nonreductive definition of myth it is a) actual narrative myth which finds the most coinage with modern pagans. For instance, what is increasingly labelled the Northern Tradition is rich in Teutonic myth, one contemporary group even calling itself the Odinic Rite. Many publications, including those of Nigel Pennick's mid-1980s *Runestaff* booklets, give the foundations of the tradition while Graham Harvey (in this volume) points out the role the Norse mythology has for present practitioners.

The likes of the Clan Dalriada integrate the Gaelic deities of the Tuatha de Danaan into their work and popular writers on Celtic shamanism like John and Caitlin Matthews are steeped in the mythological lore of early Britain and Ireland. Recently, Marion Bowman (in this volume) has placed these developments into an interesting, effectively postmodern context. Wiccans continue to use Mediterranean motifs in their practice following the initial formulations of Gerald Gardner, the key founder of modern witchcraft.

Celtic myths in particular have been consistently used in pagan reconstructive work since at least the early 18th century. The inspiration for the Druidic revivals of that century came at least as much from Celtic literature and literary concern as it did from speculations over the meaning of ancient sites. The so-called Celtic twilight period forged by the pens of the likes of James Stephens, 'A.E.' and W.B.

Yeats in the late-19th/early-20th century again burnt from that fire originally fuelled by the hands and hearts of many generations past. In the later-20th century too we are witnessing the increased burgeoning of the Arthurian mythos in a variety of media.

In my own London-based fieldwork in the 1970s I worked with more than one group that utilised Celtic myth to good effect. One instance was an allegedly hereditary Craft group and another a non-aligned pagan coterie. The former group claimed distinctiveness in a variety of ways, not the least of which was professing the possession of their own family version of the *Mabinogion* (a compilation of medieval Welsh manuscripts on mythic themes). This claim was used, on occasions, to help legitimate their hereditary craft roots and status in their own eyes and in the eyes of newcomers. It was also used to distinguish their approach to paganism from what they perceived as the Wiccan 'Johnny-cum-latelies'.

Indeed, I would suggest that the imputed legitimacy and credibility of a restored pagan grouping often rests in its appeal to 'tradition' centred around a specific culture's mythology. Aside from the Celts and the Scandinavians, and Europe more generally, examples can be drawn from other cultures–especially, perhaps, the Egyptian stretching back again to the 19th century and earlier and finding expression today in networks such as the Fellowship of Isis (given that this organisation is much broader than *just* Egyptian) and also in recent midsummer rituals involving enactments of the myth of Osiris as presented by the Pagan Federation.

In all such cases, as catalogued above, substantive myths give content (the philosophy behind and rationale for the rite), they provide impetus, they present roles for individuals in groups to play in terms of, for example, different aspects of deity. Vitally, the myths act as continuing sources of poetic and dramatic inspiration.

The Myth of Matriarchy

The interrelationship between meanings a), b) and c) of the tripartite model of myth proposed depends in any specific case on the degrees of emphasis given to each sense by the user concerned assuming that more than one sense is perceived in the first place. The controversies over the existence of early matriarchies and, to a lesser extent, issues around the allied term of matrifocality, represent well the multiple usage of the term myth in both sense b) as regards the whole hypothesis being untrue (always untrue, forever) and sense c) as regards matriarchy being a central controlling image and world view, if not now then at least in the past because based on a literalness dependent upon historical, prehistorical or archaeological factual interpretation.

The deployment of the term myth in different ways to mean different things can appear to be confusing. Yet the consistent usage of myth at only the one level of meaning, e.g. anything which is untrue, is unsophisticated and does not do justice to the rich resonance myth has held in its fullness. In respect to the debate over matriarchy we find commentators using the same word 'myth' to indicate the holding of diametrically opposing positions. The detractors broadly operate with sense b) while its proponents draw support from sense c). To complicate matters still further both parties use examples of actual substantive myths (sense a) to attempt to illustrate their case, either for or against. The usefulness of the analytical model as outlined in the Introduction should therefore by now be coming clear.

The classical definition of matriarchy as given by J.J. Bachofen (in R. Louie, *Social Organisation*, p262, Routledge, 1950) runs 'rule of the family by the mother, not the father; control of government by women, not men; and the supremacy of a female deity, the moon, not of the male sun'. It is useful to see the whole debate around matriarchy as occurring in a series of waves marked by much oppositional thinking–the first wave, interestingly perhaps, promoted by men including, as well as Bachofen himself, J.F. Mclennan and R. Briffault. The view was equally opposed by men, e.g. E. Westermarck and H. Maine. The debate featured significantly in the infancy of Victorian anthropology.[6]

A second (pro) wave can be discerned this century among classicists including J. Harrison, R. Graves, E. Neumann and M. Renault.[7] A third (again favourable) wave has emerged since the early 1970s, largely promoted by feminist writers including E.G. Davis, M. Stone and C. Spretnek amongst many others.[8] Again, there has been a significant response to this both from men and other women writers, some of whom were anthropologists, e.g. P. Webster, S. Ortner and J. Bamberger.[9]

Bachofen's work postulated three evolutionary stages that society had gone through from a general 'promiscuity', through matriarchy up to patriarchy. This view, based on a reading of classical mythic sources as history, has been roundly criticised and (apparently) relegated to an interesting curio within the history of ideas. Despite this it continues to surface from time to time. Joan Bamberger showed that in certain south-American societies the Rule of Women myth actually functioned as a way for men to retain their power–for the myth revealed how the men had stolen power from the women because they were not competent to wield it. The myth is thus used ideologically to justify male dominance and, therefore, for Bamberger, should itself be destroyed.

Others have pointed out that even the existence of mother goddesses, no matter how well it would appear they are documented within the archaeological record, does not automatically prove the existence of an entire social organisation based on women's power or fertility, or even necessarily imply a higher social status for women at that time (the upper Palaeolithic). Myths of primordial female eminence are still found today in largely male-dominated societies. Thus it might be wise not to read too much into a society in the past or in the present having myths of a creatrix, a heroine or whatever. Such cultural data need not suggest only one set of arrangements at the social structural level, for instance, egalitarianism.

Here then we have in the hands of some of its proponents a good example of a *golden age myth* resting on a somewhat idealised picture of the past and empirically on what can be called thin histories and prehistories. That is, a thinking backwards from present confusions to an alleged point of stability and organic unity in pre-feudal, pre-Dark Age, even pre-Iron Age society (*especially* pre-Iron age) and thus to miss the complex, stratified nature of earlier cultures.

However, I feel what has been particularly positive about the myth of matriarchy, in respect to the new paganism, is the way in which it has been utilised in an enhancing and visionary manner. This in respect to the construction of a feminist spirituality informed by empowering goddess figures from numerous early cultures. The goddess Innana of Sumer is a good example of this process.

The myth of Innana's voluntary descent to the underworld (seen and experienced as 'the dark') and subsequent return to this world and then to the sky is inspirationally used and essentially understood as a psychotherapeutic process to help unify those aspects of the feminine not permitted untrammelled expression in a patriarchal society. D. Wolkstein and S. Kramer provide the story,[10] S. Perera gives us the (psycho)analysis[11] and Starhawk encourages the politicisation of this process.[12]

Innana becomes a symbol for what can be done using myth as a framework for empowerment and growth. Myths of matriarchy may have started off by being historicised and for some people this may still be the preferred reading but more recently the goddess perceived as psychological and political symbol has become dominant. The impression gained is that much feminist witchcraft over the years, especially in the States, has used myth creatively in just these ways. The key issue becomes to behave *as if* the myth were indeed true.

Wicca and Myth

Throughout a consideration of this area we find fine examples of the continued interaction between myth as equated with fiction and myth operating as intensely strong controlling imagery governing approaches to the reality of the modern witchcraft perspective and its justification. At the same time as I was doing my research Margot Adler was doing hers across the length and breadth of America to eventually produce her *Drawing Down the Moon*.[13] My own findings in this country concurred very much with what she terms in that book the 'myth of wicca' of which there are numerous strands.

Perhaps the most important element posited is what I wish to call the *myth of continuity* still alleged by some to exist between early modern European witchcraft and the modern phenomenon. Such a myth has provided legitimation for the latter (as well as much stereotyping within popular culture) as regards, for instance, particular terminology, certain ritual practices, overall group structure and specific outlooks. Thus we have the vocabulary of covens, esbats and sabbats, a stress on the number 13 in principle if not in fact (e.g. the favoured number of participants in a group), an emphasis, ideally, on working couples of opposing gender in principle if not in fact, a homogeneous title of the 'Old Religion', a stress on members being effectively priests and priestesses rather than a laity, a duotheistic and universalist conception of deity, an organised cult surviving from the Bronze Age and so on.

The sources for many of the above elements are not hard to find. Much depends on a particular reading of the medieval witch trial materials as attested to in, for example, H. Pitcairn's *Criminal Trials* (1833), H.C. Lea's *History of the Inquisition* (1888) or W. Notestein's *History of Witchcraft in England* (1911) plus numerous others. Such references were brought together and drawn upon selectively by Margaret Murray in her well-known 1921 publication *The Witch-cult in Western Europe*.[14]

Since the 1980s many aspects of the myth of continuity in the above senses have begun to wobble. This has been for a number of reasons. Historical scholarship on the early modern period increasingly over the last twenty years or so has given less and less credence to the Murray thesis and put forward alternative positions of its own. A looser-limbed neo-paganism has developed over the same time period, a paganism not so in need of such legitimations or conformities to strict rubric. Finally, critical insider writers such as Aidan Kelly encourage us to view Wicca effectively as a new religious movement.[15]

The question can then be posed as to why the need for the myth of continuity in the first place? One answer might be suggested here–and this would also apply to the way that the myth of matriarchy has been approached by some–that such needs and myths arise out of the romantic imagination and what M. Eliade has called the 'nostalgia for origins'.[16] This vital psychological component should not be ignored when considering certain New Age movements for we may often discover a past-as-wished-for rather than a past-as-known. Such a nostalgia for origins may provide both feminist witchcraft and Wiccan witchcraft with a set of foundational myths from which judgements of value can then be made.

It is now recognised that the Age of Reason influenced the decline and demise of the witch trials. But one reaction to this was the Romantic movement which had its expression in many forms including art, philosophy and literature. Key literary influences on the revival of interest in witchcraft in the 19th century include Sir W. Scott, J. Michelet, H. Jennings and C.G. Leland. In magic we saw a revival of neo-platonism, the writings of F. Barrett and E. Levi plus the Golden Dawn society, to say nothing of William Blake and the anarchopantheist spirit of Henry Thoreau.

Early this century we had the development of the Cambridge myth and ritual school and in 1920 the publication of Jessie Weston's *From Ritual to Romance* analysing the Arthurian mythos along Frazerian *Golden Bough* lines. The role of such romantic roots in the shaping of contemporary paganism and witchcraft cannot be overstressed.

Also, it is wise to be aware that when one mythology shows imminent signs of collapse (in this case the myth of continuity as outlined above) then we can be sure that another myth will quickly arise to replace it performing similar functions to the earlier one for its adherents. In respect to the 'myth of wicca' overall it is worth cautioning that one person's fiction is another's controlling idea, even faith –'tread softly because you tread on my dreams' (W.B. Yeats).

A Little Note on Tradition

Within the Gardnerian construction of Wicca itself we have the Book of Shadows–the tradition's recipe book of rites, spells, chants, dances and the like. While no canonical version exists a significant body of common core elements remains (see e.g. Kelly op.cit.). If we take this text as a base then we have initially a good example of detraditionalisation. Gardner decontextualised mythic and other items from largely pre-modern cultures–in particular, Celtic, Greek, Northern, near-Eastern and Indonesian–and tied them around early modern sources from selected witch trial material. Elements range from the Key of Solomon (medieval, magical grimoire), through Eastern tantra to A. Carmichael's *Carmina Gadelica* and also Freemasonry.

Gardner thus started off in a relativising way but the results, enshrined in one version of the Book of Shadows or another, and the practices built up around it, became quite quickly absolute and authoritative. Yet the mid to late 1960s there has been some loosening and greater reliance on high magic components (e.g. use of the kabbalah) and other occult tools due, in part, to the influence of the second founding father of Wicca, Alex Sanders. Also, in more recent years an even wider eclecticism has emerged including and endorsing references to the chakras, Jungian psychology (a great prop to much New Age thought in general) and even biofeedback techniques.

However, despite all this I would want to maintain that a process of retraditionalisation took place very speedily. The Book of Shadows rubric still remains authoritative for many (albeit by no means all) covens today. This may be exemplified by, for instance:

a. the circle (sacred space) typically cast by a female
b. the stress placed on the three grade initiatory degree system
c. the Drawing Down of the Moon ritual on to a female by a male
d. such a ritual not normally performed by first degree initiates
e. the high priestess remaining the first amongst equals
f. the sequence of quarter casting in relationship to the elements
g. the place of high magic aspects more generally.

Perhaps Gardner's move re the compiling of the Book(s) of Shadows could be seen as a precursor to later New Age approaches to knowledge and practice–first detraditionalisation then retraditionalisation. Michael Harner's 'common core' shamanism comes to mind here as does the Venerable Sangharaskshita's construction of the Friends of the Western Buddhist Order out of his experiences of a variety of Buddhisms on the Indian subcontinent from the 1940s onwards.

In all three cases–modern witchcraft, neo-shamanism and the F.W.B.O. version of Buddhism we see a process of elements being taken from wider cultural and philosophical frames of reference and being woven into what its respective practitioners experience as a meaningful whole. As such an assumption of authenticity is made.

A seal of validation is provided through, for example, ordination in the F.W.B.O. or initiation in Wicca. Both may be considered New Age but not postmodern.

In essence, Wicca, and the new paganism more generally, represents an example of mythic restoration (and transformation) and functions as an arena within which the production of a modern identity can be forged via willed action on the part of the seeker in exchange with the range of representations available to him or her within the magical subculture.

Conclusion

In this chapter I have tried to make a start in answering the questions–what myths inform modern Paganism today? And why such myths and not others? I have stressed the importance of recognising the role the myths of continuity and those of the golden age play–the all-pervasive influence of substantive myths from a wide range of cultures and epochs–plus, the key role in my opinion, of an individual's personal myth and the whole activity of personal mythologizing, this process strongly underpinning much interaction between and within the social structures found in this area. I therefore urge the necessity for teasing out the myths which inform the pagan and magical subcultures–those personal myths which propel seekers towards paganism once attracted–as well as investigating those myths which maintain people in their memberships, once inside as it were.

Paganism rests on mythic foundations because of the use it makes of traditions, all of which embody mythological symbolism to a lesser or greater degree. As such these traditions offer substantive myths as building blocks for modern identity work, e.g. as a Celt, as a follower of the Northern way, as an Isian initiate and so on. Paganism can really do no other but to lean on myth in the kind of ways discussed–the resources of mythology being a very rich multicultural heritage from which to derive and develop new traditions based on seemingly ancient outlooks.

Paganism's very vitality arises from just such mythic sources as have been highlighted. But it is important that these sources be identified and recognised for what they are and the functions they serve, by practitioners and commentators alike, and that the appropriate methodologies are used to access them where they are not immediately apparent (e.g. longitudinal studies, participatory studies, in-depth preferably comparative, multiple use of key informants and so on).

Linked to this is the need to keep the historicity of modern Paganism (a complex enough area on its own) clearly defined in distinction to its more mythic undercurrents explored above. Un-fortunately, many commentators both from within and outside the subject do not always do this, thus confounding the two. One alternative then becomes that of plodding around in a morass where clarity of vision is sacrificed for ideology and mystification substituted for romanticism.

The reemergence of Paganism today administers to the symbolic poverty of our times by reactivating those centres of the mythological imagination in the receptive individual. The old legends are retold, nurturance is received once more from romance, echoes of mystery are heard anew and reassurance is provided by ritual action, symbols of place and great Nature's seasonal round.

Notes

1 Stephen Larsen, *The Mythic Imagination* (Bantam, 1990).
2 David Feinstein and Stanley Krippner, *Personal Mythology* (Unwin, 1989).
3 Stephen Larsen, *The Mythic Imagination*, ppxix, 49ff.
4 J. Campbell, *The Flight of the Wild Gander*, Part 2, Ch 3 (Harper Perennial, 1990).
5 Orrin E. Klapp, *Collective Search for Identity* (Holt, Rinehart and Winston, 1969).
6 J.J. Bachofen, *Myth, Religion and Mother Right* (Princeton, 1973); J.F. Mclennan *Primitive Marriage* (London, 1865); R. Briffault, *The Mothers* (Atheneum, 1977); E. Westermarok, *The History of Human Marriage* (London, 1891); H. Maine, *Lectures on the Early History of Institutions* (Murray, 1897).
7 J.E. Harrison, *Epilegomena to the Study of Greek Religion* (N.Y. University Books, 1962); R. Graves, *Greek Myths* (Cassell, 1958); E. Neumann, *Amor and Psyche* (Bollingen, 1960); M. Renault, *The King Must Die*, (Foursquare, 1961).
8 E.g. Davis, *The First Sex* (Penguin 1979); M. Stone, *The Paradise Papers* (Virago, 1979); C. Spretnek, *Lost Goddesses of Early Greece* (Beacon Press, 1978).
9 P. Webster, 'Matriarchy: a vision of power' in R.R. Reiter, *Toward an Anthropology of Women* (Monthly Review Press, 1975); and S. Ortner, 'Is female to male as nature is to culture?' and J. Bamberger, 'The myth of matriarchy: why men rule in primitive society', both in M.Z. Rosaldo and L. Lamphere (eds.), *Woman, Culture and Society* (Stanford, 1974).

10 D. Wolkstein and S.N. Kramer, *Inanna, Queen of Heaven and Earth* (Harper and Row, 1983).
11 S.B. Perera, *Descent to the Goddess* (N.Y. Inner City Books, 1981).
12 Starhawk, *Truth or Dare* (Harper and Row, 1990).
13 Margot Adler, *Drawing Down the Moon* (Viking Press N.Y., 1979).
14 Margaret Murray, *The Witch-cult in Western Europe* (Oxford, 1967).
15 Aidan Kelly, *Crafting the Art of Magic*, Book I (Llewellyn, 1991).
16 Mircea Eliade, *The Myth of the Eternal Return* (RKP, 1995).

Prudence Jones

PAGAN THEOLOGIES

I am using the plural here deliberately. A polytheistic religion gives many different accounts of the divine beings, and these accounts, or theologies, reflect the divine patronage of their inventors. People sometimes raise their eyebrows when they hear of *Pagan* theology, but in fact the word 'theology' dates from Pagan times and was first used concerning Pagan deities. In the *Republic* (II,375), Plato discussed the limits to be placed on poets in writing their mythologies or theologies. They must only tell the truth about the deities and must not be allowed to mislead their hearers as, Plato claimed, the ancients had done. Herodotus too (2,53) tells us that it was Homer and Hesiod who described and classified the gods. 'Theology' here, then, is a descriptive account of the divinities, often a poem or song, rather than as we now think of it, an analysis or an explication of the divinely ordered universe and of the place of human beings within it.

Here is some theology in Plato's sense from his own time, an ode by the poet Pindar, written to commemorate the Nemean Games of 463 BCE. Commentators used to say that for the Greeks the divine world was utterly separate from the human world, and that human beings had no part in the former. The Mystery schools of late antiquity belie that sentiment entirely, of course. But even as early as Pindar, the intimate kinship of deities and humans is affirmed, a thought which persisted through the Mystery religions of the ancient world and is not unfamiliar to modern Pagans:

> *Single is the race of men and of gods, from one mother (Gaia) do we both draw breath; yet a difference in power divides us, for the one is as nothing, yet for the other the brazen vault of the sky endures as a dwelling for ever.*
>
> *But we partly resemble the immortals, either in greatness of mind or in our nature, although we do not know, either by day or in the night, what course it is written that we should run.*[1]

Ancient Pagan Theologies

Theology soon moved out of poetry into sober prose. The philosophers took theology as part of natural philosophy, an account of the nature of the universe which included its divine inhabitants. Most people seem to have taken it for granted that gods and goddesses existed, since among other things people had seen them, in dreams and in the visions which were called 'epiphanies'. The Epicureans, following Democritus, understood the universe to be made up of atoms (a doctrine resurrected, like much other Pagan philosophy, in the eighteenth century, by Leibniz in his *Monadology* (2,3)). These were thought to be randomly moved by the force of gravity through a universe of empty space. Deities, like human beings, were seen as fortuitous collections of atoms, living unlike the latter in bliss in the *intermundia*, the spaces between the worlds. They took no part in the affairs of mortals, but could be of use to the latter as objects of contemplation, paradigms of the inner bliss that the wise person might attain. The pursuit of wisdom was the wise pursuit of pleasure, and in this the gods served as a model.

The second great school of the ancient world, that of the Stoics, on the other hand, saw the divine power as one and as immanent in the manifest world. Ultimately, the whole universe, both visible and invisible, was itself divine. Apparent matter and apparent spirit were simply opposite poles of a continuum. Various divinities manifested themselves according to the needs of the time, but they were all manifestations of the universal One. The universe, for the Stoics, was fated and ruled by the laws of Nature, the manifestation of divine Mind. These laws, *logoi* for the Greeks, *rationes* for the Romans, expressed the nature of things and were the same as what people ordinarily call fate. The aim of the good person was to live in accord with Nature. The whole universe was seen as good; bad or unfortunate events only seemed to be so by an error of perception. Similarly, any being which followed the laws of its own nature could do no harm, whatever appearances might suggest. In modern times, the Stoic ontology of a deterministic Nature which has no supernatural beings outside itself has appeared again in the materialistic universe of Newtonian science. But modern scientists have no deities, whereas for the Stoics, as later for Spinoza, another seminal thinker of the Enlightenment,[2] Nature *was* divinity. Stoicism became immensely popular among educated Romans in the first two centuries CE, but it faded before the otherworldly appeal of later Platonism.

Such philosophies of the ancient world contained the theologies of Pagan thought. Their influence on embryonic Christian theology was immense, affecting this at least as much as the Jewish method of rabbinical analysis on which it also drew.[3] It was from these Pagan theologies, as much as from the Jewish method of textual analysis, that Christian theology took its form. The word 'dogma' referred originally to a conclusion of Pagan philosophy.

'Pagan' Defined

Let me state what I mean by 'Pagan'. A Pagan religion has three characteristics. It is polytheistic, recognising a plurality of divine beings, which may or may not be reducible to an underlying One–or Two, or Three, etc. It sees the material world and its laws (again reaffirmed for the modern age by Spinoza as *natura naturata* and *natural naturans*[4]) as a theophany, a manifestation of divinity. Although the Platonic school, like some schools of modern Hinduism, believed in a definite mind-body dualism, there is no indication that they saw the material world as in itself harmful or 'evil' until the Christian influence of late antiquity, around the time of lamblichus (*d.*330). Finally, Pagan religions recognise the female face of divinity, called by modern Pagans the Goddess; taken for granted in Her many manifestations by the Pagans of the ancient world. A religion that does not accept that divinity may manifest in female form is not, on this definition, Pagan.

Pagan thought thus contains the religious world of European antiquity, it contains tribal religions worldwide, both ancient and modern, and it contains modern Hinduism, Shinto and other sophisticated polytheistic faiths. It is the theology, the reflective thought, of this religious outlook that I am examining here, and I am skimming through the broad trends of ancient thought in order to put modern thought in context.

Late Antiquity and the Bridge to Modern Paganism

The philosophy of Plato always contained a tension between that philosopher's desire, perhaps conditioned by the troubled times in which he was living, to believe in an absolute unchangeable world of permanent beings–the Forms, Ideas or, as they were later called, archetypes, which he saw as the pattern behind imperfect reality–and his method, the ruthless question-and-answer dialectic of his master Socrates. Following Plato's death, it was the sceptical method that won, and Platonists became famous (or notorious) for producing arguments like those of modern philosophers which show that a table is not really solid. Indeed, in 155 BCE, the then head of the Academy, Carneades, on a visit to Rome, was expelled from Italy for being a subversive influence on civic life, rather as Socrates had been executed some 250 years previously for corrupting the youth of Athens.

But the significant development for modern Paganism was the swing towards dogmatic philosophy beginning around 80 CE. The Middle Platonists, as they were called, people such as Plutarch, the assiduous ethnologist of the first century CE, and Celsus, the second-century author of *True Reason*, bitterly attacked by Origen the Christian, had been at pains to develop an ordered theory of the universe. The theory that the universe emanates in increasing layers of density from the immaterial and universal One seems to have initially been codified, interestingly enough, not by an Athenian but by the Alexandrian Jewish philosopher, Philo of Megara (fl.30 CE). His theory of the divine emanations from the universal Mind was absorbed into Jewish thought and may eventually have emerged as the four symbolic worlds of the Cabbalistic Tree of Life. We see a similar system of graded emanations, derived this time from Hindu and Buddhist thought, in the modern philosophy of the New Age. In the ancient world the cosmology of emanations from the One was firmly taken out of the realm of empirical research by the mystic Plotinus (204–70), who claimed he had certain and subjective proof of the subtle unity of all things by his visionary insights, reached after disciplined meditation.[5] Thereafter Neoplatonism (as it was called) became a personal discipline rather than a subject of religious debate, much less of scientific experiment. As a private contemplative praxis, it was able to survive Christian laws against Pagan ceremonial, and its account of the universe was preserved in literature to re-emerge in the Pagan flowering of the Renaissance and eventually find public expression via the literary conceit of the Great Chain of Being.[6]

Dogmatic, contemplative Neoplatonism was syncretic. It tried to assimilate all pantheons into the One. In its (literally) Byzantine convolutions it became inaccessible to any but professional religious specialists. Here is an account of the nature of the divine Sun by the Emperor Julian (360–3), the famous reviver of official Paganism, in his *Hymn to Helios*:

> *This divine and wholly beautiful universe ... is held together by the continuous providence (pronoia) of the god [the One, or Form of the Good] ... and is guarded immediately by nothing other than the Fifth Substance [ether], whose culmination is the beams of the sun. And in the second and higher degree, so to speak, [it is guarded] by the intelligible world but in a still loftier sense it is guarded by the King of the whole universe, who is the centre of all things that exist ... the supra-Intelligible ... the idea of Being ... or the One ... [who] produced, as middle among the middle and intellectual, creative, causes, Helios the most mighty god, proceeding from itself and in all things like unto itself.*[7]

Interestingly, for Julian, the god of the visible Sun, Helios, is not a supreme being but exists only in the middle realm, the world of intellectual creative causes. In the primary realm, the realm of Forms, exists the Mother of the Gods, together with Zeus the Father of the Gods, who create all creatures visible and invisible (see his *Hymn to the Mother of the Gods*). Once more we become aware of the feminine face of divinity in Pagan thought.

Julian's is the Paganism of a professional theologian, not of an ordinary worshipper. Ordinary Pagan religion, less self-reflective, was not so much syncretistic as pluralistic. The gods existed, they were invisible inhabitants of the natural world (theories about *creation* belong to the philosophers), every family and every community had to enter into relationship with them. Sacrifices were communal feasts, and there was no full-time priesthood. Religious duties were part of household and civic duties, a kind of psychic housekeeping, but as we have seen, the various deities of all the nations were eventually gathered under the patronage first of Zeus/Jupiter, then of the (Roman) Emperor's guardian spirit, and finally of the Sun-god (whom we see again, in a slightly different role, in Julian's system). This was not monotheism; this was henotheism, the belief in a chief, tutelary deity presiding over many deities, and in the system of Julian, as in the cult of Isis and Serapis, which I have no room to mention here, it was ditheism, the belief in a supreme Father and Mother.

There is plenty to say about ancient henotheism and the concept of the One, its possible reformulation as monotheism as early as Heracleitus (fr.16), but that is not my topic here. My concern is everyday Paganism apart from the debates of the philosophers. I shall close this section by coming back down to earth with the words of a non-specialist Pagan of late antiquity, the Roman senator Symmachus. It was he who, at the end of the fourth century, after some eighty years of official Christianity, defended the Old Ways against the reforming Christian emperor:

> *For each has his own customs, each his own rites. The divine mind has allotted different cults to guard the different cities. As souls are distributed among the newborn, so guardian spirits are distributed among different peoples ...*
>
> *It is only right that what all people worship should be thought of as one. We all look at the same stars, the heaven is common to us all, the same universe contains us. Of what use is it to ask by which way a person may seek for truth? A single road cannot lead to so great a secret, though among the leisured classes these ways are debated.*[8]

The existence of many deities for many sorts of people and nations, so obvious to Symmachus, is not obvious to monotheists, to philosophers or to atheists. But it does seem to be typical of mainstream Pagan thought.

Modern Paganism

The path of articulated Pagan thought from the late School of Athens via the centuries of official Christianity and Islam to the Italian Renaissance is a tangled one. It has been traced elsewhere,[9] and I shall now leap ahead to comment on some current Pagan assumptions, approaches and outlooks concerning the relationship between humanity and the divine. Many of these are not formulated and not debated by the Pagan community, but form a taken-for-granted background to religious practice.

Experiential Basis

Modern Paganism is not a doctrinaire movement like that of the Emperor Julian. But it is nevertheless a reforming movement, and it bases its argument for reform on experience rather than on blind faith. By experience we know that we can be transported into rapture by the beauty of Nature, by the birth of a child, by the fulfilment of love, or by the opposite, by a harrowing emotional experience which transforms itself into its opposite, the vision of cosmic order. So for Pagans the divine, transcendent powers seem to be present within Nature itself, and by deliberate ritual and contemplation the devout Pagan can make contact with these. Some modern Pagans even call their way the path of 'individually experienced religion'.

This attitude contrasts with religions of revealed authority, where the revelations of one prophet alone must be accepted at second hand by the faithful, and coincides with that of other Pagan religions, with their openness to epiphany. Such empiricism tends to be anti-authoritarian, with the evidence of each adherent's own senses standing as the test of any general principles–dogmas–put forward by anyone else. How this attitude will accommodate the need for religious communities to have some general attitudes to divinity in common, is something to be worked out as the Pagan community grows. Both Wicca and the Order of Bards, Ovates and Druids are already negotiating this compromise. Within Mystery schools such as Wicca and certain Druid orders, personal revelation is provoked according to a more or less set method, and is expected to conform more or less to a general norm. The revelations of initiates of the Mystery schools will eventually be weighed against those of individual practitioners of shamanism and *seidr*, and against those of ordinary 'lay' Pagans who assert their right to their own revealed truth.

Experiential religion outside a general framework of interpretation also runs a further risk. When the world is seen as filled with the gods, however, it can be easy to lose one's inner locus of control. Superstition results: the synchronicities of the world are seen as controlling everything, and the human being seems to have no power faced with the enveloping multitude of otherwordly forces whose influence can be read in every portent. Perhaps this is an argument for restricting communion with the divine world to ritual occasions, not allowing it to flood everyday life. For most of the time we can forget about the Otherworld and lead our own lives, as Pagan civilisations such as ancient Rome seemed to do quite successfully. It is clear that problems of lack of self-direction never troubled the ancient Romans. Conversely, modern atheists among others can be entirely outer-directed: the sub-Marxist belief for example that the human will is helpless before the great tides of class and history; or the sub-psychoanalytic view that human action is never freely chosen, but merely a mechanical reaction to early traumas. The question of fate (or divine power) versus freewill goes deeper than that of Nature as a theophany versus the desacralised cosmos, and there I intend to leave it.[10]

Magical Religion

In assuming that there are hidden powers behind the manifest world which are worthy of veneration–the religious outlook–Pagans also assume a two-way traffic between the worlds. Not only communion and seership (a receptivity to messages from the hidden world) but also magic (an active wielding of the hidden powers) is taken as a normal part of life. Individuals are thought to be able to influence the visible tangible world by manipulating the invisible, intangible world, which flies in the face of modern physics, yet is true to the experience of many otherwise sophisticated modern Pagans.

One of the roots of modern Paganism is the ritual magic tradition, derived in part from the Greek and Egyptian Paganism of late antiquity. As has been mentioned Paganism became privatised during the early centuries of official Christianity. Public practices such as the seeking of augury (from the flight of birds) and auspices (from the entrails of slaughtered animals), the expectation that the deity would make itself manifest by a sign during a ceremony, the consecration of votive objects such as the spoils of victory, all took on a new shade of meaning in private worship. Private mediumship replaced public augury, private conjuration replaced public epiphany, and the private making of talismans replaced the public consecration of dedicated objects. Looked at in this way, there is nothing mysterious, much less degenerate, about how the Paganism of late antiquity became magical. The difference between a magician and a public Pagan celebrant, in this respect, is one of intensity and seclusion, not of kind. In the days of official Paganism a publicly sanctioned private world of ritual and experience had existed as well. There had been nothing remarkable about private individuals seeing visions in their dreams, preserving sacred objects in the shrine of their family Lares, wearing the protective bulla (or amulet) until adulthood, and venerating sacred places and their Otherworldly guardians. Laws against magic, in officially Pagan societies, are laws against private ceremonies for private gain, against the interests of the community.

In public life, then, Pagan religion is magical. When we read of the sleeping cures at shrines of Æsculapius in the ancient world, are we learning of psychosomatic medicine, of magic, or of a religious retreat? At every sacrifice, the entrails of the slaughtered animal were examined to look for omens. Before a major political decision, omens were also taken. As Cicero wrote, during the birth pangs of the Roman Empire: 'This whole state is created and maintained and expanded by the power of the gods'. The divine and human worlds were in constant communication.

However, a magical outlook runs directly counter to modern accounts of causality and of personal responsibility. When anything goes wrong in our lives, it is too easy to accuse our nearest enemy of bringing this about by magical means, and if necessary to take magical revenge against them. Such an attitude of blame without proof can trap people in a constant cycle of vendetta and fear of vendetta, leaching energy from ordinary life. It can also call up the ugliest kind of mass scapegoating, in which no evidence can possibly acquit the accused, for publicly verifiable standards of evidence do not apply.

However, look again at the sophisticated Pagan cultures of old. Mass vendettas did not happen (by contrast with village cultures, of whatever official philosophy), because public institutions protected the individual and public law defended them. Private vendettas certainly did happen–the number of votive curses thrown into sacred shrines proves that–but in a magical as in a materialistic society the rule of proportion applies. Individuals are quite able to waste their time on vendettas in the physical world entirely without magical beliefs. The attitude of vendettas has nothing to do with magic, but everything to do with a closed society and an external locus of control. It is the inability to walk away from a situation in favour of a more rewarding activity which leads enemies to consume their resources in mayhem and revenge.

Nevertheless I remain uneasy about the necessity, in Pagan communities, of having laws against magical assault. If people believe in magic, then they must legislate against its misuse. Yet what laws of evidence can apply? The skilled magician may not need ceremonies or paraphernalia; so the way is left open for the persecution of an innocent person who has not even performed any magic yet cannot prove this.

However the same dilemma applies in the materialist world to cases of psychological assault. In her most recent work, ex-psychoanalyst Alice Miller argues for drastic intervention on the part of social workers, to prevent psychological damage to children by parents, believing–and here I agree with her–that such damage leads to compulsive criminal behaviour in adult life. Yet psychological theories change from year to year. We may agree in principle that children are susceptible to crucial imprinting in early life, yet psychodynamic theories are opaque to normal empirical tests. How do you measure the degree of hatred in a glance, or the healing quality of a hug? The experiment cannot be done. So how can we judge a parent for doing this or that subtle action to a child? This is the difficult decision that child care professionals have to face every day of their lives, and in this it seems to me they are in much the same position as the Inquisitors of old. In legislating about intangibles, we are treading on slippery ground, and a belief in magic is no different in kind from a belief in psychodynamic processes. It brings us hard up against the limits of the rules of evidence, rules which are already being tested in the social services.

Goddess Religion

A third feature of modern Pagan belief, which some branches of Paganism take as the primary feature, is the presence of the Goddess, the feminine face of divinity. Like its ancient predecessor and unlike the latter's philosophical systemisation, modern Paganism springs from preference and practice rather than from argument. It simply feels right to relate to a mother divinity; and her proper name *Goddess* is used: she is not called, as some feminist Christians try to do, Mother God. To test the difference, just take any passage referring to the supreme spiritual source as a male god, replace the gender-specific words with Goddess words, and see how you react.

> ***The Lady's Prayer***
> *Our Mother Which are in Heaven,*
> *Hallowed be Thy Name,*
> *Thy Kingdom Come,*
> *Thy Will be done,*
> *On earth ... etc.*

The difference we feel highlights our unconscious assumptions about the two sexes, which may or may not be accurate, but when denied in the mistaken belief that one gender can stand for both, simply confuse our attitude to deity. For Pagans, 'Goddess' is a word of dignity, just as 'God' is, and nowadays many Pagans personify the supreme Source, which we have already seen hypothesised in antiquity, not as 'the One' but as 'Goddess'. Here is a modern Goddess prayer:

> *May the Great Goddess watch over all peoples and bring them to the flowering of their fulfilment. May She nourish and protect them, who are all, unknowing, Her children.*
>
> *May She bring to them the knowledge of their fellowship within her hall, in which all races live, of their companionship at Her table, from which all nations eat.*
>
> *May all the men and women of Earth take up the stewardship of their inheritance. May joy and fulfilment come to those who care*

for this bright globe, may understanding come to those who labour unaware.

Let the grace of the Goddess be born within us all, the children of earth and Heaven. Let the knowledge of Her fellowship guide our actions and our lives.[11]

If the feminine gender is replaced by the masculine gender, once more, the effect is not quite the same. People's interpretations of Goddess-henotheism vary, and are probably best not crystallised into dogma, which will always contain inaccuracies and impose sexist restrictions. But among some ideas of a supreme source which exists and is called 'Goddess' are: that we belong in the universe as of right; that things left unsaid or inexplicit are as important as things that are explicitly formulated; that beauty is as important as strength ... and so on. Before attempting to formulate universal, non-gender-specific language, it is important to catch ourselves in the act of making androcentric assumptions and experiment with a universe that is gynocentric.

Bipolar Universe

Other Pagans by contrast see the universe as fluidly moving between two equal and opposite poles: the female principle, the Goddess, and the male principle, the God. This is rather different from Julian's model of a dual creative principle, the Great Mother and the Great Father, creating a series of subordinate levels of being.[12] The two interactive principles operate in all areas of existence, as in Chinese Taoism, with its principles of Yin and Yang, or perhaps as in the Empedoclean world-view, with its erotic/argumentative metaphor of the twin principles of Love and Strife. This gives a creative universe based on encounter and transformation, rather than a hierarchical one based on dominance and control. The metaphor of a fight to death or subordination, is the obvious one here. To move beyond the dominance–submission model is a radical move, one which involves dropping our habit of dominating our own rejected aspects and so leaves us vulnerable to the negative judgement of the patriarchal command-ego.

Command and control have their uses in the right place however (in Paganism there is no absolute evil), and the right place is not restricted to the primitive Indo-European war-band. All kinds of practical skills involve mastery over one's materials and the environment, and Pagans in the Northern Tradition in particular lay some stress on this. Honour and the heroic mentality too are highly valued. But I would dissent from any rigid attempt to promote any of these models as the One Truth. Creativity, craftsmanship and control lie on a continuum: no one of them will serve us for the whole of our lives. To repeat the words of Symmachus: 'How can a *single* road lead to so great a secret?'

Pluralism

The tolerance and flexibility of a polytheistic outlook, allowing many ways, many goddesses and gods, many philosophical schools in keen dispute with one another, is that of a religion that is suitable for our multicultural, postmodernist age. But like that age itself–and like the earlier age when the Hellenistic and then Roman empires were faced with assimilating peoples of widely differing cultures from their own–it can lack a centre. At this stage of its development, modern Paganism has not even begun to approach that problem. The cults of the different divinities are still being developed by their adherents, and the intellectual presuppositions of exclusive monotheism are still being identified and disempowered by those whose conscious minds are moving beyond them. To try to impose a planned-out official Paganism would not only be impossible, given the many Pagan paths at present, but probably undesirable, since it would play into the hands of the background monotheism of modern culture.

I distinguish the *strong pluralism* of the Pagan outlook with the *weak pluralism* of mere tolerance, itself perhaps a watered-down effect of Classical Pagan influences brought into European civilisation at the Enlightenment. Weak pluralism permits others to hold opinions that the pluralist does not share, but does not address the question of the rightful place of these differing opinions in the universe. It has difficulty standing up against zealous monotheists or dualists, because it cannot argue forcefully why there should be many paths rather than only one. Strong pluralism on the other hand argues in favour of the essential diversity of Nature. The strong pluralist will make claims such as that different ways of life are brought into being spontaneously as occasion demands, that what suits one community at one time will not suit another and hence should be defended by the one and resisted by the other, that an alien influence which is persistent expresses something in the nature of things that the host community has undervalued, and so on. There are various versions of strong pluralism, of which we have already seen one in the speech of Symmachus, referring to the unity of Nature which underlies the diversity we perceive. Another version might refer to the evolutionary strength of a diverse gene pool, arguing by analogy that what is good for the species is good for society. Diversity is welcomed by strong pluralism, but it is organised by some second-order ordering principle such as the unity of Nature, strength in diversity, etc. There is no room to discuss the various pluralistic outlooks here. Their relevant feature is that they find a comfortable home in a Pagan, polytheistic universe which is open to revelation, or at least to surprises, whereas they have the utmost difficulty making their way in a world whose official philosophy is that of the One Truth.

There is enormous scope for developing a philosophy of strong pluralism within the Pagan community, but at present two images seem to inspire Pagan tolerance. These are the ideas of *synergy* and the *circle*. The concept of synergy was developed by Peter Russell[13] and it has rapidly become a commonplace. There is great faith among Pagans of an underlying unity in the cosmos, whereby distinct and separate individuals find that their separate wills act in common, for the benefit of the whole. There is an assumption that commonality does not suppress individuality, and that individuals' interests are not automatically pitted against one another. This assumption is thought to rely on a certain maturity of outlook, which can take individual identity for granted and can identify with something larger, whether this is called 'goddess', 'process', or 'Nature'. This outlook is seen not just as a quality of the mature, enlightened individual but as an automatic process within Nature, which can simply be helped on its way by intelligent participation. Here again Paganism follows Nature rather than imposes structure upon it.

The circle, infinitely expansible, contractible to zero, in which all members are equal, is an image of this kind of synergy. Many Pagan groups hold their gatherings in a circular format, like the sacrifices of ancient Greece with their central altar, rather than following the polarised model of officiants facing a congregation. Sometimes this is seen as an unthinking imitation of Wicca, which has been the highest-profile Pagan path in recent years. But the Druid Order, which has celebrated at Stonehenge since long before the emergence of Wicca, uses this format in its public ceremonies, and as mentioned, ancient Greek public sacrifices took this shape. Post-war consciousness-raising groups also adopt a circular format in order to make every participant feel equally entitled to participate in the proceedings. Wiccan-derived Paganism is quite explicit about the circle as a containing structure, a symbol of the Goddess, and as an enabling structure to which all participants (actively) contribute and within which all are (passively) contained in equal measure.[14] Like the concept of synergy and by contrast with the control model, it unites the opposites of activity and passivity and it abolishes the more overt demonstrations of hierarchy. In this sense it is an active image in the formation of a distinctive Pagan outlook. At present it is the embodiment of a particular idea of pluralism.

Conclusions

Paganism then can be described as a religious outlook which is Nature-venerating, polytheistic and recognisant of the Goddess. It is not primarily a dogmatic religion, resting on belief in certain propositions, although it used the word 'dogma' before the religions of the Book, referring to conclusions its adherents had drawn from reflection on their experience. In its modern European form it depends on certain generally agreed assumptions, taken for granted by its followers but not, on the whole, debated. These form the basis of a distinctive religious outlook which has its own guidelines for approaching and perceiving divinity. I have presented five of these, which seem to me basic, and look forward to their further development in future debate.

Notes

1 *Poems of Pindar*, Trans. J.E. Sandys, Loeb classical series, Heinemann, 1968.

2 Spinoza's famous phrase, 'Dues sive Natura' ('God, otherwise known as Nature'), is often quoted by commentators and its implications are clear throughout his text, cf. note 4 below, but I cannot place an exact reference here.

3 The point was established by A. Harnack, tr. Neil Buchanan, *A History of Dogma*, Williams & Norgate, 1894. More recently Nick Campion, *The Great Year*, Penguin Arkana, 1994, has argued convincingly for a near-fusion of Greek and Jewish ideas throughout the Hellenistic period.

4 *Spinoza's Ethics*, trans. A. Boyle, I.29, scholium, Everyman, London, 1910.

5 *Plotinus' Enneads*, trans. A.H. Armstrong, VI.7.35, 36, Loeb classical series, Heinemann, 1988.

6 The epistemological terminology of the French logicians of Port-Royal, together with their contemporary Descartes, investigating the 'clarity and distinction' of ideas, and later of course Spinoza, another

Francophone philosopher, is also worth considering in this tradition. A. Hart, *Spinoza's Ethics*, Brill, 1983, has already analysed the thoroughly Platonic format of the late philosopher's argumentation.

7 Translation by Wilmer Cave Wright, Loeb edition of *The Works of the Emperor Julian*, vol. I, Heinemann, 1962.

8 Symmachus, *Relatio* 3.8,10, translation mine.

9 Prudence Jones and Nigel Pennick, *A History of Pagan Europe*, Routledge, 1995.

10 See the excellent discussion of the religious origins of substantialist historicism in Campion, *op. cit.*

11 Goddess prayer by Prudence Jones published in John Matthews (ed.) *Paths to Peace*, Century Hutchinson, 1992.

12 Such a model, derived from Theosophy with its seven levels of existence, is however proposed in Janet and Stewart Farrar *The Witches' Way*, Hale, pp106–14, 1984, in addition to the model of polarity described here.

13 Peter Russell, *The Awakening Earth*, RKP, London, 1982.

14 See for example Starhawk, *The Spiral Dance*, Harper and Row, 1979.

II

THE MAIN TRADITIONS IN CONTEMPORARY PAGANISM

Graham Harvey

HEATHENISM:

a North European Pagan Tradition

While most modern Pagans claim Celtic origins for their tradition, many of the ancestors of the people of Britain were Germanic or Scandinavian in origin. A growing number of groups and individuals are drawn to the traditions and history of these people(s) for inspiration. Many (though not all) such people and groups prefer to name themselves Heathen rather than Pagan. (Heathen is a north-European equivalent of the Latin-derived name 'Pagan' having similar connotations for those who use it). In this chapter I will use the terms 'Heathen' and 'Heathenism', but will make it clear that other self-designations are also used (e.g. 'Odinist'/'Odinism', 'Asatrú', 'Northern Tradition').

Along with other Pagan traditions Heathenism is growing numerically and in coherence. Heathenism shares many of the same characteristics, interests and problems as other Pagan traditions. It also has distinguishing features.

The significant groups in Britain are: two named The Odinic Rite; The Odinshof; the Rune Gild and the Ring of Troth (closely related); and *Hammarens Ordens Sällskap*. Each of these groups has different emphases and not all of them are mutually exclusive (i.e. some people belong to more than one organisation). I will say something more about these groups later. It should also be noted that there is a wider audience (not only among Pagans) for those things which are of central significance to Heathens. Books on Runes and Norse mythology abound and appear to be gaining extra space in the relevant sections (especially 'Religion' or 'Mind, Body, Spirit') of many bookshops. At present I do not have enough information for a useful discussion of a couple of the smaller groups.

Northern Cosmology

Here I only sketch the Cosmology that *many* Heathens (again note that this is not all-inclusive) consider to be their inheritance.

The world in which we live is but one of nine. These worlds are linked to the World Tree (Yggdrasil)–the exact manner of this linking varies in both the ancient sources and in the modern retellings. Our world, Midgard (popularised by Tolkien as Middle Earth), can be presumed to be central to the other worlds: some being above it, others below, though sometimes other worlds are said to revolve around it.

Each world is predominantly populated by one race or type of being: human in the case of our world, giants in one world, elves in another, divinities in two others and so on. There is continual movement between these worlds by those who are able to travel, particularly the divinities and the giants. Not all is peace and harmony; indeed there is usually conflict between giants and divinities. There is also movement up and down the World Tree which is itself continually being gnawed at and nibbled away by the various creatures inhabiting its roots, trunk or branches. The tree, however, is not only continually renewing itself but also nourishes those who devour it. The World Tree (and indeed much of this cosmology) is a 'memorable image of perpetual movement, destruction and renewal'.[1]

The divinities of these worlds are of two races: the Æsir and the Vanir. The Vanir are 'fertility deities of the earth, with Freyr and Njord and the goddesses Freyja and Frigg as the main powers' while the Æsir are 'gods of sovereignty, magic and warfare'.[2] Both groups have their own world or home. A primeval conflict between the two was resolved after an exchange of hostages who became significant allies, friends and marriage partners. The number of divinities of either or both groups is hard to calculate. Some are given more than one name, Odin has considerably more. It is possible that some names apparently applied to separate divinities may in fact refer to a hypostasis of a more well-known deity.

The difference between the two divine races is not one of gender. There are both Goddesses and Gods among the Æsir and the Vanir. Nor are Goddesses second-class citizens in this cosmology. Whilst Northern mythology is interested (obsessed at times) with fighting and breeding, the Goddesses are not all fertility symbols nor are all the Gods macho warriors. Unlike the deities of classical Rome, the northern Gods and Goddesses often performed many functions–they had many abilities or talents. This multi-functionality along with the conscious and expansive polytheism (there is no hint that anyone ever attempted to encapsulate the pantheon in one great God or Principle) are significant indicators of the wider diversities of north European history, cultures, cosmologies and so on. Even the broad unities (of place or language) are offset by many diversities (especially of clan and kin loyalties).

Polytheism enables the celebration of our everyday 'mundane' lives whereas monotheism tends to diminish these in favour of the exaltation of an afterlife of divine worship. Northern religion, Paganism and other polytheistic traditions in general, find meaning and value in the diverse ordinary lives of human beings. The deities introduce us to ourselves and do not only demand allegiance and worship.[3]

Additionally, these deities are not eternal. As with everything else in Nature (i.e. the totality of that which exists) Gods and Goddesses have beginnings (albeit long before human memory) and their deaths can be remembered in some cases (e.g. Balder) and anticipated in others.

At the foot of the World Tree are three sisters–the Norns or Weird Sisters. They are now popularly considered to be the only three spinners of Fate in all the worlds and are thought of as 'Past, Present and Future'. The *Edda*, however, presents a more complex situation in which 'fate' is a web spun out by the combined actions of many (perhaps all) beings. The *hamingja* (more than 'luck' but not quite 'destiny', and also something more poetic and mythic than 'genetic inheritance') of the group and sometimes of the individual is also significant. The three Norns are certainly central to this web. Their names might be better rendered by 'Past, Becoming, Unfolding'. Northern mythology and history suggest a great ambivalence between fatalism and complete free will. Fate was striven against more than it was meekly accepted.

There are many other significant other-than-human[4] inhabitants of the nine worlds. A group who were particularly important to the many migrating and settling folk of early medieval Europe (and much earlier too) were the 'hooded men' or 'land-spirits'. These have survived into northern English folklore as 'boggarts' and 'Brownies'. Hilda Davidson suggests that they now survive (in a cunning disguise or ignominious belittling) as garden gnomes.[5] 'Land-spirits' are those who help (but sometimes hinder) those humans who give them respect and share the same territory. They are inhabitants of this world and in some way mediate between the land and human inhabitants. Such other-than-human people illustrate an important feature of this cosmology: human relationships with other-than-human beings were a matter of contract and cohabitation (relationship and proximity, or 'neighbourliness' perhaps). While they were clearly polytheistic ancient Heathens might choose to show especial honour (or 'trust') to one or several of the deities (especially Odin, Thor and Freyr) and to their local land-spirits.

Hearth and home were central locations for religious ceremony in the past. There were temples and sacred sites (e.g. trees, rocks) which were foci for large public gatherings. Generally, though, priestly functions could be enacted by anyone. In a tradition for which there was no great barrier between 'the sacred' and 'the profane' and in which everyday events (birth, death, sex, cooking, etc.) were of interest to other-than-human people, the honouring of deities was not an unusual or specialised activity.

These are some of the features of the cosmology of pre-Christian northern Europe. Many of them remain significant in contemporary Heathenism.

Asatrú and Odinism

Before looking at the groups which constitute contemporary Heathenism I want to say a little about self-designations and self-presentations.

There is in Paganism and Heathenism a fluidity in the way people name themselves. This is not a dogmatic or static tradition. It is very much a tradition of finding yourself and finding a tradition or spirituality which expresses yourself. No dogmatic or central authority exists to insist on the use of any particular self-designation–this too is up to the individual. However, some names have become more common currency than others.

In Britain many people are happy with the name Heathen as a self-designation. It means to them much the same as the name Pagan means to those who use it, i.e. one who honours Nature and pre- or non-Christian divinities. Odinshof leader, Martyn Taylor, suggests that Heathenism also involves 'an element of ancestor worship' too.[6] However, many outsiders (even Pagan ones) are evidently unfamiliar with this usage. When I distributed a questionnaire including a question, 'do you name yourself a Pagan or Heathen?', some 'Pagans' were upset, believing that 'Heathen' was an insulting word. So, if Heathen is an 'insider's' name (though its usage has been spreading recently), what other names do Heathens use?

The Odinic Rite (both groups) and some members of The Odinshof consider 'Odinism' to be the most useful designation for their religion. They do not intend to suggest that Odin is the only deity, but do consider the name of Odin to be useful to summarise a pantheon over which that God presided during a significant period of time and in a significant number of places. That Odin was not always head of the pantheon, and never in the same way that Zeus or Yahweh ruled their pantheons, does not affect his undoubted importance in much of the literature. More to the point it does not affect the validity of the choice made by these people to give central place to Odin *now*. Pete Jennings says that one of the aims of Odinshof is 'to promote the ancient teachings and philosophy of Odin (Odintru or Asatru)'.[7] Some 'Odinists' are also happy to use this self-designation while having a closer relationship with other deities of the pantheon. The name also stresses continuity with the revivers of the tradition who chose to use it. It is also especially useful as Odin is perhaps the northern deity best known to 'outsiders' and thus might 'mean more' to them than a name drawn from German or Norse languages.

The Ring of Troth prefers to name their tradition 'the Elder Troth', defining 'Troth' as 'trust, loyalty, a promise ... or "belief" in the sense of "to trust in someone/something" '.[8] It also refers to 'True Folk', 'Troth Folk' and to 'Asatrú' ('trust in the [Germanic] Deities'). It recognises that some people prefer to name themselves 'Vanatrú' rather than 'Asatrú'.[9]

Asatrú refers to 'trust in the Aesir' but is frequently used (in English speaking countries as well as in Iceland where it is a recognised religion) synonymously with these other names. Those who name themselves Vanatrú, 'trusting in the Vanir', presumably hold that 'Asatrú' refers only to the Aesir. This is not to say that Vanatrú reject the Aesir, but that they give more attention to the Vanir deities. I should note that I am at present unaware of anyone in Britain who names their tradition Vanatrú. Similarly, there are people, in America at least, who name themselves Disírtrú, wishing to particularly stress their relationship with the Goddesses.

The *Hammarens Ordens Sällskap* have a longstanding close relationship with the God Thor but are no less polytheistic than other Heathen groups. They might accept the designation Asatrú but have problems with the name 'Odinist'. They 'do not believe in Odin', and note that Wodan is 'War' itself (literally and in as much as the God personifies war) and therefore not something by which to name yourself.[10] While the other Heathen groups do sometimes refer to themselves as 'Pagan', *Hammarens Ordens Sällskap* do not. They consider Paganism to be at least one step removed from the land, Nature or Earth in that many Pagans use some sort of altar. Whether this is a correct or completely adequate characterisation of Paganism or not, clearly it indicates the group's central concern with the land.

Another name used by some Heathens for their religion is 'the Northern Tradition'. Whilst this name can refer to magical or meditative practices on the analogy of 'the Western Tradition', it is also used with reference to the religion others prefer to call 'Odinism', 'Asatrú', 'Heathenism' and so on. For example, in an article entitled 'The Northern Tradition' Pete Jennings writes,

> *In using the words Northern Tradition, I imply the religious beliefs derived from the Scandinavian/Norse areas, including the places they colonised such as England, Ireland and Iceland, etc. I also include the related beliefs of the Anglo-Saxons, who derived from the same Germanic tribes.*[11]

That is to say, the phrase is synonymous with the other names noted.

Heathen groups in Britain

In the following sections I briefly introduce the groups named above. I deal first with the two Odinic Rites, then with Odinshof, the Rune Gild and Ring of Troth (together), and finally with *Hammarens Ordens Sällskap*. Please note that by treating one Odinic Rite before the other I do not express any view of the dispute between them or of which has most right to the name.[12]

The Odinic Rite

The first, 'The Odinic Rite'[13] has a ruling council called the Court of Gothar (*Gothar* being the plural of *Gothi*, a priest). The current director of the Court of Gothar is Ingvar. The Court has nine members including the Director and meets once every calendar month to conduct its business (which includes both priestly and administrative functions).[14] Stubba, a key figure in the development of modern Odinism, a previous director of the Court and editor of the *Book of Blots*, remains a significant member of the Court.

The Book of Blots[15] contains the official form and words for the Rite's monthly celebrations. There are also ceremonies for Baels (funerals),[16] handfastings (weddings), becoming a member of the Court of Gothar, various naming ceremonies and the oath of profession (on joining the Odinic Rite). All these ceremonies previously appeared as sheets printed for the relevant *blot*, ceremony, but are published here in their 'finalised, definitive and authoritative' form.[17]

The Odinic Rite does not celebrate the eight festivals common to most Pagan groups but does have closely-related ceremonies. In the Odinist calendar (published annually in *Rímstock*) the solstices and equinoxes are celebrated. The twelve months are given different names (e.g. September is Shedding) and each contains one major festive occasion with its associated ceremony, or *Blot*. Other significant dates are mentioned too. Following soon after the *Blot* of Hengest, celebrating the English settlement in Britain, on 12 Hunting/October, is the commemoration of the reclamation of the White Horse Stone in Kent. The stone is said to be the burial place of Horsa, who died during the battle in which he had co-led the English army. In 1985 the Odinic Rite restored the site as a place of worship and since then has conducted professions, *blots*, handfastings and the scattering of ashes of the dead there. They have also attempted to protect the site from the threat posed by the London–Paris rail link by, for example, a letter-writing campaign, meetings with the railway company concerned and with local councillors, and a TV appearance by Ingvar.

In addition to the publications referred to so far the Odinic Rite also produces a members' newsletter, *The Moot Horn*, and a magazine *Odinism Today* which contains news, articles, reviews and advertisements of interest to its readers. A number of booklets have also been produced both for members and for interested members of the public (e.g. *This is Odinism*, *Hidden Gods*, *The Language Tree*, *The Odinist Hearth*, and *Odinism and Christianity under the Third Reich*).

The Odinic Rite

The second Odinic Rite[18] are keen to say that the division between them and the other Odinic Rite was not 'a split'. Their organisation is much the same. The current Director of the Court of Gothar, Heimgest, was Director of the pre-division united Odinic Rite from 1989. This Odinic Rite has produced *The Book of Blotar of the Odinic Rite* in which it carefully makes clear that the ceremonies given are guidelines and not necessarily to be followed word for word. These ceremonies also include developments from earlier versions, including those published in the earlier *Book of Blots*, and are expected to continue evolving in the future.

This Odinic Rite's calendar is the same as that discussed above. Its main monthly *blotar*, festivals, are on the same dates and have the same names as those of the other Odinic Rite. In addition, new and full moons are listed among the 'other notable dates'[19] although there is no suggested ceremony in the *Book of Blotar* for these occasions. One difference between the structure of the ceremonies in the *Book of Blots* and those in the *Book of Blotar* is in a section labelled 'the Jarls' Rally'. In the *Book of Blots* this is a prayer for the Queen who is referred to as 'seed of Odin's royal line'. The *Book of Blotar* here reads, 'may those who lead be true, may those who follow be loyal'. This Odinic Rite prefers to express honour to leaders of their own faith rather than to 'hail the leader of an alien creed as our leader'.[20]

As with the other Odinic Rite the (Runic) Odinic Rite has local groups called Hearths. At present it has eleven functioning Hearths in Britain, several more in embryonic stage and more in Europe and America.

In addition to the publications already referred to they also produce *OR Briefing* and *The North Wind*, a yearbook containing news, articles, poetry and art work of a high standard.

A major stress of this Odinic Rite is summed up in the words beneath their logo: 'Faith, Folk, Family'. Along with other Heathen groups they are keen to stress that they are not racist but do believe that each 'race' has a tradition which people would be more fulfilled following. They encourage the development of the culture of each 'race'[21] believing that only confusion and stress can come from the mix of peoples and cultures. Odinism is considered to be the primary cultural tradition of the people of Britain descended from Germanic and Scandinavian ancestry. Nonetheless, neither this Odinic Rite nor the one previously noted, have much time for 'political correctness', and some members certainly hold views similar to those of right-wing political groups.[22] The Odinic Rite, as a charity, is not permitted to be 'political' and the Court of Gothar suggests that all shades of political opinion (though fewer to the left of centre) are represented among Odinic Rite members.

They have continued to develop their use of *Galdr*, primarily rune-chanting–the entire set of runes are often chanted near the beginning of ceremonies. Another strong and developing tradition is that of *taufr*, the making and use of talismans, especially those with runic inscriptions. Historical sources evidence some concern about *Seidr*, more shamanic practices. This Odinic Rite is contemptuous of 'what passes for Seidr today', considering it to be more a 'rehash of Crowley' than a development of the ancestral tradition.[23]

This Odinic Rite also has an interest in the White Horse Stone and continues to participate in attempts to prevent the new rail link between Paris and London from destroying, damaging or encroaching upon it. However, while the Odinic Rite is deeply concerned with

'Green' issues, they are also concerned to be seen as part of what they call 'the mainstream'. This involves a negative view not only of some of the wilder, more shamanic practices of *Seidr*, but also of homosexuality which they see as 'unnatural', 'confused' and no part of Odinism.

The Odinshof

The Odinshof[24] has approximately 200 members organised in Hearths. Its objects are 'to promote the ancient teachings and philosophy of Odin (Odintrú) and to advance education'.[25] It considers Odintrú to be analogous to Buddhism, with Odin as an enlightened teacher and wider Asatrú as being like Hinduism in relation to Buddhism.[26]

Unlike either Odinic Rite, Odinshof celebrates the eight festivals common in Paganism. There are also regular rituals (called *Maniblot*) at full moons. This has led some Odinic Rite members to consider Odinshof to be 'Wiccan' rather than Heathen.

They also consider the multi-cultural and multi-faith nature of contemporary Britain to be a good thing. They do not stress race and consider that lesbian, gay and bisexual people bring a 'special kind of spirituality into the movement'.[27]

The Odinshof is organised into local Hearths although some members prefer to follow a solitary path. Each Hearth has a Hearth Guardian, basically an overseer, and is encouraged to develop its own character and initiate its own activities. The Ipswich Hearth, for example, produces its own magazine, *Gippeswic*, in addition to the Odinshof's magazine, *Odalstone*. There are two grades of membership: Odal grade, a novitiate (named after the rune *odal*), lasting at least 13 lunar months, and above that the Oak grade. The ruling council is the Witan Assembly led by Martyn Taylor with a number of other members (currently four) of Oak grade. In addition to training *Gothar*, 'parish priests/priestesses', Odinshof is also developing the roles of *volva*, female seer, and *grimsrular*, shamanistic warrior/priests skilled in rune-lore.[28]

Odinshof is particularly concerned with ecology. They have established a 'Land Guardians' scheme which aims to buy an area of woodland to restore it to 'wildwood'. They hope that in the long term a whole series of woods can be purchased. Odinshof members are also actively involved in other ecological actions and Odinshof publications often contain news about these and information about trees and woodland.

The Rune Gild-UK and Ring of Troth

The Rune Gild-UK[29] is part of a larger organisation centred in the USA and founded by Edred Thorsson. In Britain it is led by Freya Aswynn and has developed its own character. The Rune Gild's primary approach to the northern tradition is the study and mysteries of the runes. Edred Thorsson's book *The Nine Doors of Midgard*[30] forms the curriculum for the Gild. Freya Aswynn's own book, *Leaves of Yggdrasil*,[31] is also important. While both books are about the runes and provide interpretations of their meanings and their uses, they are quite different in approach and character. Freya's book is simpler to use in the sense that it stands alone whereas Thorsson's often refers to his other works. Thorsson also expects the reader to work through the book slowly, sometimes taking weeks to practise exercises in which posture, meditation, chanting, memorisation and further reading are required. This is of course necessary in the Gild's curriculum which takes the reader through the Apprentice stage of the Gild. As with the old craft Guilds the Rune Gild has Apprentices, Fellows (or Journeymen) and Masters. Beyond the grade of Master is *Drighting* or *Drighten*, or Grandmaster. Freya Aswynn is *Drighting* and Edred Thorsson is the Gild's *Yrmin Drighten* (highest Grandmaster perhaps). Some other Heathen groups have expressed concern (and considerable opposition) to Edred Thorsson (at least partly) because of his status as a leading member of the Temple of Set, a 'Satanist' organisation.[32] Indeed his books on the Runes are frequently indistinguishable from his Temple of Set writings–e.g. he refers to Odin as 'Lord of Light and Drighten of Darkness' and uses the word 'becoming' as the Temple of Set does.[33] However, previous to their discovery of his Temple of Set connections these same groups warmly recommended Thorsson's *Futhark*, if not his other works. It seems they have fallen prey to the more widespread 'Satanism scare', now hopefully dying away.

The Rune Gild-UK has developed a distinctive character within the Gild. It has developed more communal celebrations alongside the Gild's individual Mysteries approach to the runes. It is also much more focused on the God Odin. Alongside the practice of *Galdr*, rune chanting, the Rune Gild-UK stresses *Seidr*, more shamanic practices. Freya Aswynn is a 'channel' or 'horse' for Odin and both teaches and demonstrates trance techniques.

The Gild 'rejects racist politics and views, without detracting from pride in one's own tradition' but also says that it is 'open to all who have a demonstrable "contact" with the Northern Folksoul'.[34] There is some ambiguity over race issues, the tradition is seen as appropriate for northern Europeans but Freya Aswynn is happy to acknowledge that she has learnt much from practitioners of Candomble. In common with many Pagans and other Heathens Freya Aswynn sees the Aesir and Vanir divinities (or 'God-forms') as manifestations of wider divine essences. She uses the analogy of a computer system in which the God-forms are like files in relation to the underlying deeper essence of DOS, manifested through Windows and Word.[35]

There are at present thirty members of the Rune Gild in Britain, though many more people may be studying Thorsson's book (recently reprinted) and thus be eligible to call themselves 'Apprentice' or 'Learner' of the Gild. Membership of other groups is not precluded and the 'inner' work of the Gild is seen as complementing the 'outer' work of other groups. Freya Aswynn also runs a correspondence course (from the same address) and often gives interviews and speaks at meetings of other groups.

In addition to being part of the Rune Gild this group has close links with the broader Ring of Troth movement. The Ring of Troth is a significant part of the wider Asatrú movement and is especially strong in the USA. However, its current leader or Warder of the Lore is Kveldúlfth Gundarsson who has recently completed a PhD in Cambridge on 'The Cult of Odhinn: God of Death' (under his given name, Stephan Grundy). The Ring of Troth has produced (under Gundarsson's editorship) a large work collecting articles about almost every conceivable issue of importance to Asatrúar.[36] It also includes a detailed reading list, some ceremonies and the 'Byelaws of The Troth' as a registered religious/cultural organisation in the USA. This is distributed in Britain by the Rune Gild. Stephan Grundy has clarified the group's objection to fascism and racism, saying that the Northern tradition is 'a matter of heart and soul and not of skin colour'.[37]

Hammarens Ordens Sällskap

The *Hammarens Ordens Sällskap* is now centred on the Wirral[38] though it originates among Swedish families as 'an ancient and Archaic Order of Heathen Geomann Cniths' (Yeoman Knights). The primary concern of the group, whose name translates as 'In the Company of the Order of the Hammer', is ecological and practical. They wish to re-establish a yeomanry of self-sufficient organic farmers and smallholders and are also interested in crafts and folk culture. They hope to publish a magazine called *Landfolc* to further explore and disseminate their interests.

Their 'theology' reflects these interests. They consider the Vanir deities to be most intimately connected with the land. The Aesir are more complex: they are both ancestors, actual human beings, and also the goals, aims, dreams or virtues which people work towards. They are not mere 'wishes' but achievable goals, assimilable virtues, albeit requiring some hard work. Some divinities are also described as expressions of natural phenomena or names for roles in 'real life': Balder *is* the summertime, Ullr *is* Yule and also the 'warrior hunter-gatherer', Frigga *is* the real mother. The Order does not believe in Odin, considering the things associated with that name (especially the 'all-father' theme) to be Christian additions to the northern tradition. Woden or Wotan *is* war itself and the group is therefore 'not keen on it. It brings out too many negative feelings'.[39]

The Order considers Paganism to be distinguishable from Heathenism because it stands at one step removed from the actual land. They say that the use of altars is unnecessary because they direct attention away from the land itself. The Temple at Uppsala was burnt down by Christian decree but with participation by truly Heathen groups who realised that it was an unnecessary structure for those who celebrated and actually lived from the land. On the whole, though, the Order gets on fairly well with other groups, including the Odinic Rite.

The stress on what the group considers to be 'natural', especially 'culture and land', does involve a negative view of multi-culturalism and of homosexuality. They consider that the 'mixture' of kinds (in both race and sexuality) causes confusion, unhappiness and problems especially in the cities. Their solutions are to do with family groups settling small areas of land, small-holdings, and an end to immigration. Changes and confusions are nothing new, according to their views, as the Aesir can be seen to have changed along with the movement of peoples in the past. The Vanir, however, remained largely unchanged. This serves as a moral lesson about the need to keep a strong relationship with the land and the foundations of a people's identity even though their aspirations may change. Foreign immigration into Britain can be seen as a leaving behind of the Vanir-type foundations which the Order considers damaging to people's well-being.

The group's motto, *Lif ok Lifthrasir*, 'life and survival', is said to be the key to the revitalisation of the World Tree, the deities and the people of Britain. 'Life and survival' involves organic farming, crafts, encouraging people (especially the descendants of the original Swedish families of the Order) to reconnect with the land and revitalise 'the Traditional Self-sufficient Organic Folk Culture of these our Homeland Isles'.[40] The Order uses the symbols of the Bear and the Ox for the two focuses of their tradition: land and culture. Its logo is a circle containing a tree and a horn. Different background colours indicate which branch the wearer belongs to: *Ordens*, Associate, Junior. The broader 'Landarmy' is akin to a conservation volunteers group (and works alongside several such groups) and includes both Heathens (the actual Order) and non-Heathens who share the Order's organic self-sufficient ecological principles.

Other People and Books

Before concluding I want to briefly mention a few other related people and books. A book called *The Odin Brotherhood* has been circulating which claims to be a record of contacts (in Britain and elsewhere) between Dr Mark Mirabello and a secret society called the Odin Brotherhood.[41] Whilst I have received enigmatic letters claiming to be from members of the group I have been unable to check the veracity of Mirabello's claims. No other group that I have talked to (including one that was named in a 'Brotherhood' letter as a contact) has any more knowledge of the group beyond reading the book. Most doubt its existence.

Jan Fries' book introduces another system of rune use, combining the arts of *galdr*, *taufr* and *seidr*.[42] There are valuable discussions not only of the runes themselves and of posture, chanting and meditation, but also of history and cosmology. The writer is well know among 'magickians' for other books in the magical tradition, especially his *Visual Magick*.[43] *Helrúnar* is a detailed but accessible book which will probably lead to a greater interest in the Northern Tradition, initially among those currently involved in the more high- or ritual-magical practices. It contains a particularly valuable section on the 'Seidr seething trance'.

Ivar Hafskjold runs courses under the auspices of the International Stav Association.[44] Stav means 'the knowledge of the Rune sticks' and the courses involve physical exercises and postures based on the runes, mythology, healing, martial arts, meditation and consciousness raising.

In addition to these religious and magical groups I should mention that many people in Britain are involved in groups who aim to 're-enact' aspects of Viking, English or Saxon society. Many of these are 'battle re-enactment societies' but some are developing more 'cultural' interests too.

Interest in the runes is also widespread if not always informed by the complete and complex cosmologies of some of these Heathen groups. One example of a widening and popularising of the runes among other Pagans is the use by the Dragon environmental group of a complex cosmological and magical bindrune.

Conclusion

Heathenism is in some ways distinguishable from the broader Pagan movement in Britain. Like the broader movement, however, it is growing numerically. It is also gaining increasing confidence as a religious tradition.

Wiccans and other followers of the Craft often suffer from the deeply-instilled cultural negative stereotype of the 'witch'. It is rarely possible to say 'witch' without evoking deep fears and prejudice. Druids perform open outdoor celebrations in public places such as Avebury and London's Primrose Hill (though rarely at Stonehenge) and face humour rather than hostility. Heathens stand somewhere between the two. They can be public about some of their activities and views without the barrier erected by the word 'witch', but some of their symbols (e.g. the swastika) and interests can cause alarm.

Undoubtedly many Heathens do hold views of race and sexuality which are far from 'politically correct'. A few certainly hold neo-Nazi views. This makes their relationship with other 'Earth-respecting' groups difficult. Certainly, however, some groups nuance these views carefully and others reject them altogether.

More positively, Heathenism has much to teach Pagans about the value and power of a self-consciously polytheistic tradition. Many Pagans moderate their polytheism with the somewhat confusing statement 'all Goddesses are one Goddess'. Some Heathens seem to have become increasingly involved in ecology and in celebrating their tradition out-of-doors instead of within buildings as seemed to be the case a few years ago. In short, Heathenism is changing in similar ways to the broader Pagan movement, and becoming more like that movement in some ways, without losing what is most distinctive in its own tradition.

Notes

1 Davidson, H.R.E. 'Mythical Geography in the Edda Poems' in Flood, G. (ed.) *Mapping Invisible Worlds*, pp95–106, Edinburgh University Press 1993.

2 Davidson, H.R.E. 'Hooded Men in Celtic and Germanic Tradition' in Davies, G. (ed.), *Polytheistic Systems*, Cosmos 5, pp105–24, Edinburgh University Press 1989.

3 Green, D. 'Towards a reappraisal of Polytheism' in Davies, G., *Polytheistic Systems,* Cosmos 5, pp3–11, Edinburgh University Press 1989.

4 An inclusive phrase drawn from Hallowell, A.I. 'Objibwa Ontology, Behaviour and world view' in Diamond, S. (ed.), *Culture in History: Essays in Honour of Paul Radin*, pp19–52, Columbia University Press, 1960.

5 Davidson, 'Hooded Men', p114.

6 Taylor, M., letter 18 September 1994.

7 Jennings, P. 'Odinshof' in *The Talking Stick Magical Directory*, pp10–11, Talking Stick, 1994. Pete Jennings is here quoting from the New Constitutions of the Odinshof.

8 The Ring of Troth, *Our Troth*, p1 The Ring of Troth, 1993.

9 The Ring of Troth, *Our Troth*, various pages, especially 58, 60–1.

10 Personal communication with Ingga, a leading member of the group.

11 Jennings, P. 'The Northern Tradition' in *The Talking Stick Magical Directory*, p10.

12 Both Odinic Rites use the Registered Charity number 298688, and have similar structures and origins.

13 The Odinic Rite, BM Edda, London WC1N 3XX.

14 *Constitutions of the Odinic Rite*, The Information Committee of the Odinic Rite, 1989.

15 Stubba (ed.), *Book of Blots*, Odinic Rite, 1991.

16 Discussed in my 'Death and Remembrance in Modern Paganism' in Davies, J. (ed.) *Ritual and Remembrance: Responses to Death in Human Societies*, pp103–22, Sheffield Academic Press, 1994.

17 Ralph Harrison, 'The Book of Blots: an appreciation' in *Odinism Today,* 3 (July 1991), pp1–3.

18 The Odinic Rite, BCM Runic, London WC1N 3XX.

19 *Rimstock* 1994, 2.

20 Heimgest, undated letter, October, 1994.

21 Their new 'Dragoning' ritual is said to be usable by any 'folk nation' and is offered as a 'gift for all' but is particularly applicable to the English. *Rimstock* 1994, pp7–12.

22 Thor Sannhet, 'Odinism *versus* the Occult' in *The North Wind* 3 (1993), pp41–60.

23 Heimgest, letter 12 Hunting 2244re (22 October 1994).

24 Odinshof, BCM Tercel, London WC1N 3XX.

25 *New Constitutions of Odinshof*, 17 May 1989.

26 *Odalstone 1* (1988), 2.

27 Taylor, M., letter, 15 August 1994.

28 Jennings, P. 'Working with the Northern Tradition', *Gippeswic* 3 (1993), pp18–20; and Taylor, M., letter 18 September 1994.
29 Rune Gild-UK, BM Aswynn, London WC1N 3XX.
30 Thorsson, E. *The Nine Doors of Midgard*, St Paul, MM: Llewellyn, 1991.
31 Aswynn, F. *Leaves of Yggdrasil*, St Paul, MM: Llewellyn, 1990.
32 See my article, 'Satanism in Contemporary Britain' in the *Journal of Contemporary Religion* 10, 1995.
33 Thorsson, *Nine Dorrs*, ppxxvii, xxxii.
34 Aswynn, F. 'The Rune Gild UK', *Talking Stick Magical Directory*, p11.
35 Aswynn, F., personal discussion.
36 The Ring of Troth, *Our Troth*, The Ring of Troth, 1993.
37 Stephen McNallen in 'Interface with Stephan Grundy', *Pagan Voice* 32 (September 1994), p11.
38 109 Gorsedale Road, Pulton, Wallasey, Wirral L44 4AN.
39 Ingga, personal discussion.
40 From the group's information sheet concerning the structure of the 'New Saxon Yeomanry' or 'Treowweard Organic Conservation Landarmy'.
41 Mirabello, M. *The Odin Brotherhood*, Sure Fire Press, 1992.
42 Fries, J. *Helrunar: a manual of rune magick*, Mandrake Press, 1993.
43 Fries, J. *Visual Magick*, Mandrake Press, 1992.
44 The International Stav Association, PO Box 915, Hull HU7 5XP.

Philip Shallcrass

DRUIDRY TODAY

When people find out that I am a Druid, the question which usually follows is, 'What do Druids do then?' Unfortunately, this is not a question which lends itself to a short answer, so it is good to have this opportunity to deal with it a little more fully.

The popular image of the Druid is that of a harmless and colourful eccentric in the finest English tradition, dressed in a white robe and doing amusing things for the tourists at Stonehenge. This impression of Druids is not entirely divorced from reality. In my experience, most Druids who have robes do tend to opt for white ones, albeit in a number of different styles. However, with the addition of blue, green or red tabards, black cloaks, and even the occasional orange silk kaftan, Druid gatherings are usually quite colourful. As for being eccentric, in my experience the majority of followers of the tradition are decent, kind, intelligent people pursuing their chosen spiritual path for the fulfilment they find within it. If this is deemed eccentric, then so be it.

To call Druidry a 'spiritual path' immediately raises the thorny question of whether or not it is, in fact, a religion. To some the answer may seem obvious; the pagan Celts practised Druidry as their religion, therefore modern Druidry must also be a religion. Unfortunately, things are not quite that simple. For a start, the Druid caste, which included Bards (poets, story-tellers and singers) and Ovates (philosophers, diviners), comprised only a small section of pagan Celtic society, and it is by no means clear that their religious practices were the same as those of the rest of the population. It seems likely that they functioned something like the Brahmin caste of India, that is, that they had their own sets of beliefs, rites, duties and obligations, but they also acted as priests for their local communities, officiating at weddings, funerals, sacrifices, and so on, in whatever religious traditions prevailed in their area. For most purposes then, the term Druid may have implied something like 'priest,' 'philosopher' or 'sage' rather than denoting a follower of a particular unified religion or a specific deity.

Another problem arose during the 18th century Druid revival, most of whose leaders were devout Christians. They often went to great lengths to deny Druidry as a pagan religion, coming up with all sorts of ingenious arguments about Druids being monotheistic, of their being descendants of one of the Lost Tribes of Israel, even of their being the originators of the Judeo-Christian faith. Then, in the 1960s, young people turned away from established Churches in droves, and many became disillusioned with, and suspicious of, the very notion of religion. For a combination of these reasons, or for others of their own, many Druid groups have preferred to portray Druidry as a philosophy, an ethical code, or a way of life, rather than a religion. The Order of Bards, Ovates and Druids (O.B.O.D.), for example, for several years explicitly stated in their introductory material that Druidry was not a religion. This statement has now been dropped, after a member wrote in giving a definition of the term 'religion' which clearly included O.B.O.D.'s version of Druidry.

This leaves open the question of whether modern Druidry sees itself as a pagan religion. The only answer I can give is that some Druids are more pagan than others. Some are overtly pagan, some are avowedly Christian, others try to steer a path between the two, others simply say that being a Druid has nothing whatever to do with religion. Druidry has certainly always attracted a good number of Christians and indeed Christian ministers, many of whom might feel rather awkward about being associated with paganism, although a surprising number are very friendly towards the pagan movement. On the other hand, I attended a Druid gathering a couple of years ago at which several Druids expressed their surprise and dismay at finding pagan stallholders selling occult and magical books and paraphernalia.

Fortunately, Druidry seems to find room for adherents of many faiths within it. This is partly because Druids tend to be unusually open and tolerant in their outlook, and partly because we know so little about what Druids got up to in the past that we are free to concoct just about anything and call it Druidry today. Given this fact, it is not surprising that modern Druidry is so rich and diverse in its practices, and it is to these practices that we must now turn our attention.

There is a widespread belief that Druid ceremonies are always open and take place in public. Some Druids do indeed celebrate their major festivals in public. These festivals are usually the same eight celebrated by Wiccans, that is, the four so-called Fire Festivals of Halloween, Candlemas, May Day and Lammas, often known among both Druids and Wiccans by their Irish names; Samhain, Imbolc, Beltaine and Lughnasad, less commonly by their Welsh names; Nos Galan Gaeof, Gwyl Fair, Calan Mai and Gwyl Awst, together with the Winter and Summer Solstices and the Spring and Autumn Equinoxes.

The Summer Solstice has always been particularly enthusiastically celebrated by Druid revivalists, most publicly at Stonehenge, where Druids had regularly gathered throughout the present century, until the current sad and futile policy of exclusion zones was introduced a decade ago. The vast majority of Druids, however, celebrate the festivals and other rites in private, not because they have anything to hide, or any great desire for secrecy, but because they enjoy the peace and tranquillity of their own homes or gardens, or a quiet corner of the countryside. Many certainly find privacy more conducive to the practice of Druidry than being surrounded by hordes of tourists armed with camcorders.

A major reason for the popularity of the Summer Solstice with Druids is that it represents the triumph of Light, as represented by the sun, which reaches its greatest height at noon on that day. This points up some of the perceived differences between Druidry and the most widespread and well-known of modern pagan groupings; Wicca.[1] These are that Druids reverence the sun and perform their rites in daylight, whereas Witches revere the moon and operate at night. By the same token, Druidry is seen as rational and patriarchal, Witchcraft as intuitive and feminist. In general, these remarks are truer of Wicca than they are of modern Druidry.

Yes, Druids do reverence the sun for many reasons, primarily as a symbol of spiritual light. The great 18th-century charlatan, scholar and Druid revivalist, Edward Williams, better known by his Bardic name, Iolo Morganwg, did much to encourage this concept when he wrote that:

> *A gorsedd of the bards of the island of Britain must be held in a conspicuous place, in full view and hearing of country and aristocracy, and in the face of the sun and the eye of Light; it being unlawful to hold such meetings either under cover, at night, or under any circumstance, other than while the sun is visible in the sky: or, as otherwise expressed –*
>
> *A chair and gorsedd of the British bards shall be held conspicu-*

ously, in the face of the sun, in the eye of Light, and under the expansive freedom of the sky, that all may see and hear.[2]

Iolo's first proclamation of his Gorsedd of the Bards of Britain, spoken on Primrose Hill in London in 1792, included the words, 'We assemble face to the Sun, in the Eye of Enlightenment', which are still used by some English Druid groups and, in translation, form part of the ritual of the Welsh Gorsedd of Bards when they meet at the annual Royal National Eisteddfod.

Some modern Druids follow Morganwg and his contemporaries in seeing the light of the sun as a symbol of God, or of Christ in his glory. Others identify it with one or more of the many sun Gods in Celtic mythology, such as the Welsh Lleu Llaw Gyffes, whose name means 'Light of the Steady Hand', or his Irish counterpart, Lugh Lamhfada, 'Light of the Long Arm'.

As for being patriarchal, Druidry is no longer the exclusively male preserve some of the 18th-century revival groups tried to make it, nor does it neglect the feminine and the intuitive. I know of only one contemporary Druid group which does not admit women on an equal footing with men, and even they have women's Lodges and an active internal group lobbying for change. For the rest, men and women seem to be represented in about equal proportions, and many women have active and prominent roles within Druidry. The Council of British Druid Orders, for example, is currently chaired by Liz Murray, who is also its permanent Secretary.[3]

Several modern Druid Orders are divided into three sections or grades: Bards, Ovates and Druids, admission to which is usually through some form of initiation ceremony. In many, the Bardic grade lays great emphasis on creativity and intuition. A core concept of the medieval Welsh Bardic tradition, and one which is returning to prominence in some modern Druid groups, is that of Awen. Awen is often translated as 'inspiration', or 'muse', but its literal meaning is 'fluid essence', or 'flowing spirit'. Medieval Bards viewed it as the source of their poetic genius, and specifically associated it with the Goddess Ceridwen. In the 9th-century tale, the Hanes Taliesin, the Bard Taliesin drinks three drops of Awen in liquid form from the Cauldron of Inspiration brewed by Ceridwen. He thereby gains the gifts of poetry, clairvoyance, and shape-shifting.[4] These three gifts loosely equate with the nature of the three grades of Bard, Ovate and Druid. It could thus be argued that Druidry, far from being patriarchal, in fact derives its primary inspiration from a spiritual essence which is the gift of a Goddess.

The Hanes Taliesin represents Ceridwen partly in the guise of a shape-shifting witch, so it is perhaps not surprising that she is also popular among Witches. Perhaps this is one reason for the increasing number of crossovers between Wicca and Druidry which have been occurring in recent years. Many Wiccan groups use Celtic God-names and symbolism in their rituals, and an increasing number of modern Druid groups use Wiccan elements in their rites. My own British Druid Order grew out of a Wiccan Coven, so we began with a strong Wiccan content in our rites, although this has gradually diminished over the years. However, I recently saw a televised ritual performed (at night) by the Portsmouth-based Insular Order of Druids, in which the opening of the circle was almost pure Wicca; the consecration with salt, water, and incense; the speech beginning 'I conjure thee, O Circle of Power'; the drawing of Pentagrams at the four quarters, accompanied by the speech ending 'I do summon, stir, and call you up, to witness our rites and to guard the Circle'.[5]

I know of at least four Druid Orders which had origins in Wicca, and I have met a number of Druids who were, at one time, Witches. Curiously, I have yet to meet a Wiccan who used to be a Druid. Whether this means that the flow is all in one direction, and what that might signify were it true, I cannot say. In my own case, I became a Wiccan largely because I was unable to track down a Druid group in the late 1970s. Many of the modern Orders simply didn't exist then, while those which did exist didn't advertise the fact.

I referred above to the great diversity of practice among modern Druids. There is, however, one formula common to most modern Druid groups, and that is the prayer known either as the Gorsedd Prayer, or the Universal Druid Prayer. This was composed by Iolo Morganwg at the end of the 18th century. It goes as follows:

Grant, O God, thy protection,
And in protection, strength,
And in strength, understanding,
And in understanding, knowledge,
And in knowledge, the knowledge of justice,
And in the knowledge of justice, the love of it,
And in that love, the love of all existences,
And in the love of all existences, the love of God,
God and all goodness.

This is one of several versions given by Iolo Morganwg in his writings.[6] It should be noted, however, that many modern Druids, myself included, prefer to say Goddess rather than God, and some even say God and Goddess. Versions of this prayer are heard at most Druid festivals, including the Welsh National Eisteddfod. There is another speech which occurs fairly frequently at Druid gatherings. It is usually spoken after everyone present has linked hands in a circle.

We swear by peace and love to stand,
Heart to heart and hand in hand,
Mark, O Spirit, and hear us now,
Confirming this, our sacred vow.

Another common feature of many Druid gatherings is the Awen chant. This consists of the word Awen intoned as a prolonged, low monotone, three times in succession:

Aaa-ooo-eee-nnn, Aaa-ooo-eee-nnn, Aaa-ooo-eee-nnn.

Its purpose is to invoke the inspirational presence of the Spirit into the circle. The form which the chant now takes may have been influenced by the Hindu AUM chant which became popular in the West in the 1960s. Certainly earlier in this century, Awen was used by Druids as an equivalent to the Christian Amen, as a sort of spiritual full stop at the end of a prayer. There are, however, references in their poetry which suggest that medieval Welsh Bards may have chanted or sung the Awen, so perhaps, in this instance, modern Druids are reviving a genuine ancient tradition.

With these few exceptions, modern Druid rituals tend to differ widely from group to group, some being written for specific events, as and when the need arises. Even in groups such as O.B.O.D., who produce teaching material including rituals as part of their mail order course, members often adapt or completely rewrite the rituals for their own use.[7] Writers of Druid rituals draw on a wide variety of sources, by no means all of them Celtic. I myself have incorporated African, Native American and Hindu elements into rites where they seemed appropriate and expressed what I wanted to say.

The search for an 'authentic' Druidry is like shooting arrows at the moon: both activities are essentially futile, but are great fun for their own sake. If we take it that British Druidry existed in its purest form before the Romans came to stay in 43 CE, then we have to face the sad fact that the Druids of that time did not leave us a single written account of any of their myths or ceremonies. We are left with the fragmentary, biased and usually second- or third-hand accounts of Celtic religion given by Greek and Roman writers, and with what archaeologists can recover from physical remains.[8]

Our next best source of information is the large body of medieval Irish and Welsh manuscripts which contain Celtic myths, histories, genealogies, poetry and other fragments of the medieval Bardic and perhaps the earlier Druidic tradition.[9] The very earliest of these compositions date from the 6th century CE, while most are no older than the 9th. The manuscripts themselves date, for the most part, from the 12th to the 15th centuries. They were mainly written by Christian monks for a Christian audience, but they do preserve some genuinely pagan elements; names of deities and garbled accounts of their myths; echoes of the Celtic reverence for sacred wells, springs, trees, rivers, and so on. Many modern Druids are going back to these old texts, as did previous generations of Druid revivalists, and reinterpreting them in the light of their own understanding. In doing so they are, in effect, creating a new Druidry, based on what has gone before, but made relevant to the times in which we now live.[10]

The medieval manuscript sources contain many myths in which young heroes, who can be interpreted as sun Gods, pass through phases of life which can be identified with the yearly cycle of festivals referred to earlier. In the British Druid Order, we base our festival celebrations on the story of Lleu Llaw Gyffes, as recounted in the Mabinogion. We celebrate his birth at the Winter Solstice, his naming at Candlemas, and his arming at the Spring Equinox, all of which are overseen by his mother, the Goddess Arianrhod, whose celestial home is the constellation known as Corona Borealis, the Northern Crown. On May Eve, the maiden Blodeuedd is created from flowers of oak and broom and meadowsweet, and by the incantations of the Druids, Math and Gwydion, to be a bride for Lleu. At the Summer Solstice, he reaches the height of his powers. At Lammas, he marries Blodeuedd and we celebrate the first fruits of the harvest, the result of their union, the union of sun God and Earth Goddess. At the Autumn Equinox, we celebrate the climax of the harvest season. At Samhain, Blodeuedd leads Lleu to his death at the hands of his dark twin, the Lord of Winter. His spirit departs in the form of an eagle, only to be reborn in human shape once more at the Winter Solstice, when Gwydion finds the eagle perched high in an oak tree, and sings the following incantation:

Oak that grows between two banks;
Darkened is the sky and hill!
Shall I not tell him by his wounds,
That this is Lleu?

Oak that grows in upland ground,
Is it not wetted by the rain?
Has it not been drenched by nine score tempests?
It bears in its branches Lleu Llaw Gyffes.

Oak that grows beneath the steep;
Stately and majestic is its aspect!
Shall I not speak it?
That Lleu will come to my lap?

As he sings, Lleu descends the oak tree, until he comes to Gwydion, who restores Lleu to human form by striking him with his wand. This is the wand over which Arianrhod steps as she gives birth to Lleu. And so the cycle begins again.

As I have already indicated, Druidry today embraces many elements of non-Celtic origin. Various aspects of Native American tradition have been taken up, notably the Sweat Lodge, as practised among the Plains Indians. There is some evidence that the Celts may have used a form of Sweat Lodge themselves, although their remains are usually identified either as dwellings or as cooking pits. A variety of 'shamanic' practices such as drumming, dancing, chanting, visionary journeying, contact with 'power animals' and the use of 'power objects' such as quartz crystals for healing, are also becoming popular with some Druids.[11] Others use meditation techniques having their origins in Buddhism or Hinduism, or the Kabbalistic teachings of the Hermetic Order of the Golden Dawn.

There have been a number of recent developments in Druidry which have pointed to ways in which Druids from different Orders can come together to celebrate our essential unity and also rejoice in our diversity. One of the most important of these has been the formation of the Council of British Druid Orders.[12]

The Council was formed in 1989, originally as a forum at which heads of different Orders could come together on a regular basis for discussion. It began with four Orders attending. At the last count there were fourteen Orders regularly sending delegates to the quarterly meetings, with several more in communication and receiving copies of the Minutes. These groups cover the whole spectrum of modern Druidry, from the Ancient Order of Druids, one of the oldest of the modern Orders, founded in London in 1781 by Henry Hurle, who began as a Friendly Society, and whose membership consists predominantly of smart-blazered businessmen, through to the Insular Order of Druids, whose membership is primarily composed of young(ish) pagans.

In between there is O.B.O.D., which was formed in 1964 when its then Chosen Chief, Ross Nichols,[13] led a breakaway from the Druid Order, which claims to have been founded in 1717 by John Toland, again in London. Incidentally, Ross Nichols, as well as being Chosen Chief of O.B.O.D., was also a good friend of Gerald Gardner, the father of the modern Witchcraft movement. The Druid Order itself, currently under the leadership of David Loxley,[14] is one of the few British groups not to have joined the Council of British Druid Orders, although an open invitation to it and all other groups still stands.

Other Druid groups were formed by 1960s survivors such as myself, Rollo Maughfling and Tim Sebastian. Tim's Secular Order of Druids have recently taken Druidry to 'raves' with great success. Rollo, as well as being Archdruid of the Glastonbury Order of Druids, has also been Stonehenge Officer of the Council for the past few years, in which capacity he has been lobbying for the renewal of Druidic rights of access to the site. The Loyal Arthurian Warband,[15] under the leadership of King Arthur Pendragon, are also represented on the Council. They too are actively campaigning for access to Stonehenge, and against damaging road schemes through sites like Twyford Down and Solsbury Hill. They often join with the Secular Order and the Glastonbury Order for joint celebrations.

Other member Orders include the Grove of the Four Elements, which is the London Grove of the Druid Clan of Dana,[16] which in turn comes under the aegis of the Irish-based Fellowship of Isis; and the London Druid Group, founded at some point prior to 1939, when W.B. Crow[17] was appointed its Arch Druid, which holds regular open meetings at the Conway Hall in London. There are also groups which specialise in the Bardic aspect of Druidry, such as Aos Dana, which is based in Scotland, the Taliesin Foundation, the Bardic Order Group, and the Iolo Morganwg Fellowship. This last represents another very hopeful development, bringing together both Welsh and English Druids and scholars through their shared interest in the life and works of Iolo, who did so much to inspire the Druid revival in both countries. The Council has also established links with a number of active Druid groups overseas, in France, Holland, Ireland, America, Australia and elsewhere.

For the last two years, the Council has also published a twice-yearly journal, *The Druids' Voice*, which features articles on Druidry and related topics, and details of the Council's member Orders.[18] These member Orders represent between them about 8,000 people, of whom about 3,000 live in Britain. Of that 3,000, perhaps less than half would consider themselves pagan. Of the remainder, the majority might describe themselves as humanists or atheists, while a significant minority are Christian, with a smattering of other faiths. The number of Druids not represented on the Council is difficult to estimate. They include the members of the Welsh and Cornish Gorsedds of Bards, the Druid Order, the College of Druidism in Edinburgh, the Free Gorsedd of Druid Bards, and one or two other groups. These groups between them account for perhaps another 1,000 members. Then there are individual Druids who are not affiliated to any particular group, and all those others who practise some form of Celtic magic or spirituality based on writings by such authors as John and Caitlin Matthews and Bob Stewart. Their numbers are impossible to estimate, but may run into thousands, many of whom might not think of themselves as Druids. All the figures given here are estimates based on personal observation rather than statistical survey.

The Council is represented on the Pagan Federation, and some member Orders take an interest in the Federation's Anti-Defamation League. Druids have not suffered the same sort of tabloid and Christian fundamentalist onslaught which has been directed against Wicca. After all, it is difficult for these people to attack a movement which includes the Queen and the Prince of Wales among its membership. They are both Ovates in the Welsh Gorsedd, while the Ancient Order boasts Winston Churchill among its past members. Even so, Druidry has not been immune to attack, which has sometimes taken very unpleasant forms. The head of one Order had a crossbow bolt fired at him through his front window, and also had one of his cats killed and left on his doorstep. Another Druid had screws inserted in the tyres of his car on several occasions, which resulted in a tyre blowing while he was doing 60mph on the M3. The reason for these attacks seemed to be that he had spoken to his local newspaper in favour of school children being allowed to celebrate Halloween. A Druid couple with three children were reported to Social Services by their neighbour for meditating in their garden. These incidents are pretty sickening in themselves, but almost equally sickening is that the idiots responsible for perpetrating them probably think that they are 'good' Christians, and that their poor victims are 'evil'. Fortunately, this kind of madness is fairly rare where Druids are concerned. What our response to it should be is open to debate. My personal preference is for holding more open public gatherings, so that people can see that we are doing is entirely laudable.

One of the most exciting long-term plans of the Council is the setting up of an annual National Eisteddfod based in England, and to this end the Council has recently been promoting interest and active participation in the Bardic arts.[19] Part of this policy has involved encouraging the establishment of Gorsedds of Bards centred on ancient sacred sites. The term Gorsedd literally means 'a high seat', and originally applied to ancient mounds on which Celtic kings were inaugurated and at which tribal gatherings were held. The term was later extended to apply to gatherings of Bards meeting at such mounds. I am delighted to have been involved in setting up one such Gorsedd which meets to celebrate some of the seasonal festivals within the magnificent stone circles of Avebury in Wiltshire.[20]

But all this leaves a number of questions unanswered. For instance, what do Druids believe? Well, there are probably as many answers to this question as there are Druids. There is no set Druid theology. Some Orders use teaching material embodying certain attitudes which could be called religious, but these are usually implicit rather than explicit in the texts. Christian Druids obviously have a Christian theology, but what about the pagans? Do they believe that the multitude of Celtic deities exist in the same way that Christians believe their God exists? Do they believe, as pre-Christian Druids seem to have done, that there are spirits inhabiting natural phenomena such as sun and moon, stones, trees and water? And if so, how do they regard those spirits? There is surprisingly little open debate within Druidry, or indeed, within the broader pagan movement, on theological issues, but a few general observations can be made.

Some Christian, and most Pagan, Druids share with other pagan groups a belief in a power or energy resident in the Earth, or in Nature, often represented as a Mother. But individuals are usually left to decide for themselves whether they choose to look upon this Mother as a living spiritual entity capable of directly affecting human lives, as a Jungian archetype, as a poetic fancy, as an aspect of the individual psyche, or whatever. Similarly, there are many different views on the nature of Earth energies. Ley lines are popular among Druids, although there is little clear agreement as to what these actually are and how they function. Most Druids also believe in some kind of unified spiritual force underlying the manifest world, but again, this force is defined by each individual.

For myself, my own form of Druidry is based on a combination of a lifetime of research and direct experience. In my personal theology, there is a point of unity which I envisage something like the Wakan Tanka, or 'Great Spirit' of the Plains Indians, that is, as a spiritual power which permeates all creation, but which is stronger in some people and things. I call this Spirit Celi, from a Welsh word meaning 'Heaven', 'Deity', or 'Creator'. I believe that this power resides at the heart of all things, and that it is the indestructible spark which is at the core of each human spirit. I see the other deities in the Celtic pantheon as manifestations of this power. It manifests in human consciousness as the feminine power, Awen, referred to above, which seems to be similar to the Hindu Shakti in conception and in activity.

This is all very well, but what does it mean in practice? What does it mean to be a Druid? Well, I would say that Druidry provides a framework in which to develop; physically, mentally, emotionally, morally, and spiritually. It is a way to learn about oneself and one's relationship to the Universe; a forge in which to temper the self. Perhaps I can best illustrate this by describing three significant events from my own life.

The first goes back more than twenty years, to a night when I walked among trees, trying to merge the notes I played on my recorder with the deeper tones of the trees themselves. That night culminated in a dawn which drew back the darkness like a velvet curtain. I stood at the edge of the trees and looked out across a flat calm shimmering sea. To one side were the moon and stars, to the other the red-gold sun just cresting the horizon. Day and night held for what seemed an eternity in balance, the beauty of the two combining to produce an effect of awesome grandeur. This climactic visual experience finally brought me to a realisation of the real power of Nature, a realisation which had been half-formed by a thousand lesser experiences in the past.

Years later, I was travelling back from a festival at Polgooth in Cornwall. I had hitched a lift in a lorry, and was gently nodding in the cab, in that receptive state between sleep and waking, which psychologists call the hypnogogic state, when I saw a huge figure made of leaves and branches rise out of the tree-tops which blanketed the valley floor to the north of the ridge on which the motorway ran. He lifted his head and looked at me, and his arms reached out, both greeting and beckoning. He gave the impression of immense strength, dignity, and benevolence, tinged with an intoxicating hint of danger. The first experience was essentially passive, albeit exhilarating. The second showed the active power of Nature, as manifested in storm, earthquake, and tidal wave.

These two events helped to awaken in me an awareness of the power inherent in natural phenomena; a power which lies at the heart of my understanding of what Druidry is about.

The third incident happened more recently, when I emerged from my first Sweat Lodge and lay exhausted on the wet grass and the cool earth beneath the stars. As I lay there, face down, I felt something digging into my solar plexus. It felt like a small stone, and I thought that I should pick it up and add it to my collection of power objects, gathered over the years at various sacred or special times and places. But when I rolled over and tried to lift it, I found that it was a tough, deep-rooted and thoroughly immovable tuft of grass. I admit that I was a little disappointed, but then the Great Mother spoke to me, and she said, 'The Earth itself is a power object. What more do you want?' This finally demonstrated to me that Nature is not just an abstract notion, but a living spiritual entity; one capable of direct communication, and what's more, one with a sense of humour! I pass Her message on to you. It exemplifies to me the urgent need that we have as modern Druids, to re-establish our links with the sacred places of the Earth, before they are all laid waste by the ignorance and greed which are foisted on us in the spurious name of progress.

As a pagan Druid, I am aware that whatever power I possess comes from the Earth, from the air, from fire and water, or rather, from the Great Spirit which empowers them all. I know too, that if we do harm to the Earth, then we harm ourselves and our children.

Black Elk, a holy man of the Oglala Sioux, told a story of how the sacred pipe was brought to his tribe by a beautiful woman who sang this song:[21]

With visible breath I am walking.
A voice I am sending as I walk.
In a sacred manner I am walking.
With visible tracks I am walking.
In a sacred manner I walk.

If modern Druids, can learn how to walk in a sacred manner, with reverence for the Earth, and respect for all Her creatures, and can then teach others to do the same, then our time will not have been wasted, and our tradition will have relevance, not only for today, but for all time. This, to me, is the most vital task of Druidry today.[22]

Notes

1 For a Druid's view of the links between Druidry and Wicca, see: Philip Carr-Gomm, 'Druids and Witches', in *The Druids' Voice*, Issue 2. A debate on the same subject took place at the Order of Bards, Ovates and Druids (O.B.O.D.) Summer Camp in July 1994. It was jointly

chaired by Philip Carr-Gomm, who is Chosen Chief of O.B.O.D., and Ronald Hutton. A report of it can be found in Issue 4 of *The Druids' Voice* (see 18 below).

2 Edward Williams (translated by his son, Taliesin Williams ab Iolo), *The Iolo Manuscripts*, I. Foulkes, Liverpool, 1888. For a good introductory essay on the life and work of Iolo, see: Dr. D. Elwyn Davies, 'Iolo Morganwg (1747–1826): Bardism and Unitarianism', in Issue 3 of *The Druids' Voice* (see 18 below).

3 Liz Murray, with her late husband, Colin, co-authored *The Celtic Tree Oracle*, Rider, London, 1988, which is a card divination system widely used by modern Druids and based on the Ogham tree alphabet.

4 For the full text of Hanes Taliesin, see *The Mabinogion*, translated by Lady Charlotte Guest, originally published in 1849, but reprinted many times since and frequently found in second-hand bookshops. Most modern versions of the Mabinogion sadly omit the Story of Taliesin.

5 Probably the best books on Wicca are: *Eight Sabbats for Witches*, and *The Witches' Way*, both of which are by Janet and Stewart Farrar, and are published by Robert Hale, London, 1981 and 1985 respectively. Between them they give the whole of the Book of Shadows, often giving both Gardnerian and Alexandrian versions, and much else besides.

6 Five different versions are given in: Edward Williams, *The Iolo Manuscripts*, I. Foulkes, Liverpool, 1888, pp469–70.

7 For details of the O.B.O.D. postal course, send a large s.a.e. to: O.B.O.D., P.O. Box 1333, Lewes, East Sussex BN7 37G.

8 For a reasonably comprehensive survey of Druidic pre-history and history, see: Peter Beresford Ellis, *The Druids*, Constable, London, 1994.

9 Good introductions to Celtic mythology are; Charles Squire, *Celtic Myth and Legend*, Gresham, London, n.d.; T.W. Rolleston, *Myths and Legends of the Celtic Race*, George G. Harrap, London, 1911. Translations of original Welsh texts will be found in *The Mabinogion*, of which there are now a number of translations available, including Lady Charlotte Guest's (see 4 above), which I like for its King-James-Bible sonority, and more modern ones such as: Jeffrey Gantz, *The Mabinogion*, Penguin Books, Harmondsworth, 1976; Gwyn Jones and Thomas Jones, *The Mabinogion*, J. M. Dent & Sons, London, 1974; W.F. Skene, *The Four Ancient Books of Wales*, 2 vols., Edmonston & Douglas, Edinburgh, 1868, includes text and English translations of the poems contained in the *Black Book of Caermarthen*, the *Red Book of Hengest*, the *Book of Taliesin*, and the *Book of Aneurin*; and Rachel Bromwich, *The Welsh Triads*, University of Wales Press, 1978. Translations of Irish myths can be found in *Early Irish Myths and Sagas*, translated by Jeffrey Gantz, Penguin Books, Harmondsworth, 1981; *The Tain*, translated by Thomas

Kinsella, Oxford University Press, 1970; *Cuchulain of Muirthemne*, translated by Lady Gregory, Colin Smythe, Gerrards Cross, 1970; *Gods and Fighting Men*, trans. Lady Gregory, Colin Smythe, 1976; S. H. O'Grady, *Silva Gadelica*, 2 vols., Williams & Norgate, London, 1892.

10 The best of the recent crop of books on Druidry are Philip Carr-Gomm, *Elements of the Druid Tradition*, and *The Druid Way*, both published by Element Books, Shaftesbury, 1991 and 1993 respectively. *The Druid Way* contains texts of three Druid ceremonies; for Naming, Marriage and Parting. The works of John and Caitlin Matthews are also well worth checking out. In particular: John Matthews, *Taliesin: Shamanism and the Bardic Mysteries in Britain and Ireland*, Aquarian Press, London, 1991. R. J. Stewart has also written a number of illuminating books on aspects of Celtic tradition, notably, *The Underworld Initiation*, published by Aquarian Press, Wellingborough, 1985.

11 For details of the Sweat Lodge see *The Sacred Pipe: Black Elk's Account of the Seven Rites of the Oglala Sioux*, edited by Joseph Epes Brown, Penguin Books, Harmondsworth, 1971. For a good practical guide to a variety of 'shamanic' techniques, see *The Way of the Shaman*, Michael Harner, Bantam Books, New York, 1982.

12 To contact the Council of British Druid Orders, write (enclosing s.a.e.) to The Membership Secretary, C.O.B.D.O., 125 Magyar Crescent, Nuneaton, Warwickwhire, CV11 4SJ. Full details of the Council, its member Orders and many other Druid groups can be found in Philip Shallcrass (ed.) *A Druid Directory* (B.D.O.; St Leonards-on-Sea, 1995) available from B.D.O., PO Box 29, St.Leonards-on-Sea, East Sussex TH37 7YP.

13 Many of Ross Nichols' writings have recently been gathered together and published as *The Book of Druidry*, Aquarian Press, 1990. It includes, among much else, a version of the O.B.O.D. Beltaine ritual.

14 There is a rambling and curious book entitled *The Mind of the Druid*, by Dr. E. Graham Howe, published by Skoob Books, London, 1989, which contains a brief introduction by David Loxley.

15 The Loyal Arthurian Warband publish an excellent quarterly Newsletter called *AWEN*. For details write enclosing s.a.e. to The Loyal Arthurian Warband, 10 Sine Close, Farnborough, Hampshire, GU14 8HG.

16 The Grove of the Four Elements publish a splendid quarterly magazine, *Aisling*, which covers many aspects of the Druid tradition. For details write enclosing s.a.e. to: Caroline Wise, P.O.Box 196, London WC1A 2DY.

17 The late Dr. W. B. Crow was author of *A History of Magic, Witchcraft and Occultism*, Aquarian Press, Wellingborough, 1968, and several other works on both orthodox science and occultism.

18 For subscription details or back issues, write enclosing S.A.E. to: The

Druids' Voice, P. O. Box 29, St. Leonards-on-Sea, East Sussex TN37 7YP.

19 For a brief introduction to the Bardic tradition, including some historical background and a modern Gorsedd ritual, see Philip Shallcrass, 'The Bardic Tradition in Britain', in *The Druids' Voice*, issue no.3 (see 18 above). For a fuller account of modern Bardism in practice see Philip Shallcrass, *Elements of The Bardic Tradition*, forthcoming; and for an in-depth study of the history, literature, and institutions of Bardism, see Philip Shallcrass, *The Bardic Tradition in Britain and Ireland*, forthcoming.

20 For details of the Avebury Gorsedd and its activities, write enclosing A5 s.a.e. to: Caer Abiri Gorsedd, c/o B.D.O., P.O. Box 29, St. Leonards-on-Sea, East Sussex TN37 7YP.

21 The story is told in *Black Elk Speaks*, edited by John G. Neihardt, Abacus, 1974, p.14–15.

22 Several Druid groups are involved in ecology in a variety of ways. O.B.O.D., for example, have recently launched a cassette; *Barddas 1: By Star and Stone*, featuring music by Derek Bell of the Chieftains among others, all proceeds from which will go towards buying areas of woodland currently being sold off by the Forestry Commission under yet another scandalous Government policy, and opening them up to Druid groups who will also manage them. For details of the cassette, write enclosing s.a.e. to O.B.O.D. at the address given at 7 above, and tell them I sent you.

Vivianne Crowley

WICCA AS MODERN-DAY MYSTERY RELIGION

The latter half of the twentieth century has been characterized by a growth of interest and participation in humanistic and transpersonal psychotherapies. These seek not to cure the abnormal but to improve the psychological functioning of normal human beings and to foster what can be termed inner-centredness and inner peace.

These newer movements have aims and goals that are similar to those of much older traditions of thought; namely those found in the esoteric branches of all religions, for example Christian and Buddhist monasticism, Yoga, Tantra, Sufism and the Pagan mysteries such as those of Eleusis, Mithras and Isis. These goals are self-knowledge, inner harmony and, in many traditions, the realization of a stable core of the personality–the *Self*–which can sustain us through life and endures beyond death.

In Wicca, a modern-day mystery religion, the approach to the Self is made through an external expression of the inner psychological process–religious ritual–often using images, languages and forms that are unusual in a modern Western religious context. This chapter explores the psychology and symbolism of the rites of Wicca and their impact on those who participate.

What is Wicca?

Within many Pagan societies there were two levels or aspects of religion–the exoteric aspects which dealt with the religious needs of society, including maintaining social cohesion and providing meaningful rites of passage for individuals transiting different social statuses–and the esoteric aspects of religion which are concerned with mystical and psychological matters of personal and inner transformation.

Within modern Paganism we have seen initially a revival of the inner esoteric aspects of Pagan tradition. These are small, closed groups to which entry is solely by initiation ceremonies that are designed to produce profound psychological effects on those who undergo them. More recently we have seen the growth of exoteric Paganism, whereby modern Pagans have devised rites and ceremonies, held more and more often in public, to celebrate marriage, the birth of children and death, and whereby Pagans have sought to develop religious teaching for their children and to extend ministry to those of the community who are in need, whether in hospital, hospice or prison.

This chapter is concerned with revival of Pagan mystery religion, and, in particular, personal transformation within one particular Pagan tradition, that of *Wicca*.

Wicca is practised as a Pagan mystery religion, which is Goddess-centred and includes both men and women. It has three major strands–religion, magic, and mystery tradition. Wicca is described by many of its practitioners as *the religion of witchcraft*, but the word *witchcraft* is in many ways misleading. Wiccans do not define witchcraft as would an anthropologist, taking as a model the practice of witchcraft in tribal societies, nor in the same way as witchcraft is perceived in popular culture. I will therefore use the terms *Wicca* and *Wiccan* rather than *witchcraft* and *witch* and will focus on Wicca as religion and mystery tradition.

Wicca as Religion and Mystery Tradition

As a religion, Wicca worships some of the earliest forms of deity–the Great Mother Goddess and her consort the Horned God. The Goddess and the God are seen as sexual. The Goddess is the Great Mother who gives birth to the world. The Horned God is seen as part animal, part human and part spirit. He is usually depicted as phallic. Wicca worships the gods through a seasonal cycle of eight festivals and also at the thirteen full moons.

As a mystery tradition, Wicca's preoccupations are essentially mystical and psychological. It uses rites of initiation to trigger personal transformation. The mystery cults have often been treated with some ambivalence within ancient Pagan societies. Their secretiveness and inaccessibility, like that of modern freemasonry, can generate suspicion, rumour and fear. Early Christianity suffered similar problems. Wicca may also be met with suspicion in modern society because its attitudes to certain issues differ from that of recent Western religious practice and, in particular, because of its attitude to sexuality.

To explain the Wiccan attitude to sexuality, I need to say something about the Pagan view of the relationship between matter and spirit. The divine in Wicca is perceived as energy. Energy is movement and change. Where there is movement and change, there is action and reaction, transmitter and receiver, passive and active, ebb and flow. Within the divine is a duality which is seen as female and male, Goddess and God. Most Wiccans believe that these deities are reconciled ultimately in a divinity which is one and beyond male and female. However, some very Goddess-oriented groups might choose to call the ultimate divine force *Goddess*, seeing the male force, the God, as the child of the Goddess, rather than male and female as the joint product of an impersonal unity.

Pagans worship many different gods, but a common thread in modern Paganism, which distinguishes it from most other Western religions, is in where modern Pagan traditions place their deities. In the exoteric manifestations of monotheistic religion (though not usually in their esoteric and mystical aspects), deity is often seen as separate and removed from the earth and humankind. The deity is *out there* in some insubstantial realm of the beyond and there is an emphasis on the distinction between spirit and flesh, matter and divinity.

In Wicca, the divine is seen as both immanent and transcendent. It pre-exists the universe and creates it; but it is also in-dwelling in matter. It is an energy which permeates all living things. Material creation is an expression of the divine, through which it is seeking to understand and to know itself by manifesting in as many myriad forms as possible. The material realm is not different in substance from spirit, but another expression of divine energy. Here, Wicca's concepts have similarities with Hinduism. The esoteric writer Dion Fortune, who wrote mainly in the 1930s, captures this attitude.

The ignorant and impure man gazeth upon the face of Nature,
and it is to him darkness of darkness.
But the initiated and illumined gazeth thereon
and seeth the features of God.
Be ye far from us, O ye profane,
while we adore God made manifest in Nature.[1]

In Wicca, the Goddess is immanent in matter, therefore the whole of material creation–the earth itself and the life forms which inhabit it–is sanctified and holy. This includes the human body. The divine is seen as present within human beings. There is a prayer which conveys this.

Prayer of praise to the Goddess
Blessed Be the Great Mother,
without beginning and without ending,
Blessed Be her temple of pure white marble,
Blessed Be the stillness of her holy place.

Blessed Be the babe who cries to her,
Blessed Be the deer who lift their heads for her,
Blessed Be the birds who fly the skies for her,
Blessed Be the trees which shake and sigh for her,
Blessed Be the leaf which falls for her and nourishes the soil.

Blessed Be the wave which caresses the shore for her,
Blessed Be the sand which succumbs to its embrace,
Blessed Be the shell that is cast up from her,
Blessed Be She, the Mother of Pearl.

Blessed Be the stars which shine like jewels for her,
Blessed Be the Moon in which we see her face,
Blessed Be my spirit which soars the heights for her,
Blessed Be my soul which expands in joy for her,
Blessed Be my body, the temple of her being.[2]

Far from being seen as unclean, the body (and for women this is particularly important) is seen as sacred and holy, a gift from the gods, the vessel of the divine self.

Women in Wicca

The role of women is important in all modern Pagan traditions. Women are usually seen as essential in the priesthood. Since the divine expresses itself as female and male, the gods are best served by priestess and priest.

Monotheistic religions, which are primarily created by men, are ambivalent towards sexuality, particularly women's sexuality, often regarding it as sinful. This may lead to the view that anything that arouses sexual feelings is sinful. For man, it is woman who arouses sexual feelings. Men who have been taught that sexuality is wrong often wish to find something or someone to blame for the unwelcome sexual feelings they experience: women are to blame. It is women who lead them astray; therefore women are evil. The solution is to segregate men and women for religious purposes. Men and women worship in different parts of the temple; spiritual development is carried out in single-sex groups. Monasticism is a logical extension of this.

The Pagan view is different. Separation of the sexes for the purposes of religious worship or spiritual development is seen neither as necessary nor desirable. In Wicca, men and women mix freely in religious gatherings and, in many Wiccan groups, the rites are performed by couples who are seen as representing the divine in its aspects of male and female. The rites may also be performed *skyclad* or naked.

Sexual Symbolism

In Wicca, sexuality is not viewed as contrary to spirituality. Indeed, sexuality may be harnessed to achieve spiritual ends. Woman is revered rather than feared. Implicit and explicit sexual symbolism is found in many aspects of Wicca. I have already mentioned the sexual nature of the deities. The myths of the seasonal cycle describe a fertility cycle by which the God is born at Winter Solstice; mates with the Goddess in the Spring; is sacrificed, dies and resurrects in the late Summer and Autumn; to be reborn again in the form of his son, at the Winter Solstice. Sexuality is also found in the higher initiation rites of the Wiccan tradition, which involve the enactment of the sacred marriage.

The fundamental importance of the concept of sexuality in Wicca can also be glimpsed in its creation myths. In the middle and near-Eastern monotheisms, the world is believed to have been created by a male deity operating alone. The creation myths of Wicca vary between traditions, but share a common concept–that the world was created by the Mother Goddess and they frequently contain imagery that is explicitly sexual. The image is biological–of a Mother Goddess who gives birth–rather than mechanistic–of a male God as engineer or architect of the universe.

Unity with the Divine

One of the fundamental spiritual needs of human beings is the need for union or reunion with the divine. Often, the spiritual self is considered to be part of the divine whole or to find its home in contemplation of the divine unity. While separation from the whole is necessary in order for the Self to experience the lessons of material existence, this separation is also a spiritual exile and a source of great loneliness.

The return to oneness with the divine source is a preoccupation of mysticism and also of the mystery cults. Mysticism seeks union through introversion and contemplative prayer. Mystery cults seek to externalize the inner journey of the spirit to the divine by representing it through symbolism and ritual.

Wicca as Mystery Religion

Within Wicca, the mysteries are taught primarily through two sets of ceremonies–a seasonal cycle of festivals in which the focus of the ceremony is on the group as a whole–and initiation rites for an individual or a couple. Initiation rites serve as admission rites but they are also catalysts for psycho-spiritual change. They work on the unconscious mind through symbols that have a profound impact on the psyche.

On the external level, the initiation rites mark status transitions within the Wiccan community. Like many mystery cults, Wicca practises three degrees of initiation. At the first degree, the initiate enters the world of the Goddess. Training and preparation are then carried out for the second degree, during which the initiate undergoes a symbolic heroic quest and returns to take up status as a group elder and learn from the High Priestess and High Priest those skills necessary to set up an independent group.

On the inner level, the initiation rites have other psycho-spiritual meanings. The aims of Wicca as a mystery religion are the same as those of the mystery cults of the classical world, namely *to know thyself* and to attain some form of permanent psycho-spiritual transformation involving a moving of the centre of the personality from the *ego* (what I think of as myself), to the *Self* (what I truly am when the contents of the unconscious are revealed and reconciled). Interestingly, these aims are similar to those of many of the more spiritually-oriented psychotherapy movements, of which Carl Jung's psychology is the best-known. Therapy can be seen, however, as more akin to the introverted mystical approach, with the therapist taking the role of confessor or spiritual teacher.

In their endeavours to provide routes to psycho-spiritual transformation, the mystery cults are more akin to shamanism. Whereas in shamanism, however, the psyche experiences trauma and is overwhelmed by the contents of the unconscious which precipitate a change that is uncontrolled, usually unsought and possibly unwelcome, the mysteries seek their transformational goals in more controlled ways. Otherwise, the psychological upheaval is too great. It can leave the conscious mind swamped, no longer able to distinguish fantasy from reality.

Carl Jung believed that within the psyche are symbolic representations of unrealized aspects of ourselves that must be acknowledged and reconciled if we are to attain the goal of inner unity. Jung saw the inner transformation as proceeding through a series of inner encounters with these archetypes which involves casting aside the *persona* or mask to encounter the *shadow*, the *anima* or *animus* (the contrasexual side of our personality) and the *Self*. The *persona* is the mask which we present to the world–of fun-loving party person, of ambitious executive, of parent, of radical environmental protester. Such faces help oil the wheels of society by creating sets of mutual expectations of conduct. Acknowledged as such they are beneficial. If, to extend the metaphor, they become *stuck to the face*, they suffocate us.

The *shadow* can be explained if we can visualize ourselves as two: the half which we consider acceptable and the half that we do not, the white and the black. The unacceptable half is the shadow. People often think of the shadow as negative, but the shadow is what we *think of* as negative and this is not the same thing. It includes aspects of ourselves that can be very positive but which do not accord with what we normally think of as our personalities.

Another unrecognized part of ourselves in Jung's theories is a powerful archetype of the opposite sex: for a woman the *animus*–the male part of herself; for a man the *anima*–the female part of himself. The animus and anima represent qualities which society teaches us are associated with the opposite sex: for women drive, ambition, leadership; for men caring, nurturing, the power to give way. In earlier generations, these qualities were difficult to express in socially acceptable ways.

Jung describes the *Self* as *the wholeness that transcends consciousness.*[3] The ego extends only as far as the conscious mind. The Self is the whole of the personality, which includes the unconscious as well as the conscious mind. The Self can be defined as what we really are as opposed to what we think we are or what society, teachers, parents, friends, lovers, tell us we are. Giving birth to the Self represents a transition in the focus of our consciousness away from the ego to a new vantage point. This is accompanied by a great influx of creativity; for the Self lies on the borders of the collective unconscious, the source of myth, dream, poetry and creative inspiration. It is becoming at one with the Self that is the aim of full human development, in Jung's terms *individuation*. Wiccan initiation rites echo these processes in their symbolism.

First Degree Initiation

What happens at a Wiccan first degree initiation? The rituals of Wicca take place within sacred space known as a *circle*. This is created by ritual words, gestures and actions that have a shared symbolic meaning for the participants. The initiate is placed on the outside of this circle while it is prepared and the deities of the Great Mother Goddess and the Horned God are invoked or incarnated into the high priestess and high priest for the duration of the rite. A doorway is left for the initiate to enter.

An unusual feature of the initiation rite in a modern Western religious context (though not in ancient Paganism) is that the rite is usually performed *skyclad* or naked. In initiation the removal of clothes has a symbolic meaning–that of exposure. To be initiated, we have to be willing to cast aside our *persona*, the mask which we present to the world, and to enter the circle as we first entered the world–naked and vulnerable. The symbolism has an important message for personal transformation. If we are to journey into ourselves, we must be prepared to let go of our defences, postures and disguises.

The initiate is also blindfold and bound by ritual cords. All this is designed to cause fear, but the initiate is also supported, welcomed and honoured. Within the rite, the initiator formally greets the initiate with the words:

> *In other religions the postulant kneels while the priest towers above him, but in the Art Magical we are taught to be humble and so we kneel to welcome thee and say:*
>
> *Blessed Be thy feet that have brought thee in these ways.*
> *Blessed Be thy knees that shall kneel at the sacred altar.*
> *Blessed Be thy phallus/womb without which we should not be.*
> *Blessed Be thy breasts formed in beauty and in strength.*
> *Blessed Be thy lips that shall utter the sacred names.*[4]

The body is honoured and reverenced. The symbolic message is about acceptance–that what we are and may become once free of our persona, our mask, is acceptable and welcomed.

The message is also that if we are prepared to endure the fear of self-exposure and to go through it, we will find that there was nothing to fear. Why are we afraid? To attain the goal of to *Know Thyself*, we must first encounter the frightening shadow.

The shadow personifies everything that the subject refuses to acknowledge about himself and yet is always thrusting itself upon him directly or indirectly–for instance, inferior traits of character and other incompatible tendencies.[5]

Another important message is that the mystery is found within. This message is conveyed through what is known as the Great Mother Charge. This is considered to be the words of the Goddess.

I who am the beauty of the green Earth,
and the white Moon amongst the stars,
and the mystery of the waters,
and the desire of the heart of woman and of man,
say unto thy soul:
arise and come unto me.[6]

It welcomes the Initiate into the world of the Goddess, but also invites the initiate to go further and to understand that:

If that which thou seekest,
thou findest not within thee,
thou will never find it without thee;
for behold, I have been with thee from the beginning,
and I am that which is attained at the end of desire.[7]

The Second Initiation

If the initiate learns the lessons of the first degree, he or she will undertake the second degree. This involves a journey into the underworld, symbolic of the unconscious, to meet a powerful figure–the deity of the opposite sex. Psychologically, the opposite sex deity carries much of the projection of our own contra-sexual side of the psyche–the animus for a woman and anima for a man.

The second degree initiation contains many similarities to the first, but the second degree rite also includes a mystery play called the *Legend of the Goddess*. In this, the initiate and others enact the descent of the Goddess into the Underworld, the Land of Death, where she meets with the God as the Dark Lord of Death.

In the *Legend*, the God awaits the coming of the Goddess. The message of the second degree reverses many of the messages of conventional society. The message for a man is that in order to find his true Self he must come into right relationship with the feminine. He must let go of stereotypes of male roles and striving for external goals. The answer is not to be found in books, or in gurus, or in some esoteric group. He must wait in the silence and darkness for his inner feminine to bring him the answer.

For a woman, the message is also a reversal of stereotyped roles. She is challenged to go forth and to seek experience. She is not to wait at home for the perfect male, the white knight on a shining steed, to do it for her.

Much of the imagery associated with mysticism is sexual, but there are also strong images of death. The Goddess goes into the underworld to seek the answer to the question:

> *Why dost thou causeth all things that I love and take delight in to fade and die?*[8]

After trials and tribulations, the Goddess learns that death is a necessary part of the life cycle; but that it is only a stage in incarnation. Death is frightening, but the initiatory message is about overcoming fear. In the first degree, this is fear of exposure–finding out what lies behind the mask, which is not what we pretend we are. In the second degree, the message is about overcoming the fear of annihilation. On one level, this is the fear of physical death. On another, it is the fear of the death of the ego, of what we think we are. From the perspective of the ego, giving up its central position in the psyche to the Self is a form of death. The annihilation of the ego was seen by Jung as a crucial stage in the individuation process, the process by which we become a true individual, truly unique. The esoteric writer Dion Fortune wrote:

> *There are two deaths by which men die,*
> *the greater and the lesser:*
> *the death of the body and the death of initiation.*
> *And of these two,*
> *the death of the body is the lesser.*[9]

We seek to *know ourselves*, but this means change and we are all afraid of change. We are afraid to let go of that centre that hitherto has always been me. We desire it, yet flee from it. The courtship of the ego by the Self is therefore often depicted as a chase or a game of hide and seek.

> *I flee from thee, but lure thee on,*
> *I seek for thee, but hide my face,*
> *I call to thee, but my words are silent.*[10]

At the end of the *Legend of the Goddess*, the seeker is given a new message: that from the dark world of the unconscious and the Land of Death may come rebirth. The *Legend* ends with the God and Goddess teaching one another the mysteries of rebirth. She teaches him 'her mystery of the sacred cup which is the cauldron of rebirth' and he gives to her 'the necklace which is the circle of rebirth'.

The Third Initiation

The third initiation involves the Great Rite or sacred marriage. This can be enacted either by a couple as an act of ritual sex or symbolically without physical union. (This is akin to Tantra, which does not necessarily involve physical sex.)

In earlier Paganism, the sacred marriage was not available to all, but only to a chosen few. In some societies, this might be the king, who was married with a priestess who represented the Goddess of the land. There are echoes of this in many ancient societies, including that of the Egyptians and the Celts. The sacred marriage was the core of the third initiation of the Egyptian Isis Mysteries and was also reputed to be the ultimate religious experience in the Greek Eleusinian Mysteries:

> *Is not there the dark descent, and is not the solemn communion of hierophant and priestess between him and her alone? Are not the torches doused, and does not the great multitude see their salvation in that which is consummated by the two in darkness?*[11]

The sacred marriage performed as a sexual rite is found more commonly in Goddess-oriented religious traditions that conceive of the divine as both male and female. The sacred marriage has not been favoured in the West during the Christian era, which has developed a different and more solitary approach to sexuality and spirituality–a mystical tradition in which the physical expression of sexuality is foregone and sexuality is transmuted within the individual to achieve a higher state of consciousness. Sexuality is absorbed into oneself rather than being expressed with another. However, echoes of the sacred marriage are found in Christian spirituality in the symbolism of the inner marriage of the soul to the divine, which is at the core of much mystical writing, such as that of the Carmelite nun Saint Teresa of Avila.[12]

At the third Wiccan initiation the crisis between ego and Self has passed. The perilous quest has been undertaken and the difficulties of the journey overcome. Jung used imagery from Homer's Odyssey and saw the journey as sailing between Scylla and Charybdis, the dangers of ego inflation and being swamped by feelings of inferiority. Once, as Jung put it, these have been successfully circumnavigated:

> *This leads to ... a possible synthesis of conscious and unconscious elements of knowledge and action. This in turn leads to a shifting of the centre of personality from the ego to the self.*[13]

The third initiation takes up the messages of life and rebirth hinted at in the second initiation. Anima and animus have been reconciled and from this can come the synthesis of which Jung speaks–the birth of the Self. For the birth of the Self, there must be a conception and for conception a sexual union. In the third degree of Wicca, the couple to be initiated take on the role of the Goddess and God and enact the *Great Rite* or *sacred marriage* – sexual union with the deity. The couple take the role of the God and Goddess and, as Goddess and God, they unite. This is the end of the initiatory journey. There is no longer separation between self and other, I and Thou: 'I and the other are One.'

Conclusion

The aims of the Pagan mysteries are manifold. They include achievement of psychological and spiritual understanding, conveying to participants a certitude that life is eternal and that the spirit endures beyond the mortality of the body, and providing a foretaste, through sacred rites, of the unity with the divine which is achieved ultimately only in death. In Wicca, these lessons are conveyed through the practice of a three-fold system of initiation. The initiation rites provide 'a sip of the wine of the Grail', until at last there is neither sipper or supped. The initiate becomes the Grail and realizes the truth revealed in the first initiation:

> *If that which thou seekest,*
> *thou findest not within thee,*
> *thou will never find it without thee*
> *for behold, I have been with thee from the beginning,*
> *and I am that which is attained at the end of desire.*[14]

Notes

1 Dion Fortune, *The Sea Priestess*, p124, Star Books, Wyndham Publications, London, 1976.

2 Vivianne Crowley, *Phoenix from the Flame: Pagan Spirituality in the Western World*, p109, Aquarian, London, 1994.
3 Carl G. Jung, *The Collected Works of C. G. Jung*, Vol 9, Part 1, *Archetypes of the Collective Unconscious*, p164, para 278, Routledge & Kegan Paul, London, second edition 1968.
4 Quoted in Vivianne Crowley, *Wicca: The Old Religion in the New Age*, p75, Aquarian, London, 1989.
5 Carl G. Jung, *The Collected Works of C. G. Jung*, Vol 5, *Symbols of Transformation*, p86–7, para 130, Routledge & Kegan Paul, London, second edition, 1967.
6 Quoted in Vivianne Crowley, *Wicca: The Old Religion in the New Age*, p161.
7 Quoted in Vivianne Crowley, *Wicca: The Old Religion in the New Age*, p161.
8 Vivianne Crowley, *Wicca: The Old Religion in the New Age*, p211.
9 Dion Fortune, *The Sea Priestess*, p125.
10 Vivianne Crowley, *Wicca: The Old Religion in the New Age*, p173.
11 Asterius, Bishop of Amasea, *Homilia X, Sanctos Martyres* in J.P. Migne, *Patriologie Graeca 40: Patres Ægyptis*, pp323–4, Garnier, Paris, 1863.
12 See J. Welch, O. Carm, *Spiritual Pilgrims: Carl Jung and Saint Teresa of Avila*, p165–89, Paulist Press, NY, 1982.
13 Carl Jung, *Archetypes of the Collective Unconscious*, p180–1, para 304.
14 Quoted in Vivianne Crowley, *Wicca: The Old Religion in the New Age*, p161.

Lynne Morgan

WOMEN AND THE GODDESS TODAY

Perceiving the Divine as female can have an enormous effect upon a woman's psyche. It can bring to women a whole new assessment of our personal role within relationships whether as mother, daughter, lover, work colleague or friend and particularly in our relationship with ourselves, because we see ourselves as something greater than ourselves. It can liberate us from our own stereotypical perceptions of ourselves and of our role in society, it can take us further than our own view of ourselves to build upon achievements already made, and motivate us to achieve things greater than the sum of ourselves by enhancing our perception of our potential as women. The Goddess can be a crucial role model giving us new and fresh ideas about women as creatrix and the goals which we are capable of achieving. Her images give the possibility for concepts which we have never considered before, she can inspire us with self-belief because of her potency and powerful presence; once we start to integrate her into our lives. The Goddess at a subliminal level of our awareness is a very powerful force for motivation and change, with the ability to enhance and give meaning to everything we do; by studying the significance of being female we can bring value and self-worth into our lives at a fresh level.

In sociological terms women are a minority–our values and attitudes secondary to the prevailing view, therefore women are inclined to undervalue themselves as they have formerly looked outside themselves for an estimation of their value. When we look to masculine imagery we rarely see reality because the view is often stylised, fantasised, unrealistic or worse still derogatory, added to which women are normally viewers of culture rather than makers of it.

> *In most popular representations it seems that men look and women are looked at. In film, on television, in the press and in most pop-*

ular narratives men are shown to be in control of the gaze, women are controlled by it. Men act; women are acted upon.[1]

As we have been looking at ourselves through male eyes for something like two thousand years we are bound to have a distorted view of how we are. So it is time for a reassessment and women's spirituality allows us to do that, offering us views which are distinctly feminine and based within our own values and attitudes. Since these views are subjective, imaginative and creative we have often been accused of irrationality:

> *A woman cannot grasp that one must act from principle; as she has no continuity she does not experience the necessity for logical support of her mental processes ... she may be regarded as 'logically insane'.*
>
> OTTO WEININGER IN SEX AND CHARACTER 1906

> *Women's intuition is the result of millions of years of not thinking.*
>
> RUPERT HUGHES 1872–1956

> *Whimsey, not reason, is the female guide.*
>
> GEORGE GRANVILLE THE VISION 1667–1735

> *Women are generally shy, capricious and whimsical, and are easily carried off by their emotions, and thus their study of the situation is hardly objective.*
>
> MUHAMMAD IMRAN, IDEAL WOMEN IN ISLAM 1979

> *Woman: with allusion to qualities generally attributed to the female sex, as mutability, capriciousness, proneness to tears; also to their position of inferiority or subjection (phr. to make a woman of, to bring to submission).*
>
> OXFORD ENGLISH DICTIONARY[2]

These are just some ideas of how our unique femaleness has been viewed: it is crucial that we do not internalise these views and live our lives as though we believed them.

We need to do more than that: we need to re-evaluate and to celebrate these unique qualities so that we may have equality not submission as an inferior species. If we believe these views we will feel vulnerable, helpless and powerless. Instead of feeling this uncomfortable with ourselves we can find in the Goddess and in female spirituality a fresh assessment of ourselves which informs and enhances our lives.

The earliest knowledge of the Goddess is passed down to us in pictorial images; carved upon the walls of caves in Palaeolithic times around 25,000 years ago, and in figurines such as the 'Venus of Lespugue' carved from mammoth ivory around 24,000 years ago. The commonest imagery portrays a woman with enormous breasts and belly representing the fact that the Goddess is the giver of all life and represents this facility in all women. In those times life was precious and valuable since we needed to increase our numbers on earth and the environment was very harsh and hazardous.

Goddess worship was the first and primary religious experience.

> *Modern connotations vastly differ from those of the ancients, to whom the Goddess was a full-fledged cosmic parent figure who created the universe and its laws, ruler of Nature, Fate, Time, Eternity, Truth, Wisdom, Justice, Love, Birth, Death, etc.*
>
> *Perhaps one should take more seriously the ancients' often repeated opinion that their Goddess had a thousand names. Every female divinity in the present Encyclopedia may be correctly regarded as only another aspect of the core concept of a female Supreme Being. No modern temples perpetuate this core concept. Men long since tore down the Goddess's shrines, as christian gospels commanded them to do* (Acts 19:27). *Yet even in a society that trivialised and vilified it, the core concept lives on.*[3]

Goddess worship was universal; whenever people created a community they established the female principle to watch over them and each had their own name and significant meaning for her; based within their individual culture and need. With the rise of dualistic religious concepts, i.e. religions which propose two opposing forces–god and devil–there is increased evidence of weaponry and colonisation, with societies changing their value systems from those grounded within female ones to male ones. Authoritarian values are more in evidence when ideas about living in natural harmony with Earth Mother no longer underpin religious thought.

The concept of Earth as Mother of all creatures was a natural response to what our ancestors saw all around them and consistent with the changing seasons and a harmonious society based on an agricultural existence. In ancient Greece they developed a myth to explain seasonal changes and to make sense of what they could not control. The female-based values which existed in ancient Greece highlight the ability of women to make connections and live in an interconnected way with all around. Today we should celebrate these qualities rather than denigrate them.

The Greek myth which explained seasonal changes was enacted by the women of ancient Greece as the Elysian Mystery. The myth focussed on the mother/daughter relationship: the virgin or untried girl (Persephone or Core) is described as entering the underworld–deep earth or clonic space; where life evolves and is cyclical. This represents the opposite of the sky which is life everlasting, where there is no beginning or end. The mother (Demeter) then responds in her grief by withholding her gift of fruitfulness until the spring when the daughter returns to walk upon the earth. Thus winter is explained and coldness and barrenness given meaning. When the daughter re-emerges in the spring she has been seeding the new growth within the earth and now brings it to birth and fulfilment.

Religious thought is an answer to humanity's need for meaning in their lives and with an Earth-based religion there is a strong experiential component. This enables a community living within cooperation to enact the spiritual myth, thereby creating a holistic religious experience and validating their society's belief system.

The mother's name Demeter means Meter, mother, and De is the delta or triangle (in the Greek sacred alphabet), the letter of the vulva, the female genital sign; when speaking of Demeter you are indicating the life-enhancing concept of birth, death and sexual paradise. Hence She is the doorway to the mysterious feminine and the root from which heaven and earth spring. The idea of the name being significant to religious experience has become familiar to us through Christianity. The term virgin originally meant a sexually autonomous women; Holy Virgin was the title given to the Harlot-Priestesses of Ishtar, Ashteroth and Aphrodite. Since Goddesses represent universal realities their concepts mean similar things in different parts of the world. This means that aspects of the central Goddess deification are represented at different times and places but essentially have the same meaning as a women's story. Since this joy of life is a central principle within female-centred religions, the Harlot-Priestesses served in the Temples of the Goddess to initiate young men into the joy and celebration of the life-fulfilling principle. The young men were enabled to grow up, to grow beyond the external need for a mother figure since through this process they were able to internalise their own feminine self; what Jung called the anima. They were then real men with gentleness and strength combined, to create a whole person.

The feminine principle of Mary is derived from the Persian Al-Mah, the unmated Moon Goddess. Her Latin name is Alma 'Living Soul of the World'. Mary's many names include Mari, shown wearing a blue robe and pearl necklace, classic symbols of the sea, Ishtar,

Juno and Isis as Stella Maris; Star of the Sea. The Holy Virgins or Harlot-Priestesses were 'Soul Teachers' or 'Soul Mothers'–the Alma Mater. Thus women were respected and their wisdom, as coming from the Goddess, was revered, their spirituality was totally integrated with their sexuality because they represented the life force which was Holy.

The Mother Goddess represents and celebrates the sensuality of mothering and the sensory delight in giving birth and breast feeding. This can be a symbolic celebration rather than an actual one. It can also pertain to all productive outlets and does not need to be actualised by the existence of a child. Since all women are divinely creative we give birth from our wombs and nurture our projects, crafts and skills. Our breasts are the organs from which we give forth nourishment in sincere care for others' welfare, but if we neglect to nurture and nourish ourselves our wombs may not be fruitful and our breasts dry. This can happen when our perceptions of ourselves are based within a false self-image. To give out constantly can be very harmful, particularly when our role models, such as the aspects of the Goddess and her representations, are withheld and denied to us. She gives to us the nurturing and nourishing so crucial in connecting, cooperating with, and relating to others around us, a woman's relationship with her inner sense of divinity is important to the way she functions in the world.

In *The Women's Encyclopedia of Myths and Secrets* Barbara Walker describes a notion that the ancients called Karuna and how it is central to our way of relating to the world.[4] Karuna is the Tantric term for the fundamental quality of mother love; directly experienced in infancy and radiated in adulthood to embrace all forms of the expression of love: touching, tenderness, compassion, sensual enjoyment and eroticism. Many centuries before Freudian Psychology 'discovered' infantile sexuality, Tantric sages called Karuna the essence of religion; a gut feeling of loving kindness learnt through physical and sensual comforting contact by infants and adults alike. This brings a force of innocent, sexual, warmly loving and moral behaviour patterns from deep within the individual from which they can always act appropriately. The ancients well knew that the experience of being in love reanimates the mother/child relationship in its intimate physical attachment, trust and dependency. Recognition of one particular love subject evolved from the instinctive drive that binds together mother and offspring. In order that men should understand the wisdom of the anima (Jung's definition of the female principle), Sacred Whores were the special teachers of Karuna, which may have been the root of the Italian word *carogna*–whore. Pagan Rome gave the Great Goddess the title Mater Cara–Mother Beloved. She combined all the qualities of sexuality, motherhood, marital bliss, friendship, generosity and mercy, that is *caritas*. The Christian Church later purged caritas of its sensual implications and changed it into charity. According to Barbara Walker, the Greek definition of Karuna was embodied in The Three Graces–the naked Triple Goddess whose quality of grace was changed by Christianity as the meaning of caritas was changed. She explains how in Babylon the Great Mother, whose name was Ishtar, was also the Great Whore and the lover of all men and She expressed the qualities of Karuna in Her self-description: 'A prostitute am I'. The Christian version of Mari-Ishtar is Mary Magdalene, the sacred harlot who said harlots are 'Compassionate of all the race of mankind'. Gnostic gospels mentioned Mary Magdaleneas, the original female pope, embodying the true Christian spirit kept secret from the male apostles, while it was passed directly from Jesus through his unsurpassable love for Mary. Significantly, Christian iconographers often confused Mary the Mother with Mary the Harlot.[5]

Motherhood, sensual enjoyment and kindly feelings were associated with the spirit of the Goddess under all Her names, and therefore with women as Her earthly representative. The integrated idea of Karuna with all its sophistication has virtually disappeared from modern Western society, where it is difficult to explain its meaning.

Probably the hardest part for the modern mind to understand is the emphasis on sensuality and sexuality with its basis in the instinctual. Because of the modern emphasis on the mind (and psyche has come to mean mind rather than it's actual meaning of soul), its biochemistry, and connection or not to the brain, there tends to be a scientific and reductionist attitude to the idea of individuality; so that we are all rapidly becoming clones. Only the outer conditioned self is given credence, as though only the personality which we can express, and which is seen by others, has validity:

> *Despite the materialistic tendency to understand the psyche as mere reflection or imprint of physical and chemical process, there is not a single proof of this hypothesis. Quite the contrary, innumerable facts prove that the psyche translates physical processes into sequences of images which have hardly any recognisable connection with the objective process. The materialistic hypothesis is much too bold and flies in the face of experience with almost metaphysical presumption.*[6]

Although what Jung says is wordy he is referring to the fact that we have an inner life not necessarily defined by outer experience and, when translated into symbol, metaphor and image, not immediately understandable by left-brain language patterns. So we need to learn this new language in order to have a relationship with ourselves. Pre-industrialised peoples understood this language so by referring to them it helps us to know our inner selves. They used archetypal images such as Gods and Goddesses symbolically to express spiritual concepts not amenable to left-brain language; what are called ineffable concepts. In modern times, in cities, we tend to use our five senses much less than our ancestors did; they touched the land, the soil more and were in touch with their own roots within it. Their sense of smell was more acute, and where we may block out the smell of pollution as it is, rightly, disturbing to us, we now have more emphasis on smell with the use of incenses and aromatherapy, to help awaken this sense. Their horizons were broader so they could see more, they travelled less so what they saw made more impact upon them, and was felt in a deeper way. They had smaller communities, more intimate contact with each other so touch was more appropriate. Because there was more danger from animals they needed to hear with more awareness of the danger around; there again we tend to block out noise because it is more pollutive than natural. What they ate was not treated with chemicals and tasted of freshness and good clean earth, and even today older people often refer to the way food tasted much better when they were young! I have telescoped thousands of years and hundreds of different types of cultures together to illustrate things that were lost through industrialisation and materialistic values.

This illustration is to define what is meant by sensual in the above text on Karuna; that it pertains to the five senses, is instinctual and, whilst aligned to sexuality because it is fundamental, is not synonymous with it.

If we take the line that there are fundamental differences between women and men, and obviously there are biological ones, the question is, to what extent does the way we look and function have an effect upon our psychology? In many pre-industrial societies there have been women's and men's mysteries which revolved around the differences in female and male experience. From the female experience of gathering and the male experience of hunting both to supply food and clothing, differences arose; women gathered in order to stay close to the fire, the heart of the community where children were socialised, and men hunted because they were physically stronger.

Because of the over-simplification of this example it has now become stereotyped, but the point is, there was equality of status, equal emphasis placed on each task. Female mysteries revolved around cultural experiences such as child-care and the female sexual cycle; of menarche (first period), menstruation, childbirth and the menopause. Male mysteries revolved around strength and achievement, focussing on virility and seeding the next generation. Both sexes could have pride and dignity in their particular contribution to the society they lived in. Problems arose when differences ceased to be celebrated, when there was a perceived inequality in the power balance, and this most obviously occurred when a religious experience was introduced which took the emphasis from the earth to the sky. Rather than the earth and sky being equal, which is evident in many creation myths, for some reason the sky became dominant, represented by the superiority of the mind and intellect; the earth and all things instinctive and sensatory became devalued. It is ironic that the human quality of competition came into play at some point in our story; perhaps as societies expanded, travelled and met different cultures. It is for male animals that competition is important: they have to attract the female to take his sperm and reproduce his kind in his likeness, it is with her that the choice lies; and she has plenty to choose from. In most animals, and birds are a good example, the male is much more colourful and attractive; the female can afford to be plain, her ability to generate, carry and give birth to the young gives her unassailable power. The Goddess represents abundance and with the loss of Her awareness both as a cultural and individual symbol, poverty follows. But it only follows for the vulnerable minorities who are perceived as powerless to hold onto their rights when faced with a status quo; who are so insecure they need to abuse others to get what they want.

Because religions deal with the spiritual and the spiritual should not be disconnected from the intellectual, emotional, sexual and physical, if one wants a truly holistic experience grounded in individuality rather than conditioning, it is wise to bear in mind that power is an important ingredient in all religions. An examination of where that power lies is a good indication of how that religion will nourish and nurture us. Following male-centred religions will feed our male part–animus in Jung's terms–which is very positive, but we often have to take some denigration of the female as part of the religious experience. This often takes the form of abusing our intimate female experience, and in being the temptresses of men because of our appearance and their inability to control themselves;

Even seeing Tanha, Arati, and Raga [the daughters of Mara], there was not the least wish in me for sexual intercourse. What is this, thy daughter's body, but a thing full of water and excrement? I do not even want to touch it with my foot.

BUDDHA IN CONVERSATION WITH MAGANDIYA MAGANDIYASUTTA ATTHAKAVAGGA (BUDDHIST TEXT)

Take her skin from her face and thou shalt see all loathsomeness under it ... within she is full of phlegm, stinking, putrid excremental stuff.

ST JOHN CHRYSOSTOM (MEANING 'GOLDEN MOUTH') C.AD 347–407

Woman ... A dunghill covered with white and red.

PHILIP STUBBES D. 1593, ANATOMIE OF ABUSES

Woman is an all-devouring curse. In her body the evil cycle of life begins afresh, born out of lust engendered by blood and semen. Man emerges mixed with excrement and water, fouled with the impurities of woman. A wise man will avoid the contaminating society of women as he would the touch of bodies infested with vermin.

MAHAHBARATA (HINDU TEXT)

But if you are sick, or on a journey, or one of you come from the privy, or if ye have touched a woman, and ye cannot find water, then use a good surface of sand and wipe your faces and your hands therewith; verily God pardons and forgives.

QU'RAN (ISLAMIC TEXT)[7]

With attitudes like these it is surprising that the human race did not die out, but then there are an equal number of rationalisations from men who wanted to copulate and then turn to religion to excuse him, or biology to explain his drives. These things were said a long time ago and are so enculturated that many men could not say why they are sexist and/or misogynist. Mysogynus, by the way, was a seventeenth-century playwright and such a hater of women that his name has become notorious.

Such attitudes mean that women need to do a radical rethink, and the rise of feminist thinking has given us the opportunity. Whilst the most ancient of religious experiences–The Goddess in all Her manifestations–has become virtually lost to us, or heavily cloaked in other religions doctrines, e.g. The Sea Goddess as Virgin Mary, so we need to reclaim Her. This is why in Women's Spirituality the focus is exclusively on Her. Having been abused, denied and negated we need models to enable inner actualisation; for the Goddess is there in every woman and a little search will find Her. It is partly because of its importance for women and for the earth that a religion which focuses directly upon Her energies to the exclusion of others is so crucial at this time in our story. This is perceived by people deeply indoctrinated in the competitive ethic as a direct denial of other spiritual energies, they believe that, in not mentioning the God or in mentioning Him only in passing as Son/Lover, his energy is being denied, and this indicates that old and stale religious concepts are being foisted onto an ancient religion made new and fresh within modern urban needs.

So what can emphasis on The Goddess bring to modern women's lives? She is in this context primarily a role model, an indication to us of what She means and what by believing in Her we can achieve in our lives. It is Her energy flowing within us which can enable us to take great strength in denying anyone's right to oppress or abuse us.

The Goddess manifestations used in this chapter are predominantly white, mostly Greek, because this culture offers us immediate access to these Female Deities, ironically because of the respect ancient Greece is held in by male writers in the sixteenth and seventeenth centuries, the 'age of enlightenment', when Greek culture at the time of Athens' period of power was held in great esteem by white, male writers. The myths adapted from that period when Zeus was going around raping every woman he met, actually are representative of the period in our story when in this part of the world patriarchal religions were replacing matriarchal ones. This is also the period when the idea of slavery was making an impact because of white imperialist dominant ideologies.

It is hard therefore to gain easy access to Black Goddess archetypes though they exist even in churches in France and Spain.

> *... Chatres, Le Puy and Rocamadour in France, Einsiedeln in Switzerland, Oropa in Piedmont, Our Lady of the Pillar in Zaragoza and Our Lady of Guadalupe and all the Spains. These are a few of the most famous among scores of Black Virgins that have survived centuries of war and revolution, some in great basilicas, some in tiny village churches, others in museums and private collections.*[8]

These come from the early years of christianity when the feminine aspect was revered and hostility to women was unknown. Goddesses from Africa and other threatened continents such as Oceania can be found in *Larousse Encyclopedia of Mythology* which, though seen through white, male eyes could be a starting point for women from other cultures interested in researching and reclaiming their individual archetypes.

Below is an outline of the significance of some of the major Greek Goddesses and the qualities and attributes they represent. They represent ideals, suggestions of what might be achieved if their energy were focused upon an inner work undertaken to harmonise these qualities within oneself. I am not speaking about perfection which is a very difficult concept given the socialisation which we as women have undergone, nor is there any place here for guilt, the great bug bear of us all, rather these qualities are a brief guide to our potential. They are given as suggestions of what can be achieved by moving from a stereotypical perception of oneself to an archetypal awareness of the importance and significance of what being female means. They serve to outline a totally creative, spontaneous and imaginative perception of womankind, her abilities and attributes. They suggest living with oneself happily; free from self-criticism and self-blame and therefore with self-respect and self-confidence.

At a deeper level each Goddess aligns with a Chakra; so that Hestia is the seventh Chakra with violet as Her colour, Artemis the sixth with indigo as Her colour, Athena is the fifth Chakra with blue as Her colour, Demeter is the fourth Chakra with green as Her colour, Persephone is the third Chakra with yellow as Her colour, Aphrodite is the second Chakra with orange as Her colour and Hera is the base Chakra with red as Her colour. If you wish you can focus on that colour when visualising the Goddess that you wish to invoke. Remember when invoking that you are channelling a very powerful and strong energy and always treat Her with the deepest of respect; remember also that you have moved beyond ego into the dimension of Her Realm and behave appropriately when communicating with Her. If you don't feel confident to do this just yet, it is better to wait until you have grown in confidence and/or have more knowledge through study of the energy that you are working with. Wearing the appropriate colour can enable closer alignment with Her particular energy. You may find that a particular colour better represents a particular Goddess for you, if so then that is the colour for you, as nothing that I have written is the definitive version. You can also choose different Goddesses, maybe Egyptian and Celtic who are also well researched, and assign colours as appropriate to your personality:

Hestia

Wise, serene, tranquil, full of peace and inspiration. Her eyes are the windows of the soul. She is intuitive because she listens to her inner voices and courageously follows the wisdom of her own heart. She creates and follows her own path with integrity and dignity. She is prudent, discriminating, discerning and she knows what is best for her. She questions societal messages as not necessarily appropriate for her as an individual; because she lives by her own standards she does not betray anyone else. She makes up her own mind based on deep quiet thought, she trusts that she is the only one who can know about herself. Because she follows her heart's desires she has the genius of knowing her own needs and through this understanding she is more fully aware of others needs. Hestia: Roman Vesta, is the Goddess of the hearth, the inner centre, the warm centre of inner self-knowledge.

Artemis

She is the Huntress, explorer of the unknown, unbound and free. As she is self-regulating she may be thought of as wild, as a law unto herself. She creates her own space and her own boundaries, being inhibited by none. She is quick-witted, sharp and intelligent; because she is clear-sighted she sees hypocrisy for what it is, and will not allow herself to go along with it: she is a seeker after truth. She is in tune with nature, with the natural laws of the universe, with the cycles which rule women's lives; she flows with the harshness of nature: the crashing seas, the roaring winds; because she is totally aligned with the ebbs and flows she is never uncomfortable or out of her depth. Artemis is a Moon Goddess, hence her relationship with water and the flows of Mother Nature. She represents psychic exploration, inner journeying, self-realisation and lights up the dark spaces within us.

Athena

She is the Goddess of creativity and craft; expressing herself in inspired and inventive works. She makes imaginative concepts, turning them into reality and giving birth to new projects. Whilst she has a fighting spirit she is assertive rather than aggressive; she takes a stand for what she believes in and follows through with gentle strength. Also the Goddess of craft and skill she oversees such activities as weaving, knitting, sewing, cookery, design and writing. Connected with the sun, she is brilliant and glowing, illuminating all around her. She brings dreams into fulfilment because she is swift-moving, not allowing herself to get side-tracked or bogged down.

Demeter

She is the archetypal Earth Mother, she represents unconditional love with the ability to leave others alone when they need it or to be understanding and supportive if that is the need. She is too wise to neglect her own needs since her knowledge of others' needs comes from the wisdom and connection with her own. Demeter represents qualities such as receptivity, caring, nurturing, nourishing, kindness, consideration and gentleness.

She often carries a Cornucopia symbol of the abundance of the earth and of the prosperity available to all who are in harmony with her. She represents cooperation, harmony and involvement, uniting humankind in a web of peace and creativity. She understands the cycles of birth, life and death and is wise to the ever-changing nature of humanity.

Persephone

She represents the wise child in all of us, she is spontaneous, creative, imaginative, wide-eyed, artless, fresh and naive. Her openness brings her to experiences free from prejudices of the past and eager to discover new worlds of experience. She is wise in understanding the laws of nature and that play is a serious business. As Persephone travelled into the underworld and became a Queen so also she has another darker side, where she travels into the realm of the unconscious where she is willing to experience the transforming power of self-knowledge. She understands ego death and is able to come face to face with her monsters to confront them and in transmuting them she dies and is reborn herself but irrevocably changed. She is capable of using her power with dignity and grace.

Aphrodite

The Roman Goddess Venus; the Goddess of love. In women's spirituality she is sexually autonomous, making her own decisions based within her own sexual needs. Because she is comfortable with her physical body and is intimately aware of the singular nature of her sexual needs she is enabled to confirm all her valid needs and seek to fulfil them independently. She is fully in tune with the importance of women's erotic desires and is incapable of losing herself within them, within a sexual encounter she remains true to herself and capable of satisfying both people's needs. She holds her sexual needs within herself and does not give herself away in the sexual act; as with all the Goddesses she is capable of paradoxes such as this: to give of herself freely whilst holding on to the integrity of her own being. She has both self-respect and respect for others because she shares her body out of the joy and celebration of being female whether in polarity or similarity. Her energy is magnetic, alluring, attractive and enchanting, her glamour comes from deep inner enjoyment of herself and who she is. Because she relates from deep inside herself she has great personal power and gives space for self-expression and sharing.

Hera

Hera represents the foundations on which we build whether in work, relationships or in making ideas concrete. Her energy is embryonic, full-blooded and powerful–bursting forth to make an impact on all around, she is very much in the world and can be the catalyst for new beginnings. Through her passion for initiating ideas and carrying people along with her she is able to put new projects into operation, and being the driving force in completing them through her determination, she achieves what she set out to do with warmth, power and energy. Because she trusts those around her she is incapable of alienating them but is able to move them with her to achieve joint drives and objects. She is a born leader and prime mover in activating projects, relationships of all kinds and in getting the most out of her life. Because she is committed in relationships and has a great sense of responsibility both to herself and to others she is incapable of betraying anyone's trust, therefore people will always follow her to work in cooperation with her. She is scrupulous in her dealings with other people and constant in her regard and respect for others, her sense of justice is acute and she represents qualities such as honour, fidelity, truth and honesty.

The qualities outlined above redefine women and their energies so that the things which we have abased within ourselves are totally transformed into what they rightly are: positive, creative and life-affirming. These qualities are just the same; it is the emphasis, with the help of the Goddess in all Her dimensions, that has changed for the better, so that we as women can claim our rights and just deserts as beautiful, charismatic and powerful beings.

Notes

1 Lorraine Gamman and Margaret Marshment (eds.), *The Female Gaze* (The Women's Press, 1988) Introduction, page 1.
2 Fidelis Morgan, *A Misogynist's SourceBook* (Jonathan Cape, 1989), page 59.
3 Barbara G. Walker, *The Women's Encyclopedia of Myths and Secrets* (Harper & Row, 1983) pages 346–7.
4 As above, page 495.
5 As above.
6 C. G. Jung, *The Archetypes of the Collective Unconscious* (Routledge, 1959) page 57.
7 Fidelis Morgan, *A Misogynist's SourceBook* (Jonathan Cape, 1989), pages 116 and 117.
8 Ean Begg, *The Cult of the Black Virgin* (Arkana, 1985) Introduction, page 1.

Bibliography

Margot Adler, *Drawing Down The Moon* (Beacon Press, 1986).
Z. Budapest, *The Grandmother of Time* (HarperCollins, 1989).
Mary Daly, *Gyn/Ecology* (The Woman's Press, 1979).
Anne Dickson, *A Woman In Your Own Right* (Quartet Books, 1982).
Anne Dickson, *The Mirror Within* (Quartet Books, 1985).
Caitlin Matthews, *The Elements of The Goddess* (Element Books, 1989).
Naomi Ozaniec, *Daughter of the Goddess, The Sacred Priestess* (Aquarian, 1993).
Monica Sjoo and Barbara Mor, *The Great Cosmic Mother* (Harper & Row, 1987).
Jean Shinoda Bolen, *Goddesses in Everywoman* (Harper & Row, 1984).
Starhawk, *The Spiral Dance* (Harper & Row, 1979).
Diane Stein, *The Women's Spirituality Book* (Llewellyn Publications, 1987).

Richard Sutcliffe

LEFT-HAND PATH RITUAL MAGICK: An Historical and Philosophical Overview

Introduction

In this chapter I provide an overview of 'Left-Hand Path' magick in contemporary Britain. The archaic spelling of 'magick' used herein follows the usage of contemporary Left-Hand practitioners after its reintroduction by Aleister Crowley (1875–1947). Although my emphasis in this overview is on contemporary magickal groups and practitioners of the Left-Hand Path, these groups will be treated partly in terms of their historico-philosophical context. Such an approach is necessary because contemporary Left-Hand Path magick, in both its philosophical and practical aspects, is inextricably and *concretely* bound up with the nineteenth-century 'occult revival' (McIntosh 1972) of ceremonial ritual magic that culminated, at least in terms of subsequent renown, with the formation of the 'Hermetic Order of the Golden Dawn' in 1888. Consequently, any adequate evaluation of this magical current, and its specific place within the broader spectrum of Paganism in the 1990s, cannot afford to neglect the relevant historical background. Additionally, an historically-informed survey should lend itself to any future analysis of the vicissitudes of magic and Paganism in twentieth-century Britain. In this chapter I will first outline some of the beliefs and ideas which characterise Left-Hand Path magick in general, before considering briefly some of the main groups with which I am familiar. I would emphasize, however, that this study is not intended to be exhaustive. Left-Hand Path magick is an amorphous phenomenon and, like all human praxis, is characterised by incessant transformation and *recreation*. Dissemination of information within the magickal scene takes place largely on a one-to-one basis or through a variety of magazines which frequently have very short lifespans of between one or two years. Accordingly, my emphasis here on historical continuity is not intended to be either reductive or homogenizing, but rather to provide the necessary basis from which a consideration of the specifities and innovations of contemporary magick could proceed.

My theoretical approach to magickal notions and practices in this study is phenomenological. By this I mean that it is essentially descriptive and, furthermore, that this description is grounded in the self-understanding of the practitioners themselves. Apart from some elucidation of the fundamental religiophilosophical and ontological tenets underlying magickal practice, greater attention to theoretical analysis will be reserved for a different context. This descriptive approach to the phenomenon of magick incorporates Henry Corbin's cogent assertion that the

> ... *phenomenology of religious experience ought not to deduce it from something else, nor reduce it to something else by illusory causal explanations. It ought to discover which form of consciousness is presupposed by the perceptions of events and worlds inaccessible to the common consciousness.*
>
> CORBIN 1966, P403

The term 'Left-Hand Path' has become an umbrella term of self-designation used by certain contemporary ritual magicians and is usually taken to incorporate practitioners of Thelemic magick (beginning with Aleister Crowley), Tantric magick, and Chaos Magick (inspired by both Crowley and the magickal techniques devised by the occult artist Austin O. Spare, 1886–1956).[1] The notion of the Left-Hand Path is derived from the Tantric term *vama-marga* ('left-path'), i.e. the Left-Hand Path in Tantrism. The core practices of this occult path, known as the *pancamakara*, or 'five *m*'s' (*madya, mamsa, matsya, mudra* and *maithuna*, i.e. wine, flesh, fish, parched grain and intercourse), involves the ritual transgression of certain taboos and incorporates ritual sexual intercourse. The use of this term by contemporary magicians in part reflects the fact that contemporary occultism has incorporated many ideas and techniques from both Tantrism and Yoga. More importantly, perhaps, its usage represents a deliberate attempt by Left-Hand Path magicians to transcend the outmoded and value-laden dichotomy of 'black' versus 'white' magic. This schema, in which black magic is alleged to be of exclusively destructive and malevolent intent, while white magic is used for healing, goodness, and 'light' purposes, is rejected because it is held to reflect the 'moronic oversimplicity of the judeo-xtian [Judaeo-Christian] distinction between good and evil' (MacGregor, et al, 1994 pii). According to Katon Shu'al, the term has 'nothing to do with "evil" practices but seems to originate from the magic associated with the left or more "occult" face of the god Shiva' (Katon Shu'al 1995 pvii n3). These ideas are significant because they reflect an intrinsic aspect of Left-Hand Path magick, i.e. the specific moral and ethical implications which it can have for the individual. To some extent, these are expressed in an emphasis placed on the questioning of authority and conventional morality, but this itself points to a more radical goal of magick, i.e. the liberation of the individual through deconditioning and, ultimately, gnosis. I would emphasize, however, that while there is undoubtedly an antinomian ethos in Left-Hand Path magick, the transgression of mores and taboos has more to do with the overcoming of one's own inhibitions and limitations, which are seen to be bound up with socialisation, than with any ill-conceived anarchism. Magick *is* radically individualistic, and in this sense it can be seen as a particular expression of the individualism which is part of modern ideology (on which, see Dumont 1986). But magick is also more than this; it is aimed at self-transmutation through the experience of the *totality* of being. In Crowley's terms, magick is about the realization of one's own 'True Will'. Further elaboration of some of the main ideas and characteristics of Left-Hand Path magick will be reserved for later in this chapter. Before proceeding any further, however, some clarification of the particular shades of meaning of certain terms is essential. This is necessitated by the frequent invocation of these terms without any attempt at definition, and the consequent rendering of their meanings as somewhat opaque.

The term 'magic' is itself notoriously difficult to define. This is not altogether surprising, however, since even in classical Greece the terms *mageia* and *magikos* originally meant nothing more specific than the 'arts of the magi', i.e. the religion, learning and occult practices of the *magoi*, the Median priestly caste known in Persia as specialists in ritual and religious knowledge (see Luck 1987, p6). Despite this problem, the classical scholar Georg Luck has provided a valuable definition of magic which neatly treads the boundary between generality and specificity. For Luck, magic can be defined as 'a technique grounded in a belief in powers located in the human soul and in the universe outside ourselves, a technique that aims at imposing the human will on nature or on human beings by using supersensual powers' (Luck 1987, p3). This notion of magic has several advantages. First, it is formulated on the basis of Luck's research into Graeco-Roman magic and, consequently, it avoids some of the problems engendered by the ambiguous definitions of magic rendered by medieval theologians who were frequently obsessed by demonology. Secondly, as will become clearer below, it cogently points up the degree to which modern ritual magic is grounded firmly in the Western Gnostic–Hermetic tradition. Thirdly, and this point is related to the second, via the emphasis on human will, i.e. the *intended force* of the magical act, Luck suggests that this understanding of magic predates the approach to magic which predominated during the medieval period, *viz*, a focus on the *type of power* invoked (see Kieckhefer 1989, p14). This emphasis on the intended force of magic was reformulated in sixteenth-century religious debate (*ibid*) and then became influential in early anthropological theory. Frances Yates argues that a fundamental shift in the conception of the magical will occurred during the Renaissance. According to Yates, there was a 'basic psychological reorientation towards a direction of the will which was neither Greek nor mediaeval in spirit', and which had its 'emotional source' in the 'religious excitement caused by the rediscovery of the *Hermetica*, and their attendant Magia; in the overwhelming emotions aroused by Cabala and its magico-religious techniques. *It is magic as an aid to gnosis which begins to turn the will in the new direction*' (Yates 1964, p156 italics added). The importance of the magical will in Left-Hand Path magick, beginning with Crowley's notion of *Thelema*, will be considered below. The final advantage of Luck's definition is his insistence that magic is a 'technique grounded in a belief', or preferably, a set of beliefs. This allows an entry for the notion of a magical world-view, thus recognising the ontological basis of the practice of magic as part of a specific and concrete mode of being-in-the-world.

The recognition of this ontological grounding of magical practice is fundamental to any consideration of contemporary Left-Hand Path magick because, over and above the specific techniques employed by magicians, the practice of ritual magick constitutes a specific and radical project of auto-poiesis (self-creation), which has as its ultimate aim the transmutation of the self. In this respect, I would argue, ritual magick is a particular form of gnostic spirituality within the broader spectrum of the 'Western esoteric tradition'. This existential grounding of magical practice is too often completely ignored by writers on the 'occult', who reductively conflate the widespread cultural interest in alternative forms of religiosity and spirituality with the serious practice of magic. Apart from being both superficial and misleading, this attitude to the occult fails to take account of the qualitative differences between popular enthusiasm for these ideas, and the formidable 'demands which any genuine path of spiritual development necessarily entails' (Galbreath 1971, p633/5).

The terms 'occult' and 'esoteric' are frequently used interchangeably. Etymologically, both have similar meanings: 'occult' being from the Latin for 'hidden' (or, 'to hide'), while 'esoteric' derives from the Greek for 'inner' (*eisoteros*, 'further in'; *esoterikos*, 'within'), and both have come to refer generally to something which is *supra* sense-empirical. Both also refer to a specific form of knowledge, available only to the initiated. But these vague notions are insufficient for my purpose here. More useful is the analytical differentiation, along practical versus philosophical lines, ventured by Edward Tiryakian in his seminal essay on the sociology of esoteric culture. For Tiryakian, the 'occult' is constituted by:

> *... intentional practices, techniques, or procedures which (a) draw upon hidden or concealed forces in nature or the cosmos that cannot be measured or recognized by the instruments of modern science, and (b) which have as their desired or intended consequences empirical results, such as either obtaining knowledge of the empirical course of events or altering them from what they would have been without this intervention (1972, p498).*

In contrast, Tiryakian defines the 'esoteric' as those 'religiophilosophic belief systems which underlie occult techniques and practices; that is, it refers to the more comprehensive cognitive mappings of nature and the cosmos, the epistemological and ontological reflections of ultimate reality, which mappings constitute a stock of knowledge that provides the ground for occult procedures' (*ibid*, p499). I would emphasize, however, that the actualities of magickal praxi, which are embedded in the concrete existential realities of specific individuals, rarely manifest such a clear cut dichotomy of 'theory versus practice'.

It should be noted that this differentiation of occult and esoteric is somewhat different from a more common and, it must be said, ideologically loaded understanding of the terms which reflects the Left-Hand (occult) versus Right-Hand (esoteric) approaches to ritual magic which have emerged as discrete currents of Western esotericism during the twentieth century. This Left-Hand/Right-Hand division is reflected in the organisation of the *Talking Stick Magical Directory* (1994) of magical organisations in Great Britain, which is divided into three sections: the 'pagan, occult and esoteric'. The occult section is headed by an article on 'Aleister Crowley and the Eastern Influence', thus identifying the two fundamental influences on Left-Hand Path magick. In contrast, the esoteric section is headed by an article summarising the history of the 'Western Esoteric

Tradition', and is followed by pieces on the major Right-Hand path magical orders, such as the Society of the Inner Light ('S.I.L.'; other examples of what I consider to be Right-Hand path magic can be found in Luhrmann, 1989). In terms of Tiryakian's conceptualisation, however, both aspects–the practical (occult) and religiophilosophical (esoteric)–are integral parts of *both* the Left- and Right-Hand paths. A further, rather baseless, association of this division is the notion of 'black' (Left-Hand/occult) magic versus 'white' (Right-Hand/esoteric) magic, which I have already referred to briefly. Although revealing in terms of the particular morality implicit in its invocation, usually by those seeking to label themselves 'white' and/or others 'black' (see also Martin 1989, p9), this conceptualisation of magical practice is fundamentally inappropriate in the context of contemporary occultism. On this issue, Tantric magicians sometimes refer to one of Patanjali's aphorisms on Yoga, which states that the '*karman* (action) of the *yogin* is neither black nor white; [the *karman*] of others is threefold' (Feuerstein 1989, p130, brackets in original). The implication of this is that the adept *yogin*, while abiding in a state of unified pure consciousness, becomes an *a-moral* being. In my experience, this invocation of Patanjali is used by magicians to illustrate, and legitimate, their individualistic attempt to transcend all forms of morality which are externally imposed; ultimately, it is argued, the highest morality is that which is derived through the process of self-realisation, or, in Nietzschean terms, through 'self-overcoming'.

The Western Esoteric Tradition

Before considering Left-Hand Path magick in more detail, however, it is necessary to consider the notion of the 'Western Esoteric Tradition'. This notion is gaining increasing acceptance among historians of religious ideas (see especially Faivre and Needleman, eds., 1993; Faivre 1994a) and should not be understood as referring solely to twentieth-century Right-Hand Path ritual magic. The basic premise of this notion is that there exists a relatively continuous 'tradition' of spirituality, identifiable at the philosophical rather than material–historical level, throughout the history of Western magico-religious ideas. This tradition is usually regarded as incorporating the religiophilosophical and theurgic-magical influences of Gnosticism, Hermeticism, Neoplatonism, Pythagoreanism, astrology, alchemy, and the Jewish Kabbalah (see McIntosh 1987, pp24–31; and the more detailed analyses of Faivre 1993a, 1993b, 1994a). These various esoteric currents began to coalesce in the fifteenth century, when a specific corpus of material was constituted, and the notion of an enduring 'tradition' began to be developed in the work of certain Neoplatonic philosophers during the Italian Renaissance. These scholars formulated the notion of a Christian Cabala which, along with several other currents that either emerged or gained increasing prominence from the seventeenth century onwards (such as Rosicrucianism, speculative Freemasonry, Romanticism, and modern ritual magic), can now be seen as augmentative and continuous of this Western esoteric tradition.[2]

According to Antoine Faivre, arguably the foremost scholar of the Western esoteric tradition, the 'esoteric', as a particular form of thought, can be identified through the presence of 'six fundamental characteristics distributed in varying degrees within its vast concrete historical framework' (Faivre 1993a, pxv). Four of these characteristics are held to be 'intrinsic' because their 'simultaneous presence is a necessary and sufficient condition for a material studied to be included in the field of esotericism' (ibid). These intrinsic elements are (1) correspondences, (2) living nature, (3) imagination and mediation, and (4) the experience of transmutation. A consideration of these constituents of esotericism at this point will obviate needless repetition below since, I shall argue, these elements form an essential basis of contemporary magick and, consequently, I will have recourse to refer back to them.[3]

1 Correspondences

These are 'symbolic and/or real correspondences between all parts of the visible or invisible universe' (Faivre 1993a, pxv). This idea is summed up in the alchemical edict 'that which is above is like that which is below; that which is below is like that which is above' (from the *Tabula Smaragdina*, or 'Emerald Tablet'). Examples of these correspondences include those between the 'material world and the invisible spheres of the celestial or supercelestial realms' (Faivre 1993a, pxv), and those which constitute the dialectical interrelationship between the individual human body and the totality of the cosmos. This human–cosmos homology is a particular form of the archetypal matrix of microcosmos–macrocosmos dialectics. The theory of the occult constitution of human beings derives from the notion that there is a strict equivalence between the structuration of the individual human 'embodied psyche'[4] (the microcosm), and the structure of the cosmos, or universe, as a whole (the macrocosm).

According to Faivre, esoteric correspondences are 'considered more or less veiled at first glance, and they are therefore meant to be read, to be decoded. The entire universe is a great theater of mirrors, a set of hieroglyphs to decipher; everything is a sign, everything harbors and manifests mystery' (1993a, pxv). The principle underlying the theory of correspondences is that of cosmic sympathy, or universal interdependence, i.e. that there is an implicit affinity or unity between every thing in the universe (see also Luck 1987, pp3–4; and the primary sources excerpted in *ibid*, pp118–31). Essentially, then, this conception of the universe is one of 'an organic whole under the influence of laws to be searched for in the light of analogy' (Faivre 1993b, p26).

2 *Living Nature*

This notion is inextricably bound up with the theory of correspondences in which the cosmos is regarded as complex and hierarchical. Accordingly, 'Nature occupies an essential place within it. Multilayered, rich in potential revelations of all kinds, it must be read as one reads a book' (Faivre 1993a, pxvi). This idea of nature as alive and ensouled is found in the ancient notion of the *anima mundi* ('world soul') which is described in Plato's *Timaeus*, and is also found in a great deal of alchemical thought. Contemporary versions of this idea include Lovelock's 'Gaia hypothesis', and certain aspects of Hillman's 'Archetypal Psychology'. The idea of living nature is also bound up with the notion of the inner light which 'pervades Nature to its very core' (Faivre 1994, p65), and is 'akin to the light of the soul, to the light with which God has created the universe' (*ibid*). In much esoteric thought the microcosmos–macrocosmos homology includes this essential link between the individual soul and 'Nature', or even the soul of the world or cosmos. This link is possible because both the individual and the ensouled world are imbued with the same essential substance, light, or energy.

Having considered these esoteric notions of correspondences and living nature, I would now add to the definition of magic cited earlier (from Luck 1987) Faivre's summation of magic as 'at once the knowledge of a network of sympathies or antipathies which bind the things of Nature and the concrete implementation of this knowledge' (1993a, pxvi).

3 *Imagination and Mediation*

These two ideas are integrally linked because it is the esoteric imagination, in the positive and creative sense of the term, which operates predominantly through various forms of mediation, such as rituals, the Tarot, the Kabbalistic 'Tree of Life', mandalas, systems of correspondences, and so on. In fact, this creative form of imagination is already implied in the idea of correspondences because such complex symbolical systems only become esoterically meaningful via the application of sophisticated modalities of analogical consciousness.

The magickal, esoteric imagination is a form of imagination which is accorded its own ontological positivity, i.e. it is recognised as having a real existence and is appreciated for its infinitely creative potential. Such a conception of the imagination is radically different from the impoverished ontological status of the imagination prevalent in the contemporary West, i.e. as the 'not real'. Consequently, some of the more radical theorists of the imagination have found it necessary to formulate new terminology in order to distance themselves from this reductive conception. In terms of this chapter, the most pertinent example is Henry Corbin. Corbin coined the term 'imaginal' to distinguish that most radical form of creative imagination which 'has a noetic value ... it is an organ of knowledge because it "creates" being' (Corbin 1969, p180). Based on his work on the doctrine of the imagination in Shi'ite theosophy, Corbin formulated the notion of the *Mundus Imaginalis* (the 'world of images') to specify the realm of mystic ' "cosmography" [which] designates the intermediate world or plane of being specifically corresponding to the mediating function of the Imagination, as the luminous world of Idea-Images, of apparitional figures ...'(*ibid*, p190). Faivre regards this intermediary realm as a 'mesocosm' with which visionary rapport can be established via the mediating function of the imagination as an 'organ of the soul' (1993a, pxvii; cf. Corbin 1969, p221ff). The esoteric imagination, then, is 'an imagination that allows the use of these intermediaries, symbols, and images for gnostic ends, to penetrate Nature's hieroglyphs, to put the theory of correspondences into active practice, and to discover, to see, and to know the mediating entities between the divine world and Nature' (Faivre 1993a, pxvii; on the importance of the mediating image in Gnosticism, see Filoramo 1990, pp40–1, 57).

4 The Experience of Transmutation

This notion is virtually synonymous with gnosis, which I will discuss presently, and so will only be briefly considered here. The experience of transmutation is perhaps the most significant aspect of esotericism in that it is the ultimate attainment to which the esotericist aspires. 'Transmutation' is more than just a spiritual 'transformation' since it implies the passing of a thing from one level to another, and the 'very nature of the elements constituting it [being] modified' (*ibid*, pxviii). The idea of transmutation is fundamental to alchemy, but it is also more widespread in the archetypal matrix of the spiritual initiation, and the 'metamorphosis' or rebirth which the initiate thereby undergoes. The experience of transmutation is the attainment of genuine gnosis; suffice it to note here that to attain this experience, 'one must not separate knowledge (gnosis) from interior experience, or intellectual activity from active imagination' (*ibid*).

Gnosis and the Intentional Structure of Consciousness

Having considered the four 'intrinsic' components of Western esotericism, of which magick is a contemporary form, it is necessary then to consider in some detail the central principle linking the various manifestations of this tradition, i.e. the attainment of *gnosis* (spiritual knowledge). This emphasis on gnosis is, I would suggest, no less characteristic of many contemporary Left-Hand Path magicians than it was of their historical predecessors (see, for example, Carroll 1987, p31ff); and this is despite the fact that certain historians of English occultism have tended to dismiss contemporary practitioners, particularly those who follow the Left-Hand approach, as little more than dilettantes. This attitude is disingenuous. In contrast, I would argue that the attainment of gnosis, understood in its fullest sense, is perhaps the most fundamental aim of magickal practice. This will be elucidated below, but it is first necessary to consider what, specifically, is meant by this term (gnosis). The justification for this is twofold: first, on the grounds that many of the epistemological and ontological premises of magickal practice are derived from the essence of this gnostic philosophy. Secondly, and this is consequent upon the previous justification, the religiophilosophical basis of magick cannot be properly apprehended, let alone analysed, without some attempt being made to grasp this seminal concept.

To begin with, it is essential to emphasize that gnosis, as understood here, must be distinguished from 'Gnosticism', i.e. the term used to designate the complex of religio-theological notions characteristic of the 'Gnostic' sects that flourished, for the most part, in Egypt during the second century CE (see Filoramo 1990, ch9). Additionally, gnosis, as a core component of the Western esoteric tradition, should not be confused with those trends in Western religious history which, resembling Gnosticism, have been termed 'Gnostic' by scholars surveying these phenomena from a diachronic perspective (see, for example, the recent works by Filoramo 1990, and Couliano 1992). Gnosis, as distinct from Gnosticism, can be defined initially as 'knowledge of the divine mysteries reserved for an élite' (definition from the Messina Colloquium on Gnosticism held in 1966, as cited by Filoramo 1990, p143). In classical Greek, the terms *gnosis* and *gignosko* indicate 'true knowledge of "what is" (*ta onta*) in contrast to mere sense perception (*aisthesis*)' (*ibid*, pp38–9). Significantly, the term implied the act of knowing rather than knowledge itself (*ibid*); gnosis is thus a specific modality of consciousness (the imaginal). But gnosis is far more than just a cognitive process of the intellect; it is ontological knowledge, an activity which involves the whole existential being. This was so for the historical Gnostics, in whose texts gnosis became 'synonymous with *epignosis*, recognition of one's own true reality: that is, the ontological self that constitutes and is its basis' (*ibid*, pp39–40). It is equally so according to the modern understanding of the term since, as Roberts Avens emphasizes, a fundamental aspect of gnosis is the idea that 'there is a strict correspondence between knowledge and being' (1984, p3).

At this point the radical difference between gnostic and intellectual knowledge becomes manifest. Through gnosis, there is a collapse of the traditional subject-object dichotomy that has become entrenched in the structure of Western ontology. This is because 'to know' through gnosis implies that the knower becomes immersed to the point of identity in that which is known, *viz*, the numinous realm of the *Mundus Imaginalis* (cf Filoramo 1990, p41). In terms of magickal ontology, this notion of a gnostic identification with that which is known is implicitly present in the desire for the unification of the microcosm with the macrocosm which, Crowley asserts, is 'the principal business, the essential, of all magical work' (Crowley 1969, p78). While I cannot elaborate on this point in any detail here, I would like to suggest that the esoteric system of correspondences, particularly the positing of a common substance which permeates the entire cosmos and so makes possible the union between the microcosmos and the macrocosmos, is in fact revelatory of the basic intentional structuration of human consciousness (on which, see Kapferer n.d.) which arises through the ongoing 'bodily projective fusion with and assimilation of the world' (Mimica 1991, p35). In existential phenomenological terms, human existence is always structured via the incessant irruption or transcendence into the world of consciousness from its 'originally given organismic (bodily) immanence' (*ibid.*). That is to say, human (embodied) consciousness is not separate from the world, but is always already in the world while simultaneously and perpetually bringing that world into being. As such, esoteric correspondences represent a specific form of human cosmic self-totalization, a potentiality which is emergent from the intrinsic 'openness of the human organism, its intentional orientation to the world' (*ibid.*). This mutual interrelationship of the individual and the world, which is irreducibly a dialectical interfusion of interiority and exteriority, is beautifully expressed by Merleau-Ponty, who states that both:

> *universality and the world lie at the core of individuality and the subject, and this will never be understood as long as the world is made into an object. It is understood immediately if the world is the field of our experience, and if we are nothing but a view of the world, for in that case it is seen that the most intimate vibration of our psycho-physical being already announces the world, the quality being the outline of a thing, and the thing the outline of the world.* (*1962, p406*)

The final aspect of gnosis which must be emphasized in this connection is its soteriological potential; gnosis is knowledge which transforms the knower. This is often referred to as the 'salvational' aspect of gnosis (see Avens 1984, p3ff; Filoramo 1990, p41; Faivre 1994, p64) but such a notion is inappropriate in the context of the Left-Hand path because it is overly connotative of Christian redemption. The soteriological aspect of gnosis in Left-Hand magick is more appropriately understood in relation to the idea of 'liberation' found in Indian soteriological/liberation teachings (cf Feuerstein 1989, p12). This is especially so in the case of Tantric magick. Such liberation is inextricably bound up with the ontological nature of gnosis referred to above. To know one's own true reality and the ontological self which 'constitutes and is its basis' implies knowing one's own origin (see Filoramo 1990, p41). In Left-Hand magick this knowledge becomes possible essentially through an ongoing project of individual *deconditioning* aimed at the transcendence of everything which impedes the individual from becoming his or her 'true' self, such as the process of social conditioning (see, for example, Katon Shu'al 1995, p20). Liberation, or freedom, is ultimately attained through the individual's project of realizing his or her own 'True Will'. Having considered some of the fundamental esoteric tenets upon which magick is based, it remains to outline some of the major currents of the Left-Hand path.

Thelemic Magick: The Legacy of Aleister Crowley

The most important single influence on contemporary Left-Hand Path magick is Aleister Crowley, and it was essentially through Crowley's magickal innovations that the Left-Hand Path emerged as a discrete current within the broader context of the Ritual Magic tradition in Western esotericism. Crowley received his magical training from the Hermetic Order of the Golden Dawn, founded in 1888, of which he was a member from 1898–1900 (see Howe 1985, p192; Gilbert 1986, pp159–60). It is probably fair to say that, for all Crowley's magical innovativeness, it was the Golden Dawn's complex synthesis of Hermetic lore which remained the essential structural foundation for Crowley's own system of 'Magick'. Although there is not space here to discuss the Golden Dawn in any great detail, a brief discussion is apposite given its enormous subsequent influence (which endures to this day).[5]

The Golden Dawn can be seen as the culmination of the nineteenth-century occult revival. Francis King has argued that there are 'four fundamental concepts on which the modern magical revival is based' (1975, pp18–19). Three of these were, to some extent, systematised in the influential occult works of Eliphas Lévi (1810–75),[6] viz, the doctrine of correspondences, which constitutes an example of the first 'intrinsic' component of esotericism discussed above; an emphasis on the potentially unlimited powers of the magically trained human will; and the notion of the 'Astral Light' which pervades everything in the universe. According to Lévi, the 'will of intelligent beings acts directly on this light and thereby on all Nature. It is the common mirror of all thoughts and forms' (Lévi 1968, p12 n1). Again, this notion is essentially similar to the second intrinsic component of esotericism discussed above. Lévi's work was also important in that it contained the first explicit attempt to incorporate the Tarot into an occult system of correspondences. These three concepts form an integral part of the magic of the Golden Dawn. Additionally, however, the Golden Dawn introduced the fourth component of King's schema, i.e. an explicit emphasis on the 'Magical Imagination' (King 1975, p25). The Golden Dawn theory of the imagination is elaborated in the fifth 'Flying Roll', as certain of the instructional manuscripts were known, written by Dr E.W. Berridge. According to Berridge:

> *The uninitiated interpret Imagination as something 'imaginary' in the popular sense of the word; i.e. something unreal. But imagination is a reality ... To practise magic, both the Imagination and the Will must be called into action, they are co-equal in the work. Nay more, the Imagination must precede the Will in order to produce the greatest possible effect (as cited in King, ed., 1987, p47).*

Such an understanding of the imagination was not that novel in terms of the history of Western esotericism, but was actually a revivification of a fundamental component of magico-esoteric philosophy, as I have already noted above. This does not, however, reduce the significance of the Golden Dawn's reintroduction of an explicit emphasis on the creative, noetic imagination. On the contrary, I would argue that this positive understanding of the imagination is one of the most essential distinctions between contemporary magickal ontology and the prevailing rationalism of Western society.

To understand Crowley's magickal system, then, it is necessary to recognize the influence which the Golden Dawn system had upon him. The most important components of the Golden Dawn's teaching were ceremonial magic, the study of practical Cabala, and the use of Yoga and/or Eastern meditational practices (Katon Shu'al 1995, pp23–4). In particular, Crowley was influenced by Allan Bennett (1872–1923), who was the most important instructor he had during his formative period as a magician (cf Howe 1985, p194). Bennett had almost certainly used hallucinogens as part of his magical experimentation, as Crowley would later do on numerous occasions. It is also likely that Crowley's interest in Eastern meditational techniques was influenced fundamentally by Bennett. Apart from the Golden Dawn system, there were two other integral components to Crowley's Magick, *viz*, the 'sexo-magical practices of the Order of Oriental Templars, and the religious, historical and philosophical teachings of the *Book of the Law*' (King, ed., 1974, p5). It is these two components which have most directly influenced contemporary Left-Hand Path magick.

The Book of the Law, which represents the distillation of Crowley's magickal philosophy, comprises a series of aphorisms which provide the ontological and ideological basis for the cult of *Thelema*.[7]

Crowley's notion of 'Thelema' derives from the Greek word for 'will' and was prefigured in Rabelais' satirical *Gargantua and Pantagruel* (c. 1532–4) in which there appears a monastic institution, the Abbey of Thélème, which has the injunction *Fay ce que voudras* ('Do what thou wilt'), the abbey's only law, inscribed over the entrance. The generally accepted account of the origin of *The Book of the Law* is that Crowley acted as a vehicle for its transmission during a magickal working, which took place over three days, in Egypt during April 1904 (see Crowley 1989, p393ff; King, ed., 1974, p9). The source of this transmission was claimed by Crowley to have been some form of 'praeter-human intelligence' known as 'Aiwass' (or 'Aiwaz'), whom Crowley later recognized as his 'Holy Guardian Angel', or inner guide. Of the book's content, three aphorisms in particular are generally taken to express the essence of Thelema:

> Do what thou wilt shall be the whole of the Law (*AL*.I.40).
> Love is the law, love under will (*AL*.I.57).
> Every man and every woman is a star (*AL*.I.3).

The first of these aphorisms, described by Crowley as 'the most sublimely austere ethical precept ever uttered, despite its apparent licence' (1973, p352), has been frequently misunderstood as an exhortation to gratify egoic desire, to 'Do whatever you like'; this is most emphatically not the way Crowley understood it, as he repeatedly made clear in his expositions of *The Book of the Law*. Crowley's notion of will implies a Nietzschean conception of a 'true self', which underlies the socialised ego, and which is the essential core of one's being. For Crowley, 'any True Will is of necessity in harmony with the facts of Existence' (Crowley 1973, p335n), and further, ' "Do what thou wilt" is to bid Stars to shine, Vines to bear grapes, Water to seek its level; man is the only being in Nature that has striven to set himself at odds with himself' (*ibid*, p352). Like Nietzsche's Zarathustra, who proclaimed 'Become who you are', Crowley's Aiwass expounds a radically individualistic philosophy which is essentially an ethics of self-realization. Implicit in this, however, for both Crowley and Nietzsche, is the notion that much of the time we do not act in accordance with this higher self due to our failure to question our conditioning by society and our adherence to the received morality. Accordingly, Nietzsche suggests that in order to single oneself out from the mass you should listen to your conscience, which says 'Be your self! All you are now doing, thinking, desiring, is not yourself' (Nietzsche 1983, p127). For Crowley, 'The word of Sin is Restriction' ... 'It is a lie, this folly against self' (1989, p400). The third of the aphorisms mentioned above, 'Every man and every woman is a star', Crowley explains as meaning that every individual is unique 'one, individual and eternal' (*ibid*, p401). Thus, the overarching precept of Thelema is 'to realize one's own absolute God-head and to act with the nobility which springs from that knowledge' (*ibid*). With this understanding of True Will, as an underlying dynamism inherent in the individual, in the essence of his or her true self, Crowley's well-known definition of magick, as 'the Science and Art of causing Change to occur in conformity with the Will' (Crowley 1973, p131), is more easily interpreted. Will, both for Crowley and those who are inspired by him and call themselves 'Thelemites', is a cosmic force which permeates the entire universe. Accordingly, someone who is doing their True Will has the 'inertia of the Universe' (*ibid*, p133) to assist them. Magick is less about exerting one's egoism than about transcending the ego in order to align oneself with the harmony of the cosmos. The principal aim of magickal ritual, to unite the microcosmic human with the macrocosmic Universe, expresses this notion beautifully.

Crowley understood the reception of *The Book of the Law*, in 1904, as inaugurating the 'New Aeon of Horus', of which he was the prophet. This was based on a cosmological notion of aeonic time in which each aeon lasts for approximately two thousand years and was essentially a reformulation of the astrological notion of the 'Great Year' made up of twelve 'Platonic months' (and derived from the phenomenon of the precession of the equinoxes). Crowley's scheme begins with the Aeon of Isis, characterised by the worship of the Mother, followed by the Aeon of Osiris, i.e. that of the dying-god, which is contemporaneous with the Christian era and which Crowley subsequently termed 'e.v.' ('Era Vulgaris'). According to Crowley, we 'may then expect the New Aeon to release mankind from its pretence of altruism, its obsession of fear and its consciousness of sin' (1989, p400). In very summary form, then, this is the religiophilosophical framework which forms the basis of Thelemic magick. It is in the context of this New Aeon, which is regarded as having superseded the outmoded ethics, morality, and mediated religion of the Era Vulgaris, while opening the way for each individual to seek liberation through the realization of their own True Will, that the antinomian and amoral principles of Left-Hand Path magick must first be understood.

Contemporary Thelemites, on the whole, tend to 'admire something in the spirit of Crowley rather than the word' (O.G.D.O.S. n.d.).[8] This is in keeping with the principles of Thelema, of deconditioning oneself in order to develop 'independence of spirit and ultimately to become [one's] very own self' (*ibid*). An uncritical adulation of Crowley is known in the magickal community as 'Crowleyanity', i.e. yet another form of mediated spirituality, and is usually seen to be undesirable. It remains, then, to briefly consider some of the contemporary groups which work with Crowley's ideas.

The Ordo Templi Orientis (O.T.O.)

In England there are currently two main O.T.O. groups, the O.T.O. 'Caliphate', and the O.T.O. 'Typhonian'; both claim to be the authentic successors to the English O.T.O. which Crowley headed until his death (in 1947). Additionally, there are several other O.T.O. groups in Europe and the rest of the world. The early history of the original O.T.O. is obscure. The German historian P.R. König (1991) suggests 1902–3 as the date for the earliest documentary evidence relating to the O.T.O. but, unfortunately, provides no extracts from this material. The inspiration for the order's formation can be attributed to Karl Kellner (1850–1905) and Theodor Reuss (1855–1923), both of whom were involved in German irregular masonry and were interested in Yoga techniques; Reuss in particular seems to have been interested in 'sexual yoga' (Howe and Möller 1978, pp30, 38). R.A. Gilbert (1994, p10) suggests that the O.T.O. was founded by Kellner in 1902 and that Reuss became involved soon after; again, however, no supporting documentation is provided. Accordingly, although it may have been 'founded' as early as 1902, in the absence of further evidence it does not seem unreasonable to agree with Howe and Möller's assertion that it 'seems unlikely that the O.T.O. was in any sense active as early as 1905–6 and we believe that it was not effectively launched until 1912 when Aleister Crowley became involved' (Howe and Möller 1978, p38). To some extent, the dating depends on semantics since most of the people involved at this early stage were both personally acquainted with and involved in various irregular and fringe masonic groups whose lifespan was often short and in which there was a certain degree of membership crossover; a situation which is not entirely dissimilar to Left-Hand Path magick today. Essentially, the O.T.O. was a product of the phenomenon of fringe and irregular masonry in England and Germany during the late-nineteenth and early-twentieth centuries (see Howe 1972; Howe and Möller 1978).

Originally, the rituals and grade structure of the order were pseudo-masonic, but with the important difference that the higher degrees included sexual magic. Crowley assumed the leadership of the English branch of the O.T.O. in 1912 (on which, see Gilbert 1994). Since Crowley's death various factions have emerged, each claiming to have the best claim to 'authentic' succession of Crowley's order. These disputes have involved legal proceedings in recent years but these do not concern me here. Of the two main groups in England, the Caliphate O.T.O., which has its administrative base in the USA, has maintained a quasi-masonic structure. The Typhonian O.T.O., headed by Kenneth Grant, is perhaps closer to the spirit of Crowley's own magickal order, the A.A. (*Argenteum Astrum*, or 'Silver Star', originally founded by Crowley *c.* 1907), and is structured around individual graded magical practices aimed at the attainment of adeptship; the Typhonian O.T.O. produces the occasional magazine *Starfire* (Volume 1, nn1–5, have appeared during the period 1986–94).

Oxford Golden Dawn Occult Society

Founded in 1981 by Frater Katon Shu'al, who was at that time a member of the Typhonian O.T.O., 'O.G.D.O.S.' is not a magickal order as such. Rather, it is a non-sectarian magickal sodality which 'aims to disseminate authentic information about the occult' (O.G.D.O.S. n.d.) and, accordingly, organizes speaker meetings and workshops throughout the year, usually on a monthly basis. This culminates in the National Symposium of Thelemic Magick, which has been co-ordinated by O.G.D.O.S. each year since 1986 and provides an opportunity for the congregation of people interested in the Left-Hand Path (see, for example, Morgan, ed., 1995). The organization also offers a foundation course in magick, along Tantrik-Hermetic lines, on a small-scale basis. Essentially, O.G.D.O.S. is a community of individuals who share similar interests in magick, but who usually do solitary magickal work. Additionally, there is an inner ritual group, involving some newer members and several long-term members of O.G.D.O.S., which began work early in 1994 and meets on a monthly basis. This is the latest of a series of such groups within the organization which work with a 'freestyle' approach to magick, and incorporate such interests as 'ceremonial magick, witchcraft, tantra, qabala, shamanism, runes', and Thelemic magick (O.G.D.O.S. n.d.). The ethos of the organization is radically individualistic and anti-hierarchical.

Chaos Magick: Guerrilla Ontology as World-View

Chaos Magick is one of the most recent developments of the Left-Hand tradition; it is also one of the most self-consciously 'new' forms of magick. This can be evinced from Chaos Magick's self-construction of itself as the 'emergent magical ethos' of postmodernity (Hine 1993, p120), and in some Chaoists' attempts to incorporate quantum physics and Chaos theory into their magickal systems. In one of the few critical pieces on Chaos Magic to have appeared to date, Siobhán Houston argues that 'one useful way to regard Chaos Magic is as 'postmodern shamanism'' (1995, p55). Houston rightly emphasizes the affinities between Chaos Magick and 'deconstructive postmodernism', particularly in terms of a mutual relativistic epistemology and an insistence on the fragmentation of subjectivity (cf. Hine 1993, p120) but, I would argue, Houston is not sufficiently critical of the self-constructive aspect underlying these trends in Chaos Magick (and postmodernism), i.e. a certain neo-technophilia, which is evident in the interest among Chaoists in cyberspace and virtual reality (see Hine 1993 on 'cybersorcery' and 'virtual magick'). More often than not, however, these notions represent an updating of terminology rather than any genuinely radical innovation in occult theory, as illustrated by Hine's dismissal of the notion of 'Virtual Magick' as 'any magical activity carried out within a visualized space (1993, p67). In fact, Hine is merely using an updated metaphor, fuelled by the conviction that the new is equivalent to the best, for the imaginal modality of consciousness which, I have argued above, is integral to esoteric thought. In this respect, Chaos Magick, as the latest attempt to make magick 'scientific' (Houston 1995, p56), fails to take note of the fact that scientific 'empiricism' and 'objectivity' are as much the products of the imaginary structuration of human consciousness as are esoteric models of the cosmos.

Historically, Chaos Magick emerged from the Leeds occult scene during the late 1970s primarily through the collaboration of Pete Carroll and Ray Sherwin. The 'Illuminates of Thanateros' (I.O.T.) was originally a fairly small, loose network of individuals who were experimenting with various magical techniques. The first public notice of the I.O.T. seems to have been published in 1978 in Sherwin's magazine, the *New Equinox*, which stated, 'The IOT represents a fusion of Thelemic Magick, Tantra, The Sorceries of Zos, and Tao. The non-mysteries of symbolic systems have been discarded in favor of mastery of technique' (as cited in Houston 1995, p58). The first 'organized' I.O.T. group came together in Yorkshire in late

1980 and worked for about eighteen months, until the spring of 1982. A second group was organized *c.* April 1984 and died out in late 1987. By this time the magazine, *Chaos International*, had begun to be produced (in 1986) and this is still running today. At approximately the same time that the second of the Yorkshire I.O.T. groups dissolved, the 'Magical Pact of the Illuminates of Thanateros' was formed. The 'Pact' is more like a 'traditional' magical order, with an initiatory grade structure and temples in different areas of the country (for information regarding the Pact grade structure see Carroll 1992). The Pact is still operative today and many 'Chaoists' meet annually at national or international Chaos conventions.

In terms of historical influences, Chaos magick has drawn inspiration from Crowley's system of Thelema, as well as from the solitary sorcerer and artist Austin O. Spare, who was briefly a magical pupil of Crowley (on Spare see Grant 1975; Drury and Skinner 1972, pp49–71; and the important article by Semple 1994). Spare personified the solitary magician and developed a complex personal magico-cosmology based on the dualistic conception of the 'Zos Kia Cultus', which corresponds, approximately, to 'I' and 'All-Otherness' and, Semple argues, 'Being and Nothingness' (1994, p63). Kia is the 'absolute freedom which being free is mighty enough to be "reality" at any time: therefore is not potential or manifest ... by ideas of freedom or "means", but by the Ego being free to receive it, by being free of ideas about it and not believing' (Spare, cited in Semple 1994, p58). This notion is taken up in Carroll's *Liber Null* (1987) which was one of the earliest 'grimoires', or magical manuals, of the nascent Chaos movement when it was first published in 1978.[9] For Carroll, Kia is the 'unity which appears to the mind to exert the twin functions of will and perception ... Sometimes it is called the spirit, or soul, or life force ... [it is the] 'basis of consciousness (or experience), and it has no fixed qualities which the mind can latch on to' (1987, p28). Kia is, in existential terms, the ground of the disclosure of being. In contrast, Zos is 'the body considered as a whole' (Spare n.d. p45), which Semple elucidates as 'all that is embodied or manifest–the apperceptive or "Conative" Ego that "receives" Kia, and is indeed is [*sic*] the bodying forth of the Absolute into being' (*ibid*). Additionally, Spare developed the magical technique of sigilisation, which involves forming a glyph of conjoined letters or images, the sigil taken to embody a precise statement of the magician's will, which is then projected into the 'subconscious' while in an altered state of consciousness. Ideally, this process derives its efficacy through by-passing completely one's everyday, 'rational' consciousness or egoity. Sigilisation has been very influential in Chaos Magick (for more detailed discussions of the technique see Carroll 1987; Sherwin 1992; Fries 1992; and Semple 1994).

Chaos Magick is, to some extent, characterised by an emphasis on developing magickal techniques. This is due partly to the fact that many Chaoists do not feel the need for the elaborate metaphysical schemas which are often associated with magickal systems. Through an embrace of quantum physics and the notion that the outcome of an experiment is dependent upon the observer (more accurately, on the nature of the experiment), i.e. non-objectivity, Chaoists like to play with the idea that belief shapes reality, and consequently engage in 'paradigm-shifting', i.e. the deliberate, but temporary, adoption of a particular belief in order to achieve a desired outcome, after which the belief may be discarded. Belief is thus a tool *of* magick rather than an immutable framework for its practice. This attitude is summed up in the phrase 'Nothing is True, Everything is Permitted'.[10] Such 'guerrilla ontology' (R. A. Wilson 1992, p59; cf. Younger 1991) reflects the important influence of the American 'Discordian' movement on Chaos Magick. Discordianism is iconoclastic and, to a point, anarchistic; the only prominent deity in the Discordian pantheon is Eris, goddess of chaos, discord and confusion (on Discordianism see Younger 1991; R.A. Wilson 1992; and Adler 1986, pp328–37). While this Discordian influence could be seen as representing the irreverent, satirical tradition of 'sacred clowning' in Chaos Magick (see Hine 1993, p106ff), there is also a more radical anarchist trend in the Chaos movement which is evident in such Chaos groups as the New Orleans-based 'TAZ' (the 'Temporary Autonomous Zone'). This group derives its inspiration largely from the writings of Hakim Bey, whose projects of 'ontological anarchism' and 'Immediatism' (see Bey 1991; 1994) represent a continuation of the critique of Capitalist consumerism as alienating spectacle, i.e. as enforcing a mediated experience of the world, as formulated in the works of the Situationists (such as Debord and Vaneigem) and the French Nietzscheans, Deleuze and Guattari. According to Bey, the TAZ 'envisions an intensification of everyday life, or as the Surrealists might have said, life's penetration by the Marvelous [sic]' (1991, p111). Similarly, Hine emphasizes the significance of the 'immediacy of experience' in his discussion of Chaos Magick and postmodernity (see Hine 1993, p120ff). While Chaos Magick in Britain does not seem to have such explicit links with this anarchical current, there is certainly a interrelationship between radical politics and the occult on both sides of the Atlantic and it is worth noting in this connection the reference to Bey in the most recent edition of the *Principia Discordia* (see Younger 1991, pix). While I cannot elaborate on this phenomenon here, I would emphasize the ideological parallels between Left-Hand Path magick (originating with Crowley) and certain contemporary radical theorists (frequently inspired by Nietzsche), particularly in terms of the mutual emphasis on immediate experience and the need for individual deconditioning in order to attain some form of self-transcendence or liberation (on notions of morality in Chaos Magick, see Houston 1995, p57).

This emphasis on magickal techniques, or 'Results Magic' (see S. Wilson n.d., p33), and the explicit resistance of any single metaphysical framework, has been the focus of certain criticisms of Chaos Magick. On the whole, however, these criticisms have ignored the explicit emphasis on the essential role of gnosis in magick which permeates the writings of Chaos magicians such as Carroll (1987, p31ff) and Hine (n.d.); Hine's article is particularly notable since it argues for a deeper, more spiritual understanding of gnosis by Chaoists. While it is probably true to say that Chaos Magick is the most agnostic type of magick being practised in England today, this emphasis on gnosis means that Chaoists often develop a spiritual basis for their magick, albeit in a more individual way.

The Kaula-Nath Community (including A.M.O.O.K.O.S.)

The Kaula-Nath community is perhaps the most radical synthesis of Western Esotericism with Left-Hand Path Tantrism. It has emerged out of A.M.O.O.K.O.S. (the 'Arcane and Magickal Order of the Knights of Shambhala'), which was founded in 1978 through the collaboration of Thelemic magician Mike Magee and 'Dadaji' (Shri Gurudeva Dadaji Mahendranath). Dadaji, although English-born, had gone to India in 1949 at the suggestion of Crowley, whom he had met during the 1930s. Dadaji travelled widely in the East in his quest for occult knowledge. Of his various initiations two, in particular, concern me here; in 1953 he was initiated as a sadhu in the Adinath cult by the 'last remaining Adinath Yogi in all India' (*Tantra Magick* 1990, p7), Adiguru Lokanatha. The Natha sect is a teaching lineage within Shaiva Tantrism which was probably a development of the Siddha cult (*c.* 800–1200 C.E.). The Siddhas aspired to the transubstantiation of the human body and it was within the Natha sect that *hatha-yoga* was developed (Feuerstein 1990, p234). According to a tradition of Northern India, there are nine *nathas*, or subsects, of which Adinath is one. Additionally, Dadaji was initiated by the 'last surviving Guru of the Uttara Kaulas' (*Tantra Magick* 1990, p8), Shri Pagala Baba of Ranchi. The Northern Kaula tradition is an ancient Tantric sect and:

> *... [in] consonance with the Siddha tradition, the kaulas believe that enlightenment is a bodily event and that the body's structures, if rightly manipulated, would yield Selfrealization. The central mechanism of this process is the 'serpent-power' (kundalini-shakti) ... The body-positive orientation of the kaulas included the employment of sexual rites (maithuna) ... (Feuerstein 1990, p177).*

Through these lineages, A.M.O.O.K.O.S. constitutes a direct link between the Left-Hand Path in Indian Tantrism and Thelemic magick. The affinity between these two occult paths is evident in the fact that certain Tantric traditions incorporate the ancient notion of 'doing One's own will', for which the Sanskrit term is *Svecchachara* (see *Tantra Magick* 1990, p10; Magee 1994, p25ff). It is not surprising, then, that Crowley has now been acknowledged by Feuerstein, a scholar of Yoga, as 'an adept of what in India would be called *vama-acara*, or left-hand Tantrism' (Feuerstein 1992, p62).

A.M.O.O.K.O.S. developed in England during the 1980s although, by the early 1990s, it had undergone some organisational restructuring. Currently, it consists within the more loosely organised Kaula-Nath community of initiates who take on individual students for magickal training. The grade structure and magickal curriculum of A.M.O.O.K.O.S. can be found in the anonymously co-authored *Tantra Magick* (1990). Essentially, this work is divided into three sections: communal ritual work, sexual magick and the spiritual. This curriculum aims to develop the *siddhis* (magickal powers) and, ultimately, to liberate the individual through a project of deconditioning leading to self-realization. In common with other Left-Hand Path magicians, Western Tantrics often define their magick as being concerned with knowledge rather than belief, and with really 'doing it' instead of just talking about it.

In conclusion, then, I would suggest that Left-Hand Path magick is characterized by an attempt to engage in magickal praxis which does not accept externally imposed limitations, but rather tries to celebrate the totality of human experience in all of its folly and grandeur.

Acknowledgements

This paper is part of my (currently ongoing) ethnographic fieldwork within the Pagan and Magickal subculture of Britain. My research is being financed by the Australian Postgraduate Research Council and the University of Sydney. I thank these institutions for their support. I also want to thank all those magicians and pagans who have spoken with me about their beliefs and who have generally been very supportive of my project. I particularly want to thank the members of the H.T., with whom I have worked most closely, and also K.S., Ak'Ath Ashan, Jack Daw, Alex B. and Julian Vayne, for invaluable discussions about various aspects of magick. Clive Harper, via K.S., provided me with copies of some invaluable articles at very short notice, and Dave Lee kindly discussed with me the historical origins of Chaos Magick (as did Ak'Ath Ashan); I thank all of them for their time and interest. A preliminary version of this study was presented to the Department of Anthropology at the University of Melbourne and I am grateful to the participants of that seminar for their constructive responses. Also, special thanks to Roger Just, Nick Blamey and Daniel Suggit. Finally, I would like to thank Jon Marshall and Jadran Mimica for their critical comments on an earlier draft; for their acuity helped me to clarify several ambiguous passages. Obviously I am solely responsible for any remaining shortcomings, either conceptual or stylistic, in this study. Love is the law, love under will.

Notes

1 I had originally also intended to discuss The Temple of Psychick Youth (T.O.P.Y.) but unfortunately, during the writing of this paper (early 1995), I learned that this order had recently disbanded after approximately ten years.

2 For several, slightly varying, accounts of the constituent elements of the Western Esoteric Tradition, see Avens (1984, p133n11), McIntosh (1987, pp24–31), Wilson (1994), and the valuable interview with Professor Antoine Faivre in *Gnosis* Magazine (Faivre 1994b). The best single survey of the material in English is Faivre (1994a), which is complemented by the collection, *Modern Esoteric Spirituality*, edited by Faivre and Needleman (1993).

3 For a more detailed elaboration of these components than I can attempt here see Faivre (1993a, ppxv-xx; 1994a, pp10–15). The other two components are the notions of concordance and transmission, but these lie

outside the limited scope of this study.

4 The term 'embodied psyche' is used here following Jadran Mimica (1991), who emphasises that this notion does not imply a mind/body duality, but is rather meant to emphasise the 'human totality despite the established tradition of Cartesian dualism. I [Mimica] use *psyche* especially to emphasise the concrete body-person-world structures of human experience.' (Mimica 1991, pp54–5n2)

5 The history of this magical sodality has been the subject of several valuable studies which have appeared since 1970. See especially the works of Howe (1985) and Gilbert (1983, 1986) which are admirable in their detail. Both of these authors write about magic from a non-practitioner's perspective. The basic source for the ritual practices of the Golden Dawn is Regardie (1989). On the nineteenth-century occult 'revival' more generally see also King (1972), McIntosh (1972), Eliade (1976), Laurant (1993), and the important study by Howe of the phenomenon of 'fringe' Masonry, which was in many ways an historical precursor of the Golden Dawn (Howe 1972).

6 Such as *Dogme et rituel de la haute magie* (1856) and *Histoire de la magie* (1860). On Lévi see McIntosh (1972) and Eliade (1976). Lévi exerted a considerable, if indirect, influence on nineteenth-century English occultism (see, for example, McIntosh 1972 and Howe 1972, p255).

7 *The Book of the Law* (contained in Crowley 1983) is alternatively known as *Liber Al vel Legis* or *Liber Al* or even just as *Al*.

8 O.G.D.O.S. n.d. denotes citations from various minor documents produced by the Oxford Golden Dawn Occult Society which are in the present author's collection. These 'Flying Rolls' are intended mainly for limited internal distribution amongst the organisation's membership.

9 This was also the date of the first edition of Ray Sherwin's *The Book of Results* (1992), another seminal grimoire of Chaos Magick.

10 Allegedly deriving from the leader of the Syrian Assassins, this phrase seems to have reached Chaos Magick through the work of William Burroughs who, along with Brion Gysin, has been influential on contemporary Left-Hand Path magick (particularly Chaos Magick and T.O.P.Y.).

Bibliography

Adler, Margot 1986 *Drawing Down the Moon: Witches, Druids, Goddess-Worshippers, and Other Pagans in America Today* 2nd rev. and exp. ed. (orig. 1979). Beacon Press: Boston.

Anon 1990 *Tantra Magick* Amookos and Mandrake: Oxford.

Avens, Roberts 1984 *The New Gnosis: Heidegger, Hillman, and Angels* Spring

Publications: Dallas, Texas.

Bey, Hakim 1991 *T.A.Z. The Temporary Autonomous Zone, Ontological Anarchism, Poetic Terrorism* Autonomedia: Brooklyn.

Carroll, Peter J. 1987 *Liber Null and Psychonaut* Samuel Weiser: York Beach, Maine.

Carroll, Peter J. 1992 *Liber Kaos* Samuel Weiser: York Beach, Maine.

Corbin, Henry 1966 'The Visionary Dream in Islamic Spirituality' in G.E. von Grunebaum and R. Caillois (eds.), *The Dream in Human Societies* pp381–408. University of California Press: Los Angeles and Berkeley.

Corbin, Henry 1969 *Creative Imagination in the Sufism of Ibn 'Arabi* trans. Ralph Manheim. Princeton University Press: Princeton, New Jersey.

Couliano, Ioan P. 1992 *The Tree of Gnosis: Gnostic Mythology from Early Christianity to Modern Nihilism* trans. H.S. Wiesner and I.P. Couliano. HarperSanFrancisco.

Crowley, Aleister 1969 *The Book of Thoth: A Short Essay on the Tarot of the Egyptians* Samuel Weiser: New York. (1st ed. 1944).

Crowley, Aleister 1973 *Magick* ed. John Symonds and Kenneth Grant. Routledge and Kegan Paul: London.

Crowley, Aleister 1983 *The Holy Books of Thelema* Samuel Weiser: York Beach, Maine.

Crowley, Aleister 1989 *The Confessions of Aleister Crowley: An Autohagiography* Reprint of 2nd ed. (RKP 1979), ed. John Symonds and Kenneth Grant. Arkana (Penguin Books): Harmondsworth, England.

Drury, Nevill, and Stephen Skinner 1972 *The Search for Abraxas* Neville Spearman: London.

Dumont, Louis 1986 *Essays on Individualism: Modern Ideology in Anthropological Perspective* University of Chicago Press: Chicago and London.

Eliade, Mircea 1976 'The Occult and the Modern World', in his *Occultism, Witchcraft, and Cultural Fashions: Essays in Comparative Religions* University of Chicago Press: Chicago and London, pp47–68.

Faivre, Antoine 1993a 'Introduction I', in Faivre and Needleman (eds.), *op cit* ppxi-xxii.

Faivre, Antoine 1993b 'Ancient and Medieval Sources of Modern Esoteric Movements', in Faivre and Needleman (eds.), *op cit* pp1–70.

Faivre, Antoine 1994a *Access to Western Esotericism* State University of New York Press: Albany.

Faivre, Antoine 1994b 'What is Gnosis?' Interview with Antoine Faivre in *Gnosis* 31, pp62–8.

Faivre, Antoine, and Jacob Needleman (eds.) 1993 *Modern Esoteric Spirituality* SCM Press Ltd: London. (Reprint of 1992 Crossroads ed.)

Feuerstein, Georg 1989 *The Yoga-Sutra of Patanjali: A New Translation and Commentary* Reprint (orig. 1979). Inner Traditions International:

Rochester, Vermont.

Feuerstein, Georg 1990 *Encyclopedic Dictionary of Yoga.* Unwin Hyman: London, Sydney, and Wellington.

Feuerstein, Georg 1992 *Holy Madness: The Shock Tactics and Radical Teachings of Crazy-Wise Adepts, Holy Fools, and Rascal Gurus* Arkana.

Filoramo, Giovanni 1990 *A History of Gnosticism* trans. Anthony Alcock. Blackwell: Cambridge, Massachusetts, and Oxford, England.

Fries, Jan 1992 *Visual Magick: A Manual of Freestyle Shamanism* Mandrake: Oxford.

Galbreath, Robert 1971 'Introduction: The Occult Today,' in Galbreath, ed., *The Occult: Studies and Evaluations* In-depth section of the *Journal of Popular Culture* 5(3), pp629/1–754/126.

Gilbert, R.A. 1983 *The Golden Dawn: Twilight of the Magicians* Aquarian Press: Wellingborough, Northamptonshire.

Gilbert, R.A. 1986 *The Golden Dawn Companion: A Guide to the History, Structure, and Workings of the Hermetic Order of the Golden Dawn* Aquarian Press: Wellingborough, Northamptonshire.

Gilbert, R.A. 1994 'Baphomet and Son: A little Known Chapter in the Life of 666', in Macgregor, et al., eds., *op cit*, pp10–21.

Grant, Kenneth 1975 *Images and Oracles of Austin Osman Spare* Frederick Muller: London.

Hine, Phil 1993 *Prime Chaos* Chaos International: London.

Hine, Phil n.d. 'Stirring the Cauldron of Chaos', in *Chaos International* 15, pp9–11.

Houston, Siobhán 1995 'Chaos Magic' in *Gnosis* 36 (Summer 1995) pp54–9.

Howe, Ellic 1972 'Fringe Masonry in England 1870–85', in *Ars Quatuor Coronatorum*, Transactions of the Quatuor Coronati Lodge, Vol. 85, pp242–95.

Howe, Ellic 1985 *The Magicians of the Golden Dawn: A Documentary History of a Magical Order 1887–1923* Second ed. (orig. 1972). Aquarian Press: Wellingborough, Northamptonshire.

Howe, Ellic, and Helmut Möller 1978 'Theodor Reuss: Irregular Freemasonry in Germany, 1900–23', in *Ars Quatuor Coronatorum*, Transactions of the Quatuor Coronati Lodge, Vol.91, pp28–47.

Kapferer, Bruce n.d. 'From the Edge of Death: Sorcery and the Motion of Consciousness' in A.P. Cohen (ed.) *Questions of Consciousness* (forthcoming) Routledge.

Katon Shu'al 1994 *Sexual Magick* 3rd rev. ed. Mandrake: Oxford.

Kieckhefer, Richard 1989 *Magic in the Middle Ages* Cambridge University Press: Cambridge.

King, Francis 1972 *Ritual Magic in England, 1887 to the Present Day* reprint (orig. 1970). New English Library: Holborn, London.

King, Francis 1975 *Magic: the Western Tradition* Thames and Hudson: London.

King, Francis, ed. 1974 *Crowley on Christ* 2nd ed. (orig. 1953). C.W. Daniel: London.

King, Francis 1987 *Astral Projection, Ritual Magic and Alchemy* Rev. and expanded ed. (orig. 1971). Aquarian Press: Wellingborough, Northamptonshire.

König, Peter R. 1991 'Consider the OTO Non-Existent', in *Nuit-Isis* 10, pp10–14.

Laurant, Jean-Pierre 1993 'The Primitive Characteristics of Nineteenth-Century Esotericism', in Faivre and Needleman (eds.), *op cit* pp277–87.

Lévi, Eliphas 1968 *Transcendental Magic: Its Doctrine and Ritual* Trans. A.E. Waite. Reprint of 2nd rev. ed, 1923 (orig. English ed. 1896). Rider and Company: London.

Luck, Georg 1987 *Arcana Mundi: Magic and the Occult in the Greek and Roman Worlds* Crucible: London (Reprint of 1985 ed. Johns Hopkins University Press).

Luhrmann, T.M. 1989 *Persuasions of the Witch's Craft: Ritual Magic in Contemporary England* Blackwell: Oxford, UK, and Cambridge, USA.

MacGregor, Hugo, Katon Shu'al, Ak'ath Ashan (eds.) 1993/4 *Nuit-Isis* reader. Vol. 1 of new series, includes selected articles from the old series (1986–92). Mandrake: Oxford.

McIntosh, Christopher 1972 *Eliphas Lévi and the French Occult Revival* Rider and Company: London.

McIntosh, Christopher 1987 *The Rosicrucians: The History and Mythology of an Occult Order* 2nd. rev. and expanded ed. (orig. 1980). Crucible: Wellingborough, Northamptonshire.

Magee, Mike 1994 'Factions, Fictions and Functions: AMOOKOS in a Thelemic Setting', in Macgregor, et al., eds., *op cit*, pp22–34.

Martin, Stoddard 1989 *Orthodox Heresy: The Rise of 'Magic' as Religion and its Relation to Literature* Macmillan: Basingstoke and London.

Merleau-Ponty, Maurice 1962 *Phenomenology of Perception* trans. C. Smith, Routledge: London

Mimica, Jadran 1991 'The Incest Passions: An Outline of the Logic of Iqwaye Social Organization', Part I, in *Oceania* 62, pp34–58.

Morgan, Mogg (ed.) 1995 *Thelemic Magick XC (1994): Being the Proceedings of the Ninth International Symposium of Thelemic Magick (Carfax, Oxford)* Golden Dawn Publications, Mandrake: Oxford.

Nietzsche, Friedrich 1983 *Untimely Meditations* trans. R.J. Hollingdale (orig. 1873–6). Cambridge University Press: Cambridge.

Regardie, Israel 1989 *The Golden Dawn* 6th rev. and exp. ed. Llewellyn: St.

Paul, Minnesota.

Semple, Gavin W. 1994 'Zos: The New Flesh of Desire (for the companions of the Lie)', in *Starfire* 1(5), pp54–76.

Sherwin, Ray 1992 *The Book of Results* 4th rev. ed. (orig. 1978). Revelations 23 Press: Sheffield.

Spare, Austin O. n.d. *The Book of Pleasure (Self-Love: The Psychology of Ecstasy* limited edition facsimile reprint, Morton Press.

Talking Stick, *Talking Stick Magical Directory* 1994, London.

Tiryakian, Edward A. 1972 'Toward the Sociology of Esoteric Culture', *American Journal of Sociology* 78(3), pp491–512.

Wilson, Robert Anton 1992 *Cosmic Trigger I: Final Secrets of the Illuminati* 8th printing (orig. 1977). New Falcon Publications: Scottsdale, Arizona.

Wilson, Steve 1994 'The Western Esoteric Tradition', in *Talking Stick Magical Directory* 1994, p20–1.

Wilson, Steve n.d. 'Results Mysticism', in *Chaos International* 15 pp33–4.

Yates, Frances 1964 *Giordano Bruno and the Hermetic Tradition* University of Chicago Press: Chicago and London.

Younger, Malaclypse the 1991 *Principia Discordia* IllumiNet Press: Avondale Estates, Georgia.

Gordon MacLellan

DANCING ON THE EDGE:

Shamanism in Modern Britain

I'm called 'a shaman'–maybe by people who do not know any better–or even by those who should. But since none of us seem to be able to define exactly what makes the shaman, maybe when people feel the term is the right one, that is enough of a decision and that will have to do. 'Shaman' isn't a label that is achieved: not a status that can be measured, tested and awarded. Rather, it is something that comes upon a body and its appellation depends probably more upon the role that an individual plays within a community and, to some degree, how they achieve that rather than on any personal claim upon the title. This piece sets out to try to unravel something of that role in modern Britain and the places of shamans and shamanism within the current Pagan community. And this is a personal comment; it has to be: shamanism is evasive and elusive, shaping itself to the needs of its practitioners and their communities; sooner catch mist in a jam-jar than find easy definitions within a shamanic world. As with most modern Paganism, there is no single dogma or central authority to measure things against and we are all free to, and do, disagree with each other about everything!

Traditionally, the shaman belongs to a time and to cultures where survival runs along a knife edge and where

> *... the greatest peril of life lies in the fact that human food consists entirely of souls. All the creatures that we have to kill to eat, all those that we have to strike down and destroy to make clothes for ourselves, have souls, souls that do not perish with the body...*'[1]

'All that exists lives'[2]–spirit imbues everything: all things contain a spark of the conscious Infinite: human, plant, hunter, hunted and stone. All these are alive, all hold spirit and all exist in the spiritworld as forces to be reckoned with.

That spiritworld surrounds us: we live with spirits all the time but because they have no physical form, on the whole modern humans are almost completely oblivious to their presence. Spirits touch us with premonition, a fleeting unease, an atmosphere or a passing dream, but we are close to forgetting them. The spirit world, however, is not separate from the earth we walk upon, not some convenient semi-detached housing estate down the road you can drive away from when the tone of the neighbourhood starts to crumble. The spirit-world is here beside us, always; and unseen, often unguessed, it touches and changes the world of physical forms that we live in. Our actions, in turn, change the spiritworld, and we can work to heighten our awareness of it so that we are and are not consciously aware of it at will and we learn to operate in all the worlds at once, or in specific parts of them (because there is more than one spiritworld, just as there are different forms of physical existence). So we may choose, eventually, to have our eyes open in this world, and in that world, but our choice does not prevent the spiritworld being close beside us and being able to influence what happens in our physical world. The shaman moves between the worlds and can act in all of them.

The shaman makes no promises: and certainly not that anything she says will make instant sense! The shaman's world is one of apparent contradictions, but we can return to that later. The key to a shaman's reality is quite simply: 'All that exists lives'.

In those societies where shamanism still operates, the shaman is the bridge between the worlds: the pathfinder for his people; plotting a life-course through the trails of this world and the spiritworld. The shaman communicates human needs and desires to the spirits and interprets the spirits' own needs to his community. How she does this varies tremendously. 'Shamanism' as such is not any single set of teachings or practices; I see it more as that role: the communicator. People filling that niche are found in cultures across the world belonging to different types of society and very different mythologies but from the wide reach of these peoples various general patterns of behaviour and thought do emerge and these may give us the framework by which to look at modern shamanism.

There is rarely, even within a single people, a firm shamanic dogma: a lot is open to individual interpretation within that culture's worldview. There may be rules about how you do things, about the form of a ritual or the shapes of songs, but there is also a lot of flexibility–a recognition of the individual and the need for her to establish her own relationship with the spiritworld.

The general points are very general: shamans work with spirit people, shamans work through trance. Call them guides, or totems or helpers, gods, there are spirits with whom that shaman has close links. Often that link is one of cooperation as much as coercion; shamanism can feel like a joint venture: both sides of the bridge–the human and the spirit want to work together. Other spirits may come and go as they are needed–or as they need the shaman–but there is a core group, a spirit family, who stay together and may well work together for the rest of the shaman's life. Some spirits even stay with a family from one generation to the next, establishing those deepest, most totemic of bonds that in British culture may have survived as the animals seen on coats of arms or associated in folklore with particular families.

Shamans work with trance–and ecstasy. Trance is not necessarily of the 'all fall down and twitch convincingly' school of magic (although it may be): it can just as easily involve the shaman sitting down and having an apparently rational conversation with her client while still looking into the spiritworld. 'Trance' is achieved when the shaman is conscious of, talking to and operating in all the relevant worlds of his reality at the same time. The shaman can get there by more techniques than can be readily named. Generally, these can be grouped into six main categories: music, song, dance, pain, traditional hallucinogenics and stillness. Within these, and between these can be found the shapes from which more sophisticated magics have since evolved: shamanic forms range from the very simple to the spectacular and intricate. If it works, someone will use it.

And ecstasy? The ecstasy is the passion in life that is perhaps the best measure of the shaman. It is a pain and a delight: the fire of the Otherworld that burns in our veins, the fire that makes living such an intense delight and that the shaman sees and feels running in all the living world that surrounds him. Ecstasy comes with the realisation that everything is always now.

No, it may well not appear to make sense but what a shaman says, as a shaman, is always true: knowing the where and when of that truth is not always obvious, however. And no, shamans are not always obscure for irritation's sake, although the Fool may be there to annoy you out of an expectation for neat answers. At other times, the words simply cannot fit the experience.

It can be very easy to ramble on at length about the general patterns of shamanic practice and pull examples from cultures across the world and across time. But this would stay very general: shamanism defies limitations and sprouts exceptions to every rule that anyone formulates. Those underlying principles do seem to hold up: by accepting that their expression is then shaped by the relationship between people and place to produce something distinctive wherever shamanism is found, we can begin to catch the pattern that is shamanism. There are no rights and wrongs: the test is in the effectiveness of the forms used in helping people understand, communicate with and live as part of the environment they are in. In that process, the shaman is the one caught in the middle; the spider in the web, perhaps. Or maybe the fly.

In Britain, the spiritworld–the Otherworld of the Celts–is very ancient. And the Dream it dreams is an old and very seductive one. The world of Faerie is a part of this, the land of enchantment that can carry you away, dreaming, for seven, or a hundred or a thousand years and return you, lost, confused and adrift to a time not your own. The Otherworld is the abode of spirits: there we meet the talking foxes and watch the shapes of stone people unfold from the rocks on a hillside. When most of us enter the Otherworld in dreams, nightmares or magic, it shapes itself to our imaginings: if the people of the Otherworld are going to respond, they use the images we carry in our heads to give themselves forms that we can relate to. But beyond all the personal dreams of visitors, eventually, the Otherworld, is the dream that the land itself is dreaming: the accumulated experience of the spiritforce of all who live within the land and in the earth and stones, rivers, mountains, winds and trees themselves. That Dream is like a river running behind everything that happens: this is the Dream that holds the shape of the land. When the Dream is broken, the world begins to end. And this dream defies words! It is an experience, an initiation that leaves the visitor no longer 'a visitor' but a waking part of the Dream itself, bound to the ecstasy of it and to the wholeness of it and the need of it to continue, to grow and to change. Evolution with its own sentience?

This is the shaman's world. She moves through an Otherworld that may correspond exactly with the territory she calls home, but here is midnight and a world frosted with energy like ice on every leaf, where the mist at dawn is a swirling, pouring cloud of spirals, spilling out of damp hollows. And the 'Other' is not 'other' at all, but this world, the mundane physical world. And it is our physical world that changes most, that is most vulnerable and only the Dream persists, rolling slowly over the centuries with the breathing of the hills. Everything else is illusion ...

Given the passion, and often downright strangeness of the shaman's world, it is easy to wonder if there is any place at all in modern British society for anyone that weird. But if the shaman does truly function as that 'bridge between the worlds' then the need for communication and understanding between human and other worlds is as great now as it has ever been. In a society that seems increasingly alienated from and at odds with the natural world around it, anyone who can help people bridge that gap and find connections between themselves and their environment has an important role to play. There are shamans here amongst us; and not all covered in feathers and dead bits of things in true 'witch-doctor' style, nor even named as 'shamans' in public. Our wider society does not recognise, let alone accept, that role and the most effective shamans are not usually the ones who walk through their daily life with 'I'm a shaman' on either their lips or a lapel badge. The shape modern shamans take may be apparently different from their traditional one but the task is still there. The role of guide or pathfinder or communicator has specialised a bit now, perhaps because of the nature of the individuals involved or simply because we now live in such large groups of people that the shamanic function has had to subdivide for shamans to remain effective at all. Modern shamans may be:

personal healers: shamans who help people listen to themselves
community healers: shamans who help people listen to each other
patterners: shamans who help the community listen to/relate to the world around them

That traditional role of communicator is still there but more finely tuned, perhaps, although none of us are exclusively one thing or another–we all do a bit of the other roles. Again, anyone could claim to do any of these things, but drawing upon the traditional stance, the shaman is empowered to act by the community he works with and is similarly touched by and works with the spiritworld. Shamans belong to their people. That widescreen cinematic demonic tyrant, witchfinder and general villain holding everyone in terror is unlikely. In a deep trance a shaman is vulnerable: to direct assault and to the elements, at least, and may need physical protection and support. Often to move into those deepest of trances, she will have needed the help of her community to get there: with drummers or singers, drug handlers or simply the concentrated collective will of the people to propel her from this world to the other.

The modern shaman is more isolated. With people not recognising the role, the shaman must sort out a lot of that side of things for herself. The driving need is there, it can be felt and touched but now, often, the shaman must move with it on her own both into and out of the Otherworld again, doing what must be done with never a thought from the people she is bound to. Or rather, they may see and appreciate the results and be grateful for what has changed without ever knowing the process.

I am a patterner: I work on the relationships between people and the world around them. My 'job' is to help people find their own relationship with nature and to understand and appreciate that connection. Working in environmental education and interpretation as I do, my daily work is part of the fulfilling of my shamanic function: I help people explore the world around them. I rarely do this with traditional shamanic tools: most of the people I work with would look askance at a collection of drums and rattles and trance dances. We use investigation and awareness and discovery and personal creativity, we learn to enjoy the natural world and find that wherever we are, even in the concrete heart of the city, nature is around us and we are always part of it, changing and changed by it. The 'magic'–the dances, drumming and so on–are what help to keep me connected, to move me into the depths of the Otherworld, to draw the understanding, inspiration and energy that keeps me going and makes me, hopefully, an effective educator.

A final twist comes with letting people go: we are no longer part of a community that shares a common mythology and worldview. I may see things in one way and believe in the rightness of one course of action, a movement that I see as part of the pattern, but there is no guarantee that the people who work with me will see the same thing, and I cannot bring them to do so. No matter what result I may hope for, I must respect the right of those people to draw their own conclusions from their experiences of nature: to impose my view upon them, beyond the choice of vehicles we use to get there (that is my choice as a technician), is in itself to twist the pattern that is growth and awareness. So while I am a shaman and a pagan, the people I work with can interpret what we have done in whatever mythology suits them: Christian, Jewish, Islamic or Darwinian Evolution. That does not really matter; it is the fact that a connection has been made and some of 'my' people are looking at their world with open eyes again that I accept as the achievement.

Things work the other way, too. The 'bridge' lies open to the spirits and the shaman must meet their needs and talk and dance with them and when the demand comes, help their work in the physical world. So shamans appear as protectors, initiators of action, stirrers of the storm with anything from ferocious trance dance to confront a danger, to delicate gentle supportive magic for metamorphosing toadlets, to finding people to write letters, plant trees or help a new nest-box project.

The challenge that faces shamanism in Britain now is in growing a 'new' tradition. We live in a land with a long, rich magical history and this land has layers and layers of stories upon it, that start unfolding when the shaman first moves in the Otherworld, and then never stop. Our human societies are a melting pot of mythologies and folklores with the accumulated effects of ancient Celtic and pre-Celtic cultures, later Roman, Saxon, Viking and Norman settlements and still more recent additions as other groups of people have settled here and added their experience to the whole. While my own deepest responses are to the Scottish and Irish stories of the earliest times, I cannot accept that these are the only points to work with. Among British pagans there is often an unspoken elevation of the Celts and some dismissal of everyone else since then. Regardless of the rights and wrongs of who has been doing what to whom over the centuries, all those experiences contribute to make us and the land what we are today and the shaman is likely to meet aspects of all or any of that. So, while I may reach back to Irish myth-cycles and odd Neolithic goddesses for my most profound experiences, my 'day-to-day' awareness of the Otherworld moves within a sort of composite 'British folk tradition' and I can see lots of Saxon and medieval elements in that. My everyday work has still wider multicultural elements, reflecting the diversity of the modern urban communities I am usually involved with. Given time, all this will sink into the Dream as well and the Dream will grow richer with the variety it brings.

But we do not have an extant shamanic tradition to draw upon. There are claims for surviving hedge-witch practices, some of the old covens have lasted down the centuries and there are tantalising echoes of still fuller traditions fading with our older generations. Descriptions of the Highland seers sound very like those of entranced shamans. Folk tradition is full of spirit-catchers and witch-bottles and the proper ways of living with the spiritworld of Faerie. But a lot has been lost and there is a sense of watching things receding even as one looks at or for them. What there is can be useful but may not always be appropriate for the mix and attitudes of modern people. I see the shaman's job as working with communities and while one could claim that that need only be the 'pagan' community (however one defines that!), my own definition is 'the people one lives among'. They may not want what the shaman has to offer, but the offer has to be there: the experience that a shaman can bring is not the exclusive province of people who regard themselves as animistic. Remember 'all that exists, lives', the drive is always to see the connections. The shaman's community may change with time and place, and sometimes the shaman's job seems rooted almost entirely in the needs of the Otherworld ('What is going on? What are they doing? Why?'). We are part of a society that is changing very fast and values and imagery are evolving rapidly: the shaman remains a connection to the pulse of the living world in all the running stream of change. But the shaman must also accept that the people he works with may need a new language to understand the messages and the paths that he brings.

So now, modern shamans need to find a language that modern communities will respond to. We all do this in our own ways but some of the most exciting shapes it takes have come with the environmental action of the last few years. Where people have felt angry enough, or empowered enough to go into direct confrontation with the builders of roads or the abusers of rainforests, new rituals have almost spontaneously started appearing. Brewing out of a mixture of traditional witchcraft, street theatre and odd bits of traditional shamanism but drawing their inspiration from the need the people feel in a hilltop camp to give shape to their feelings about the earth they are fighting to protect, ceremonies are taking shape. These are often decried by the magical establishment because the people are 'untrained', the material they work with incomplete, the traditions mixed, a hotchpotch. But what is overlooked is the passion that inspires them and that here are people on the edge of physical action and quite possibly personal danger. They may have been sleeping rough, or camping in a wood for days, or have just walked down from some terribly nice house up the road, but there is an earthlink there and what is sung, danced, spoken or screamed comes from the heart. Heart to heart, land and people: new magic taking shape. I believe that this is where the future of the shaman lies–in the road camps, or in city centre celebrations of people and place: a Tree Dressing Day, a Kite Festival on Chinese New Year, a Beltane Dance in a country park. Shamanism works with and for the people. It does not belong in High Magic Lodges or in a Witches' Circle: it is rooted in people, land and spirit. Maybe shamanism is just the grubby end of magic, but that is all right: we need all our variations to make for a stronger, more complete and more supportive magical community, which in its turn should feed energy and awareness back into the wider communities of human and spirit.

For me, then, shamanism is very much 'enchantment for anyone who will stop long enough to listen'–its practitioners are not elitist in who they work with, which rather goes against a lot of the current trends in shamanism. Shamanism is fashionable. If you have the money, you can go and spend hundreds on this or that weekend, or this spirit journey, or that quest to the Andes. It also appears in a wonderful array of hybrids with 'shamanic wicca' and the like. None of this is 'wrong', but equally for me it is not shamanism. To be pedantic, maybe we have here the difference between what is 'shamanic'–belonging to the principles of shamanism, and what is 'shamanistic'–using the techniques of the shaman. People I meet working in these traditions are not shamans, but they are using the techniques of shamanism: those six categories of music, song, dance, pain, drugs and stillness, to explore their world and their magic. And those practices are powerful indeed, especially with people coming from a culture that avoids excess: to move into a throbbing drum trance, or to dance until one's feet are bleeding and to go on dancing can shake the walls of your world in a way quite unlike more formal magical systems. But this does not make the drummer a shaman. As well as all the stuff above about communities and roles, when you meet a shaman you meet someone who has been claimed by the Otherworld: somewhere, sometime, some spirit person has reached out a hand, a claw, a paw, and set it on the shaman's brow as the shaman reached out to it, and together they have said: 'We are one'.

Come listen my men, while I tell you again,
The five unmistakable marks
By which you may know, wheresoever you go,
The warranted genuine Snarks.[3]

I am afraid there aren't any. The shaman's world can seem an endless round of contradictions: to dance is to understand stillness, pain can be pleasure, at your most effective no one may ever know what you do for them. Only the dream is real and in the Dream everything is real. That simple opening statement 'all that exists, lives' can unravel into a nightmare knot when you start to examine it, but to learn to 'be' and not to 'know' is part of the shaman's task: not to analyse objectively but to understand from within. By being part of the threads of that tangle, you can flow through and move on. Shamans are notoriously unpredictable on one level: they are the Tricksters who break realities, but should be bitterly consistent on a deeper one. The shaman is bound by her dream: her vision, his reality–the only one that matters is the path that leads to the heart of it all, that moves the community on–and the public expression of that may change like the surface of a pool from one day to the next. Anyone can claim all that is of the shaman and claim to be one, and they do.

But the shamans must be horribly true to themselves: they have had to see themselves taken apart and 'lick the blood fresh from your own bones'.[4]

There are no rules, but still we are bound, tied by our dream: the honour of a personal truth is inescapable and that carries safeguards for the community. In the Otherworld, the shaman must be who she really is: to face the spirits with deceit is to court disaster and this then moves in all worlds. Bound by the need to 'be who you truly are', not what your family, friends, spouse, employers, or local shaman wants you to be, the shaman who tries to convert people to fit her idea of things is tying her own shoelaces together and she is, at the least, going to fall flat on her face sooner or later. But this is not a process governed by fear and the horror of an angry spirit howling down the chimney; it is one of freedom: the freedom to dance along a storm or, as a sensible, responsible grown-up-type person, to revel in the wind at a bus stop.

Shamanism is ecstatic. My magic moves most strongly in dance and with the wild, whirling dances of the animal spirits; with others it takes other forms, but for us all the power, the strength to act, lies in an ecstasy in life–that living is such a delight! And maybe that is the best measure of a shaman: feeling the awareness, the closeness of the Otherworld like a shadow in the shaman's eyes and a passion in the life that surrounds him, that celebrates the wind and finds fascination in the reflections in the windows of an office block.

The power of it is a delight that runs like fire. When I dance, my innermost self becomes still and the movement of the dance sets me free, I become all the spirits that I work with. I see with all their eyes, we enjoy the physical form of the dance. I feel a world that thinks and its presence humbles me and sets me free. This is bliss. My eyes open in a world where 'all that exists, lives'. This is the inspiration. The pattern moves like a spider's web in many dimensions. Every step I take, every sweep of hand or arm trails energy like echoes of movement. The dance carries me across the web in a helter-skelter ride of awareness. The morning is crystal and the sunrise paints my body with green and red and gold. The Otherworld is this world–there are no barriers. It burns through me with a passion and a delight. The life of the Earth is sacred and is a part of the Infinite. To be alive is to move in celebration. The shaman is bound–how can you live and not be a part of life: 'I love you all and I cannot help myself'.[5]

And, of course, it is all a dream. The shapes of the words change, the images we work with are fluid. Our gods are liable to remind us that their shapes are illusions and dissolve in a shower of stars or prove our own illusory nature by peeling the skins from our bodies and have us lick our own bones clean. Perhaps that is the final shamanic contradiction: it is all completely true and it may all be wrong.

In the midst of the word he was trying to say,
In the midst of his laughter and glee,
He had softly and suddenly vanished away –
For the Snark was a Boojum, you see.[6]

Notes

1 Halifax, J. *Shaman, the wounded healer,* Thames and Hudson, 1982.
2 as above.
3 Carroll, Lewis *The Hunting of the Snark*, Macmillan 1948
4 Gordon the Toad *Small Acts of Magic,* Creeping Toad 1994
5 as above.
6 Carroll, Lewis *The Hunting of the Snark,* 1948.

Adrian Harris

SACRED ECOLOGY

It would be easy to spout on about environmental destruction and rant about our duty as Pagans to save the Earth. However, there has been too much 'holier than thou' preaching in the Green movement as it is.

A second option would be to look beneath the surface a little and try to uncover what it is about Paganism which speaks so clearly to those of us who care for the Earth. However, I don't want to waste your time by telling you what you already know.

So I'm going to try and dig a little bit deeper. I'm going to explore Paganism's unique role in the environmental drama, and I'm going to argue that the theology and practice of Paganism not only holds a solution to our environmental crisis, but can bring about a revolution in the way our culture makes sense of reality. Paganism puts us back in touch with the body, reconnecting our wordy analytical culture with the physical self, and bringing us back to Earth. Through that healing of ourselves we may come to heal our relationship with our planet.

Perhaps I should have titled this chapter '*Towards* a Sacred Ecology', for the ideas I am going to try and put across are still undergoing a process of development. But I trust that they will be coherent enough to make sense, and original enough not to be too obvious. I am drawing on the theoretical work of Lacan, Kristeva and Morris Berman, as well as my own personal experience and that of other Pagans.

We find ourselves in the caring decade of the Green 1990s, and in these enlightened days it is decidedly unfashionable to suggest that Nature exists purely as a resource for humankind to use. Everyone from the Pope to the Prime Minister would have us believe that we are all environmentalists now. Even multinationals mouth the gospel of Greenness, and habits once considered eccentric, like recycling your bottles, are accepted as the norm.

But despite all the Green rhetoric, nothing has fundamentally changed. For most companies 'environmental awareness' means having a Green public relations strategy. Government environmental policy is a half-baked compromise, motivated by a vote-catching mentality that avoids real change. That leads campaigners to concentrate on short-term crisis management, trying to slow the destruction of the rainforests, or urging reticent Governments to patch up the ozone layer. Such campaigns tend to be exercises in damage limitation; it is sticking-plaster environmentalism, desperately treating the symptoms of the environmental crisis, but doing very little to deal with the underlying disease.

Even Green consumerism, that much vaunted mythical saviour, is driven more by guilt and fear than by any real feeling for the ecology of our world. Ultimately, it can do no more than slow the process of destruction. Meanwhile, media predictions of Global chaos and graphic descriptions of ecological disaster serve to disempower people, encouraging despair rather than motivating action.

So how do we bring about real constructive change? There are many philosophical and theological attempts to answer that question. Green Christians, for example, tend to talk about 'Responsible Dominion'. Humankind is to act as stewards of the Earth. The ecology of the planet is to be protected because it is part of the glory of God's Creation. God loves the Earth, and therefore so must we.

In the secular field, the environmental philosophers who agonize for hours over moral imperative and definitions, generally fall into three main camps. First, the instrumentalists. These pragmatic greens argue that we should protect our environment simply because we need it to survive. Even if we manage to fend off the worst effects of Global Warming, pollution and the like with a few techno-fix miracles, trashing the world's wild places would leave us with an impoverished quality of life.

Then there are the Social Ecologists, who have a broader view of things. They argue that the environmental crisis is rooted in the structures of our society. It is the direct result of the hierarchical organisation of power and the authoritarian mentality which goes with it. Their alternative is to base our society on ecological principles: an organic unity in diversity, free of hierarchy and based on mutual respect for the interrelationship of all aspects of life. Social Ecology emphasises the social dimension of the environmental problem. We must change human society first. Our relationship with the rest of nature will become transformed as we move from a world based on domination and hierarchy to one rooted in mutual respect and cooperation.

A third position is that of the Deep Ecologists. They emphasise that human beings are only part of the ecology of the planet: Only by understanding our unity with the whole of Nature can we understand ourselves. In the philosophy of Deep Ecology all organisms are equal. Human beings have no greater value than any other creature, for we are just ordinary citizens in the biotic community, with no more rights than amoebae or bacteria.

I can only give you a very brief outline of the richness of Green thought. This is not the place to discuss the complexities of environmental philosophy. But I want to give you some idea of how other people have attempted to answer the question of how we are to achieve real change.

There are a lot of valuable insights in both Deep and Social Ecology, but they are fixed in the Western philosophical tradition which goes back beyond Aristotle and which, I would argue, is the root of the whole problem. For it is a way of making sense of the world which is profoundly cerebral and which assumes a Universe of concepts, language and logic which has no place for the mystical which lies beyond words.

Even Deep Ecologists, who appear to be proposing a kind of spiritual understanding, are trapped in the mind. Inevitably they end up producing verbose academic discussions full of careful definitions and precise principles to be followed, like a doctor's prescription or some legalistic judgement.

From my study of the subject of environmental philosophy it seems that all these Green thinkers are stuck in a common mindset. Such systems live in the head, the rational, analytical world of argument and counter-argument. What is required is another way of knowing, a Sacred Ecology which moves beyond the cerebral to bring us to a direct experience of a wholeness rooted in the body.

The Sacred Ecology which is emerging does not proscribe or provide manifestos. It does not have a carefully argued programme of principles, because it is not known intellectually, but through direct experience. Besides the cerebral knowledge we all possess, the words and ideas stored in our heads, there is a deeper knowledge held within the tissue of our bodies. It is a somatic, physical knowing which comes from direct experience. This is the knowledge of faith, of emotion, of the gut feeling.

The philosophical tradition of the West is an intellectual one founded on logic and language. It is profoundly limiting, for within it whatever cannot be said simply does not exist. What I am proposing is a radical alternative: a Somatic philosophy which respects the knowing of the body, the knowledge, memories and wisdom held within our muscles, flowing with our hormones, sparking through our nerves. A Somatic Philosophy is yet to be developed, although the seeds of it exist in the work of Wilhelm Reich and Morris Berman, in the practice of body work, massage, Rolfing and Alexander technique. But accept for a moment the possibility of such a way of knowing, for therein lies Sacred Ecology.

Our culture is based on a certain way of understanding reality which has developed over the last two thousand years or so. What passes for common sense, as obvious, actually has a history. The way we think about ourselves and our world is not 'natural', not born into us, but learnt. What we in the West have inherited from the great philosophers and theologians of the past: Plato, Aristotle, Saint Paul, and their ilk, is a split in our reality that alienates us from ourselves. Our languages, our culture, and our 'common sense' all conspire to convince us that we are self-contained entities, divided from the rest of the universe. Each of us occupies a little box, and most of us remain shut up inside our heads for our entire lives. 'Common sense' teaches us to analyse our world into discrete units. I am 'in here', and everything else is 'out there'. We are separate, unconnected, and the boundaries are set by that Sacred Cow of the West, the big 'I am', the ego.

But this analytical and divisive way of knowing the world is not the only one possible. Anyone who has been part of a powerful ritual or experienced good sex can tell you that. At such times we come to the wisdom of the body; that all things are ultimately one. Intellectually, that is a very difficult thing to prove, although research on the edge of quantum physics is moving towards such a conclusion. Yet even if we accept intellectually that the split between the self and the other can be healed, as some Deep Ecologists do, it is far more important to feel it, to experience it in our bodies. That is a far deeper knowing and a true healing.

How do we come to know this wisdom of the body? We need some way of reconnecting with our own physical selves, healing the rift between our cerebral self and our somatic self. I mentioned two ways of connecting to wholeness earlier: Ritual and sex. Good sex is the closest most people get to a truly spiritual experience, but few in the West have the cultural understanding of sexuality which such a spiritual path demands. Sadly, ours is not an erotic culture. Our attitudes to sex have been profoundly damaged, distorted by patriarchy and the

Aristotelian self/other split which locks us into isolation. Sex has become a form of consumption.

A culture of sensuality knows the sacred through the physical: it tastes, smells, touches and hears bliss, feeling wholeness in sensual delight. But we actually repress sensuality and the body, worshipping instead the concept of consumption and its ultimate insatiability. Unfortunately, the spiritual dimension of sex is all but lost to us.

A discussion of the connections between sex, ecology and the sacred would take more time than I have available. For now I want to talk specifically about reaching wholeness through the techniques and beliefs broadly called Paganism.

There has been much debate of late about what we mean by Paganism. One of the clearest and simplest expressions I have found is in a short article on 'Witches and the Earth', by Chas S. Clifton:

> *Live so that someone ignorant about Paganism would know from watching your life or visiting your home, that you followed an Earth religion.*

For me, Paganism is not so much a set of beliefs as a way of relating to the world. The wholeness I have spoken of, that oneness of everything which we experience in moments of spiritual knowing, is what I call the sacred, and Pagan ritual is both a path to the sacred and a way of honouring it. In our rituals we reconnect with ourselves, healing the rift between body and mind through ecstatic dance, chanting and the drama of ritualized myth. We lose our ego-centred selves and achieve that somatic knowing of the unity of everything. It is in these moments of spiritual ecstasy that we know the wisdom of the body.

This healing through ecstatic Pagan ritual is what lies at the heart of Sacred Ecology. It is a deep knowing of the sacredness of the Earth which is beyond intellectual awareness of the facts and figures about species decimation and habitat loss. It is a feeling of unity with the Earth that we have in our gut. At such moments there is no guilt, no fear or disempowerment. We act to protect our Earth because we know, in every cell of our bodies, that our lives, our communities and our land are sacred. We act from a grounded strength which reaches beyond intellectual awareness and yet reinforces it, rooting deep within us.

In contrast to that spiritual experience is our highly complex industrial society. Instead of the sacred at the core of our being, there is consumerism. Yet our lives demand meaning. Those who have lost the Spiritual dimension seek something to replace it. What has emerged from loss is obsessive consumerism, an ersatz religion that has reached its apotheosis in our age. The consumer object is the fetish, consumption has become the sacred rite, while advertising vampirizes our deepest needs to preach the new creed of the product. Consumerism leads us like a will-o-the-wisp to destruction, and we follow like lemmings. It is a cancer of the physical world, destroying our environment with its insatiable demands, and worse still it is a cancer of the soul, cheapening and prostituting the spirit.

Sex, food and music all have a sacredness, but in our society they are pre-packaged and freeze dried. Fast food, muzak and pornography are all expressions of our consumerist mode of being. We have sanitized once sacred acts, cut out their essence, taken the love and the care out of them: food, music and sex without qualities. It has become simply material. We stuff ourselves with this pap, somehow believing that consuming more will satisfy our need. We have come to rely on this religion of materialism. Our lives and our society are falling apart, and revisionist nonsense about social reform will achieve nothing unless we can bring the spiritual back into our lives.

The shattered shards of the sacred remain buried in many aspects of Western culture: music, sport, advertising, dance, drama and the cultural icons of art, all hold smouldering embers of the scattered fire of the sacred. The obsessional worship of pop stars and sports personalities which is manifested in the tribalism of football supporters and youth subculture, is an attempt to reach wholeness, to relate to something larger than ourselves.

Now the resurgence of Paganism is bringing together these elements. We are creating something entirely new from threads leading back into our cultural past which connect us to our physical selves and to our Earth. From our past comes a new vision for the future.

Pagans have practised Sacred Ecology throughout history and continue today across the globe. In the U.K. we are still learning, though many of those who campaign to save our land from destruction draw on this wisdom of the body. The battle to save Solsbury Hill from tarmac and bulldozers is a Pagan struggle. Twyford Down, which has become a symbol for the grass roots environmental movement of the strength of our spirit, was the birthplace of the Dongas Tribe, many of whom draw courage and inspiration from their own knowledge of Sacred Ecology. Meanwhile, Dragon Environmental Group is working on the frontline to weave this most powerful eco-magic, using Pagan ritual to empower individuals to campaign for social and environmental change.

We must tread the Pagan path to Sacred Ecology with care. There are many potential pitfalls, but one of the first questions I would consider is our role as a Priesthood. The word 'hierarchy' originates from *hierarkhes*, the late Greek for High Priest. In many religions it is the High Priest who controls the power of the sacred, and spiritual practice too easily becomes the exclusive business of a Priesthood who are all too often male, esoteric and hierarchical.

Now is the time to release the sacred from the temples and bring it back into people's lives, to plug everyone back into the ecstasy of the sacred. This must be a process of empowerment, and the role of Paganism is not to create a Priesthood caste to carefully dispense wisdom and spirit. We can best act as guides, signposts for others on the road who may well travel far beyond us.

It will take great courage to face the causes of environmental crisis. If we are to live in harmony with our Earth and know the joy of unity which is the sacred, we must abandon much of what passes for common sense. Established values and accepted principles have brought us to where we are today. I don't need to list the horrors of environmental destruction or human misery, for you already know too well the birthright bequeathed to us by the errors of the past. But there is nothing that cannot be changed. Piecemeal repairs to the environment will only postpone the crisis, for even if scientific techno-fixes can save us from global warming, ozone depletion and habitat destruction, the human crisis remains.

Ultimately we must face the need for radical change. The ecological crisis is more than a question of environmental destruction and human misery, for it is at root a spiritual crisis. Genuine alternatives, revolutionary alternatives, require remarkable, imaginative leaps. Sadly, most revolutions simply regurgitate old forms; hence their inevitable failure. We must think beyond ourselves. Not simply beyond the established consumer-driven system, but beyond language, beyond the conceptions, categories and habits which tie our minds to established ideological models. We must go beyond, to imagine what has never been conceived of, to dare to demand what contemporary thought considers impossible.

But all this is just words. What is basic to Sacred Ecology lies beyond language, for words are but a finger pointing to the moon. Sacred Ecology leaves behind words. It can only ever truly be known through experience.

Bibliography

Morris Berman, *Coming to Our Senses*, Unwin, 1990.
Rosi Braidotti, *Patterns of Dissonance*, Polity Press, 1991.
Chas S. Clifton (ed.), *Witchcraft Today* (Book One), Llewellyn, 1992.
Peter Marshall, *Nature's Web*, Simon and Schuster Ltd, 1992.
Toril Moi, *The Kristeva Reader*, Blackwell, 1986.
M. Sarup, *Introductory Guide to Postculturalism and Post Modernism*, Harvester Wheatsheaf, 1988.
Starhawk, *Truth or Dare*, Harper and Row, 1990.

Michael York

NEW AGE AND PAGANISM

Many different views are constantly expressed about Paganism in contemporary Britain–some scholarly and objective, some sectarian and some even proselytizing. My own tentative approach here is to raise questions rather than furnish cogent answers or analyses. As a sociologist, I wish simply to present some current observations, but before I do so, I confess from the start to an addiction to 'male-oriented categorizing'. As Shan Jayran once put it, 'Even words and nonsense have their place.'

When I began my research into the New Age and Neo-pagan movements some six or more years ago, New Age was in general a little known term within the public in general. Paganism, of course, was virtually unknown and equated at best with atheism and at worst with satanism. It has been interesting for me to learn of the overwhelming familiarity of nearly everyone in attendance at the Paganism in Contemporary Britain conference with the New Age movement. Moreover, the vast majority at the Newcastle conference saw this movement as one which has a positive potential, and no one expressed their feeling that New Age is something which is worthless. Of course, with the predominant pagan sympathy to be found among those attending that particular conference, contemporary paganism is likewise seen as a worthwhile and positive movement, and only the inevitable pagan joker expressed that it is otherwise. In my own original research, however, both New Age and Neo-paganism appeared as largely amorphous movements virtually elusive of any possibility of definition.

Philip Shallcrass asks in his chapter in this volume whether Druidry is a religion and, more specifically, whether it is a pagan religion. This questioning leads us to a broader consideration, and any understanding of either Paganism or New Age as a religious concern depends in the end on the constitutional basis of religion *per se*. So I propose that we begin by asking the question: 'What is religion?' And I propose to answer this question with a broad definition of what religion is.

Firstly, a religion is something which is *shared*. The etymology of the English word 'religion' is debated to this day and is still unresolved. The Latin predecessor is *religio* which carries the meaning of 'the bond between humanity and the gods'–deriving possibly from *religare* 'to bind back, to bind together'. Whether implicitly or explicitly, religion is something shared between people. A religion of one is at best a personal faith and at worst a form of schizophrenia. But when that faith is shared with another such as with one's partner, we can see already the beginnings of religion. Coupledom, with its shared ways of looking at things and its semi-private language between two persons, we can identify as 'quasi-religion'. True religion, then, is that which is shared between three or more individuals.

But our next question must of necessity become one which asks, what is it that is shared? The general term we use for this answer is that of a *world-view*. Any ideology or outlook on the world entails identifying what is the world, what is humanity and what is the supernatural as well as what is the relationship between them. Every religion makes these identities and posits the connections or interactions which are believed to exist between these three components of reality.

And, finally, a religion consists of how its particular shared world-view is applied. In other words, the completing element in any understanding of a religion involves the *application* of the tripolar conception which is shared by its adherents. This application comprises the particular acts of assigning meaning, allocating value and enacting validation which are based on the ideological underpinnings of any particular religion.

Consequently, we find there are two essential types of religion: those which we might label materialistic, and those which are transcendental or idealistic. A third type comprises a mixture of the other two.

The materialistic religions either place matter as primary or else in some way deny either the reality or the value of the supernatural. While Marxism, atheism, methodological science or scientism and certain forms of humanism reject the reality of the transcendental or magical, a form of Buddhism such as Theravada, while not denying the existence of the supernatural, devalues it as something which is relatively or ultimately unimportant. We might consider Stoicism as a religion which falls into the materialistic category as well. Certainly, certain forms of paganism belong here too–inasmuch as the physical is thought to take precedence as the matrix, the Great Mother, and the supernatural is then considered to be a subsequent derivative or evolvement.

Turning now to the transcendental religious type, we find here such expressions as the Advaitic and Vedantic forms of Hinduism, the Platonic–or Neoplatonic–based religions, gnosticism, various New Age Galactean beliefs (Keys of Enoch, Church Universal and Triumphant, etc.), New Thought and Christian Science and even in a sense Christianity itself. What these faith-identities have in common is a denial of the physical or at least a rejection of it as constituting the lowest rung on the ladder of being. Clan-mother and priestess Shan from London's House of the Goddess sums up the essential attitude here when she describes gnosticism as that expression which holds God or spirit as being utterly remote. In Shan Jayran's opinion, this comes close to 'the dominant ideology of Christianity'. This is true if the Neo-Orthodoxy of the early Peter Berger and many others within the church is accepted as the fundamental Christian position. But even Alexandrean high priestess Vivianne Crowley expresses a transcendental viewpoint when she considers that the religious search is a 'journey homeward'–a quest for *re*-union with the source of the spirit. For Crowley, the achievement of 'the ultimate destination' is the final purpose of paganism and, indeed, all religion. From the materialistic viewpoint, on the other hand, one which includes an attitude shared by many contemporary pagans, the Earth or the physical is the foundation of an ever-open and never-ending quest and evolution.

The third fundamental religious attitude is that which celebrates equally the world, humanity *and* the supernatural. To some extent, Christianity and perhaps Islam belong here–especially inasmuch as the world is considered and cherished as the creation of God. But to the degree that creation is *ex nihilo*, the ultimate priority of the supernatural is affirmed by the Judaeo-Christian tradition. On the other hand, most forms of Mahayana and Vajrayana Buddhism recognise the validating reality of the human, the physical and the spiritual. Shan expresses this last when she considers in Rinzai there to be 'no gap between the spiritual and secular'. And finally, paganism itself predominantly celebrates the enduring sacredness not only of the supernatural but also that of the earthy, the physical world, the matter-energy continuum and the human position within it.

Consequently, we can see that religions can be identified by the way they individually identify the reality, meaning and value of the world, humanity and the supernatural. For some, this last is regarded as the personal or consciousness; for others it is impersonal. Some feel that the supernatural is one, one God, perhaps the pantheistic all; for others, whatever of the supernatural is not to be identified with the monotheistic God must then be ascribed to the anti-God, the Devil. For pagans, on the other hand, the supernatural appears through many deities, many gods and goddesses.

But here, it might be appropriate for me to distinguish between the terms as I use them, namely, 'paganism' and 'Neo-paganism'. This last is essentially a sociological term–one against which even many practising pagans protest. Nevertheless, I still find it a useful designation for two reasons. Neo-pagan refers to a new religious movement, one which has re-appeared however much it is based on ancient practice and tradition. Neo-pagan indicates a religious orientation which has emerged in our times or at least in relatively recent times. As Ron Hutton so clearly points out in this volume, there is little if any continuity between the paganism of the pre-Christian classical world and that of today. Ken Rees has been known to refer to 'the myth of continuity', and he has expressed the view that the subscription to this myth is 'like various New Age creations'.

But the second distinction between the pagan and the Neo-pagan rests on the absolute plurality of the former and what I would term the bi-theism of the latter. I have often wondered if the traditional understanding of God for the better part of the last two millennia in the West does not represent in essence a projection of the collective human spirit. If this were so, then God as the 'personification' of 'mankind' should clearly be the Goddess since there are more women in today's world than there are men. But more to the point, the bi-theistic understanding of the supernatural and animating forces of the universe as *the* Goddess and *the* God which are characteristic of modern Wicca and other contemporary expressions of Neo-paganism are to me more of an updating and rectification perhaps of an essential Christian attitude which is different from the free-ranging and loosely-defined multiplicity of personalities and forces and deities which collectively constitute the pagan godhead.

Consequently, in lieu of the use of the term 'Neo-pagan' as both a new religious movement and a bi-theistic theology, the contemporary Neo-pagan 'family' may be said to include 'genuine' pagans such as the Asatru, Odinists, Vanirists and certain Druids in Britain or, further afield, the Sodalicium Romanum, the Egyptian-based religions such as the Lyceum of Venus of Healing, and the Lithuanian pagan movements of North America or Romuva in Lithuania itself.

The practices of Candomble, Santeria, Voodoo and some Native Americans conform to traditional expressions of paganism as well, though here the sociologist of religion is less likely to consider them as 'Neo-pagan'. On the other hand, though Neo-pagans may be distinguished from polytheistic paganism to various extents, as a loosely identifiable religious orientation, paganism as a whole may be said to include both traditional pagans and Neo-pagans. In other words, Neo-pagans *are* pagans though generally pagans of a different kind.

Another helpful approach I find is one which looks at our world as a whole and endeavours to understand the broad religious affiliations of its human population. For this, I have turned to and extrapolated from the *World Christian Encyclopaedia* (1982). Consequently, we can understand that nearly one-third of our planet follows a Christian faith, and two-thirds of this number belong to the Roman Catholic Church alone. Something less than one-fifth of the planet is Moslem (1985: 17.1 per cent; projected 2000: 19.2 per cent), and together the Christian and Islamic communities include one-half of all humanity.

The next largest grouping that can be identified is the non-religious/atheist community which holds a world-view shared by slightly more than one-fifth of the people living on this planet (21 per cent). Slightly less than one-fifth or 19 per cent of the world's population is Hindu or Buddhist. This leaves the pagan community as the fourth largest identifiable religious affiliation in which 5 or 6 per cent of humanity practice an overt form of animism, spiritism or polytheism. Within this number, the largest grouping is that of the Chinese folk religionists (1985: 3.9 per cent; 2000: 2.5 per cent). But the pagan coalition/non-coalition also includes tribalists, shamanists, what the *World Christian Encyclopaedia* calls both spiritists and Afro-American spiritists, and Shintoists. The Neo-pagans of both North America and Europe as well as Australia and New Zealand would number to an infinitesimally insignificant number compared to these figures.

And just to complete the picture, the *World Christian Encyclopaedia* identifies new religionists as numbering two per cent of the world's total population, while all other religions–including Judaism, Sikhism, Confucianism, Bahai and Jainism–number together less than one per cent.

Now these are at best only suggestive figures which may assist us in gaining some perspective of the religious picture of our planet. These are rough estimates and often vary considerably from numbers given in other accounts. Moreover, they are illustrative of affiliative religious *identity* and *not* necessarily religious *behaviour*. Hinduism and Buddhism alone are rife with pagan practice as indeed are most religions–including Roman Catholicism and Islam.

The 1993 centenary of the Parliament of the World's Religions in Chicago, unlike the first Parliament in 1893 whose sub rosa purpose University of Lancaster's Paul Morris tells us was the conversion of the world to Christianity, had no hidden agenda. The purpose of this present-day Parliament was simply and openly to invite leaders and delegates from all religions to come together to listen, discuss and learn whether there is the potential or possibility to solve the major world problems harmoniously and in a manner compatible with the central tenets of each religion. This was a beginning effort, and the fact that it was a beginning helps put any failures which emerged during the Parliament into a proper perspective. The upshot, however, is that any bona fide religion wishing to participate in the world forum must be able to tolerate if not celebrate the existence of all other bona fide religions. If this is to be possible, I believe there must be an eventual shift within all religions from a faith which is literalistic or fundamentalist to one which is symbolic or metaphorical, that is, to one which entertains its religious icons not as literal realities but as metaphors which are at best merely suggestive of a greater and otherwise inexpressible truth.

If this analysis is at all correct, where then do the New Age and Neo-pagan faiths fit into the overall picture? Referring to contemporary paganism, Amy Symes sees this as a religion of paradox in which groups form, collapse and leave room then for new groups to come into being, and she asks what are the satisfactory sociological models which can be used for such phenomena. In my own studies, I questioned the applicability of the church-sect typology and its various modifications to both New Age and Neo-paganism, and while I found such typology-derived models useful for different groups within the orbits of either movement, I decided that these were not helpful for approaching the movements as a whole.

Instead, I turned to Luther Gerlach and Virginia Hine's SPIN concept which sees the movements as networks comparable to those of the PLO or the Black Panthers. Western government leaders formerly complained that the PLO, for instance, did not exist since there was no one who could speak for the organisation as a whole. Gerlach and Hine argued, however, that because the segmented-polycentric-integrated-network (SPIN) was not hierarchical and structured like traditional corporate institutions, Western political figures were unable to recognise it. In other words, from a traditional viewpoint, the SPIN remains invisible. But the boundary-diffuse, reduplicating cell structure and overlapping network arrangements of the SPIN are a successful way of surviving in an otherwise hostile environment–one which Gerlach and Hine recognised in the early Christian church and the early Pentecostal movement among others. This same model seems to describe the growth of such movements as New Age, Neo-paganism, Human Potential, Goddess Spirituality and Creation-Centred Spirituality in an environment that is either antagonistic or at least entertaining of a contrary mainstream view and in a technologically advanced world in which communication is greatly facilitated through electronic progress.

The similarity or overlap between the New Age SPIN and the Neo-pagan SPIN is ubiquitously observable. This was inadvertently expressed during the Newcastle conference when someone exclaimed that in Glastonbury, 'Everything is pagan'. This may be quite true, but Glastonbury is just as equally recognised as New Age–perhaps even as *the* New Age centre for all Britain.

Following upon the heels of the Parliament of the World's Religions in which the attempt was made to bring all religions peacefully together and the consequent realisation that such a symbiotic harmony depends upon each participating religion recognising the inherent worth of those which are different and other than itself, it became clear to me that there have been various attempts to develop a religion which is based on what is perceived to be the best in other, already existing religions. Immediately such faiths as Bahai, Ramakrishna's Vedanta and especially theosophy come to mind. New Age, too, and in particular as a contemporary development or outgrowth from theosophy, may be recognised as an attempt to draw the best from all other religions. Perhaps New Age endeavours to do this in an obviously eclectic manner, but it is an attempt at trans-religious synthesis nonetheless. Neo-paganism does not fall into this category, and though also eclectic, as is New Age, it tends to be more selective and more organic.

For New Age itself, its cross-cultural eclecticism has left it with an unresolved and inherent conflict between accepting nature as real and dismissing nature as illusion. To the extent that New Age accepts the transcendental position of theosophy, its selection of what constitutes the 'best' of other religions is coloured. Neo-paganism does not enter into this situation. Though not exclusively, it remains closer to the nature as real position. It is this pagan orientation which recognises the immanence of the godhead and constitutes the this-worldly grounding of New Age–one which counterbalances the tendency otherwise to drift off into the airy-fairy realms of 'pure' and transcendent spirit. In this respect, new Age parallels what Catherine Albenese refers to as an obstinate split in American nature religion.

New Age and Neo-paganism reveal other similarities as well. If contemporary paganism both overlaps and yet is distinct from New Age but still constitutes the grounded base which anchors the otherwise esoteric mysticism of New Age, both orientations may also be seen as partial legacies of Calvinism. Though on most issues, they may not follow the position of John Calvin's Protestantism, New Age and Neo-paganism both consider the Calvinistic belief that material welfare reflects spiritual achievement. Physical well-being is not considered incommensurate with growth, enlightenment and progress in the sacred. Indeed, for the practitioner of the 'magical arts' and/or 'positive thinking', mind or the will is believed to have a direct influence on the material. While a deep distrust remains with the Neo-pagan of the New Ager's capitalistic high-price system–and, indeed, Margot Adler claims that real difference between the two is merely a decimal point, in general Neo-paganism is more socialist-oriented. Neo-paganism is less involved with capitalistic profiteering but is more honest about it, while New Age is more capitalistic but less honest about it.

Other shared traits between the two movements include an interest in Celtic heritage, the Native American, shamanism, reincarnation, ecology, and the animism of *genii loci*–whether the *devas* of Findhorn or the *elementals* of Neo-paganism. In most cases, each of these is approached differently, but the common preoccupation remains.

Among the further contrasts between the two, we find a theatrical and ritualistic side to Neo-paganism which is largely absent in New Age. Neo-paganism also embraces the idea or practice of ritual/symbolic or sacred sex. Within New Age, we find little if any use of the sexual metaphor. According to Vivianne Crowley, the mainstream will not accept overt sexuality. As one attendant at the Newcastle conference pointed out, Wiccan/pagan ritual nakedness is condemned by traditional mainstream social attitudes.

Certainly New Age has more establishment appeal. Neo-paganism is by contrast sectarian and represents a minority view-point. Art Quester illustrates the cult/sect position when he notices that unsupported child abuse accusations made against Wicca have the effect of tainting Wicca in the eyes of the general public. He compares this to the difference which arises when the same allegations are made concerning a Christian priest. Christianity itself does not suffer condemnation regardless of the erring behaviour of particular members or clergy.[1]

The greater dissenting position vis-à-vis mainstream thought is perhaps the chief distinction between Neo-paganism and the socially more acceptable position of New Age. In general, New Age may be thought of as an attempt to convert the entire *cultic milieu* into a new religious movement. New Age wishes to open all the ancient and traditional mysteries. It seeks the bringing of esoteric into the public domain.

In this sense, Neo-paganism is quite different. For the most part, paganism can be recognised as 'subliminal religion'. We must keep clearly in mind that pagan religion is not the same as pagan behaviour. This last includes not only the Moslem's bowing to a black stone in Mecca five times a day but the Westerner's unconscious and automatic tossing of a coin into a well or fountain as well as his or her perpetuation of solstitial, equinoctial and other pagan commemorations. As a subliminal religion, paganism can only become conscious or consciously recognized as such by the few, that is, by a minority. Of necessity, then, paganism is a minority or marginal religious movement. It is a religion of protest and social and/or ideational rebellion. New Age by contrast aims deliberately and consciously for the mainstream. It does not possess that same stigma by which, according to Ronald Hutton, pagans are seen as the enemies of Christianity and civilisation. Perhaps, instead, the proper role for the Neo-pagan is, following Adrian Harris, to act as guides in the ecological changes which are necessary, to recognise the greater or hidden rhythms of the natural cycle and create not a priesthood caste but a role-modelling social behaviour to encourage organic harmony.

Notes

1 See Art Quester's unpublished dissertation, University of Lancaster, 1992.

III

PAGANISM IN PRACTICE

Amy Simes

MERCIAN MOVEMENTS:

Group Transformation and Individual Choices Amongst East Midlands Pagans

I was amused to read in a recent issue of *The Cauldron* (No73, p24) an announcement concerning the formation of a new association to serve as a 'contact and social network for independent witches who work solo'–'hedgewitches', to use Rae Beth's term. According to its founder, a network such as this one has become necessary because 'there are more solitaries around than people in groups'. He has therefore organised a group for people who otherwise do not join groups. True, the members of this group will probably never meet face to face, but that in no way lessens the legitimacy of the group by Pagan standards. Modern Pagans often belong to groups which never meet, and consider such membership as valid as belonging to groups which do occasionally meet.

Paganism can be described as a religion of paradox, particularly with regard to groups and individuals. Pagans are often characteristically individualistic and are able to practise their religion alone, yet a large number of Pagan groups and organisations exist, and new ones continue to form all the time. Like bubbles in a cauldron, groups appear on the surface, usually small at first, then grow in size until they either burst into newer, smaller versions of the original group, or transform into reactions against the original group, or even disappear altogether. It is a process which often happens at a rapid pace.

In my own study which began in 1992, I became acquainted with a population of approximately 60 Pagans in the East Midlands who belong to a variety of Pagan traditions. My area of study includes parts of Nottinghamshire, Derbyshire, Lincolnshire and Leicestershire. Over a period of 2½ years I have observed and participated in various groups which have formed, or which already existed in the area, and have interviewed approximately a third of this population.[1] During my period of study I have come into contact with over 13 separate groups which have formed locally. I have also encountered regional subgroups of national organisations, such as Paganlink. I participated regularly with five local groups, and observed the changes, often radical and frequent, which took place within these groups. From my research I feel that I am able to pursue certain questions which may shed some light on the unique nature of Pagan affiliations.

What are Some of the Most Common Features of Pagan Groups?

In order to address this question it is necessary to introduce several categories into which Pagan groups may be placed. It must be stressed that these categories are my own, although broadly based on other established sociological typologies, and that any attempt to fit Pagan groups or individuals into typologies is difficult at best due to the extreme amount of variation found within Paganism. Nonetheless, it is helpful to begin a discussion such as this one with a structured framework of some sort.

Experience has led me to divide Pagan groups into three types:

a) The first type consists of *purposive* or *networking* groups. These are groups which meet for a specific purpose, usually to facilitate contact between Pagans, but also commonly to make available information, or to provide a forum for discussion of topics which would be of interest to most Pagans. Paganlink and the Pagan Federation would be examples of this type of group. These are both national secular organisations founded in order to represent British Pagans to outside bodies, as well as to serve as non-denominational networking organisations for Pagans scattered throughout Britain. Both organisations are represented in my study area by smaller, regional groups which meet regularly to organise, socialise and sometimes hold large events, such as Earth Healing days.

Another group which is included in this type is the discussion group. Pagan discussion groups exist in great quantity throughout Britain, often in association with universities[2] or with local Pagan groups, such as Talking Stick in London or Manchester's Pagan Wheel. Most discussion groups meet regularly, usually once or twice a month, and often guest speakers are invited to attend. Discussions tend to take place in an informal, sometimes social atmosphere. Other than the university societies of which I was aware, I also located several other established discussion groups in my area, including the Green Magic Collective in Leicester, several 'women's mysteries' groups in Leicester and Boston, and four independent discussion groups,[3] some of which also met to hold rituals. I participated regularly with three of these groups over a two-year period and interviewed several of the group members.

b) A second type of modern Pagan group is commonly known as a *Working* or *Ritual* group. I prefer the first term simply because it is inclusive of all groups which meet to perform magic. A ritual may not always take place when magic is performed, although this is unusual. Working groups are either 'open' or 'closed', depending upon whether outsiders or new groups members may attend and take part in the rituals. An example of a closed working group would be a Wiccan coven. Newcomers seeking to join a coven must spend a considerable amount of time, traditionally a year and a day, getting to know the established coven members, reading books and demonstrating their commitment to join the coven. If successful, they are then initiated and allowed to participate in coven rituals. This process is also sometimes carried out by Druid and Odinist groups, but more frequently by magical groups, such as the Illuminated Congregation of Melchizedek (ICOM) in Derbyshire. In my study area I encountered two closed covens (one Gardnerian, one Traditionalist) and one other closed working group which consisted primarily of Wiccans but did not call itself a coven.

An example of an open working group would be any group of Pagans who come together for the purpose of holding a ritual or doing a 'working'. In some cases, such as that of the Druid grove, the group may consist of members who share a common tradition (Druidry) and who may be following a correspondence course and therefore belong to a larger organisation, but be permitted to bring along guests who do not belong to this organisation. In other cases the group may consist of Pagans from different traditions who meet locally to celebrate festivals or hold rituals with people who they have come to know through other Pagan activities or groups. In my study area I participated with four open groups. Two of these groups were open to all traditions, but were primarily Wiccan in orientation, one group was open to all traditions but was primarily Druid in orientation, and the other group was the Druid grove which was Druid in orientation but allowed outsiders of any tradition to join in celebrating the festival sabbats.

c) A third type of Pagan group is the *Social* group. This third category could really be a sub-category of either of the above two types, as very few Pagan groups actually form exclusively as social groups. Furthermore, social groups rarely exist as formal groups with established members. The social group is more commonly a collection of ever-changing individuals who meet regularly in the same place. However, socialising is an important activity in Paganism, and I have occasionally encountered a Pagan whose only contact with other Pagans is through social groups. The best example of a social group is a pub moot. A pub moot is a regular gathering, usually held at the same pub, established to serve as a way for Pagans to make contact with each other and learn about other on-going events in the local Pagan community. In my study area there are regular pub moots held in Nottingham, Derby, Chesterfield, Sleaford, Boston, Loughborough and Leicester.

Some pub moots feature speakers or discussions, but most moots are informal affairs designed to offer those new to Paganism a safe, public entrance into the community. They may also serve as gatherings for Pagans who live too far apart from each other to get together for regular rituals. I have attended pub moots in the Nottinghamshire and Lincolnshire area for two years on a regular basis. In that amount of time four new moots have been added to the annual schedule.

Another social group which meets on a regular basis is the Pagan conference. Although such events may include speakers and discussions, and occasionally a ritual, these are primarily social events which are organised on a regular basis for an inconstant group of people. Pagans have discovered the Western business tool of networking and are aware that conferences are one of the best means of accomplishing this. At the average Pagan conference one is likely to encounter speakers, performers, authors and academics, vendors, other organisers of groups and, of course, other Pagans. Most Pagan conferences take place only once a year, but there are now enough conferences held regularly throughout Britain for most Pagans to attend more than one each year without travelling long distances. In the East Midlands there are conferences held regularly by the Pagan Federation and Paganlink. Other groups, such as Dragon, the Council of British Druid Orders and the Hedgewitch Association, are beginning to attract enough members to warrant separate events.

The above structure of group types is an interesting starting place for a discussion of Pagan group features, but by itself it paints an unrealistic picture of Paganism as being neatly divided into tidy, mutually exclusive categories. In fact the boundaries between these three types of groups frequently become blurred, and sometimes disappear altogether. For one thing, many Pagans belong to many different types of groups simultaneously and, as a result, tend to carry one type of group behaviour over into a different type of group. For example, a ritual may occasionally be spontaneously introduced into the context of a discussion group, perhaps because it is mutually agreed that such an event is needed, or because someone requires a healing or a magical 'working'. Ritual groups often meet to hold discussions about what will take place at forthcoming rituals, and so might conclude an evening's meeting without actually doing any ritual work. Sometimes festival gatherings which have been designed primarily for ritual purposes turn into social gatherings instead. If the gathering is held outside, the weather might determine a change of events.

I have not noticed that these areas of indistinctness are particularly upsetting or disturbing to Pagans. The average Pagan does not subdivide group activity into academic categories and does not need to develop a terminology for group types as I have done. It appears that for most Pagans who participate regularly with groups–and most who I have encountered do–there are only two important distinctions which are normally given some consideration prior to taking part in group activities: first, is the group specifically tradition-orientated or is it more eclectically composed; and secondly, will the activity include a 'working' or not? Sometimes even this second consideration is omitted, most often when the group consists of very close friends who are comfortable working together.

Clearly closed groups, such as covens, behave in a more structured way than do open groups because members are more likely to have distinct roles within the group (such as High Priestess or Archdruid), and meetings are more likely to be tightly organised with less opportunity for flexibility or spontaneity. This is not to suggest that such things do not occur in closed covens, but with an established membership which is slow to change and, especially in the case of Gardnerian covens, with established guidelines for ritual structure and liturgy which is often memorised, individual influences are less likely to affect the group overall. Because of their closed status, I have not been able to participate in coven meetings. However, in conversation with the High Priest of a Gardnerian coven I have been able to determine that a certain amount of inflexibility is necessary for the successful running of the coven. Spontaneity is not problematic when it does occur, but it is certainly not normally encouraged to the degree which it might be in an open ritual group.

Open groups are often very loosely structured. Activities are organised, and rituals are usually led by one or two people who volunteer to take on these roles, although the roles may alter during the course of the meeting or over the course of several meetings. The meetings themselves are usually informally planned, but sometimes written 'parts' may be distributed to those who will be speaking during the ritual. These details are normally agreed upon beforehand, often over the telephone. All group members are allowed to contribute in some way to the meeting, and are usually encouraged to do so. Personal poetry, music or dance may form part of an individual contribution. In order to help new members feel more comfortable, a certain part of the meeting or ritual is often designated as the proper time for personal contributions from members.

Sometimes group status changes over time. Often a group will form as an informal, loosely structured collection of people who live within the same area and have come to know each other through other activities. Such a group may organise events over time from all three of the above categories, and therefore have no definitive identity as, say, a ritual group. However, in time some group members may begin to more actively direct the group events to reflect a specific identity. Such behaviour almost inevitably leads to inner conflict, disputes and perhaps even temporary disbandment of the group. Then, after a period during which individual group members may have temporarily worked alone or with other groups, the group may reform under a more formal, less open structure. It may even declare itself a closed group. Usually this reformed group will be smaller due to some former members choosing not to belong to a closed group, and sometimes it will introduce new membership requirements. An example of how this sometimes happens can be seen in the following observations of the changes experienced by a local Druid group.

The Druid Grove

During 1992 I became acquainted with the members of a local grove (this is a term used to designate a formally established regional Druid group) who all belonged to a large national Druid organisation. There were five members when the grove first formed in March 1992–Kent, Beth, Gill, Mark and Leon[4] – who were all following the correspondence course of this Druid organisation at one of the three different levels of 'Bard', 'Ovate', or 'Druid'. The grove met once every fortnight for informal discussions about topics associated with the course, and in order to plan forthcoming rituals. I was invited to attend both the meetings and the rituals, which I did, even though I was not a member of this organisation.

Even at this early stage, one of the five original members, Leon, had stopped attending both meetings and rituals due to feeling 'uncomfortable' with the other four members. He felt that the other four members were too dissimilar in personality, outside interests and background for him to be able to relax around them in a group setting. He did not formally leave the group, but he did stop attending, though he continued with his coursework independently. At the same time, five new members–June, Gail, Lisa, Sue and Rae–all began to attend regularly, so Leon's departure was largely ignored by the remaining original members.

In the Autumn of 1993 two other original group members, Gill and Mark, formally announced that they were leaving the group in order to start a group of their own. This event was clearly quite upsetting to the remaining group members, but was not discussed in any detail during group meetings. Nonetheless, it was clear to new group members that Kent and Beth, the only remaining members of the original grove, were deeply distressed by Gill and Mark's departure, and I became aware of an undercurrent of uneasiness amongst the other members. This feeling was also noticed by Suni, another potential new member, who attended one meeting before deciding that he did not wish to formally join the grove.

At the end of 1993, June, Gail and Lisa all stopped attending grove meetings, although they all continued with their coursework. Gail and Lisa continued to attend other Pagan events in the local area, including open rituals. June eventually joined forces with Mark who had now left Gill. Gill and Mark had not started a new group after all, so June and Mark decided that they would start one. Together in early 1994 they started a new Druid 'seed group' (a precursor to a grove) which they organised under the authority of the national Druid organisation which the grove belonged to, but with an emphasis on individual contributions from members. The announcement of their formation read, 'Every member brings a unique voice and outlook which can be of benefit to every other member, whether they have been doing the [Druid] course for five years or five minutes. It is to be hoped that in this way we can avoid falling into the trap where inexperienced members meekly follow, feeling under-valued and ignored, and experienced members boldly lead, feeling increasingly self-important and wonderful'. Clearly the formation of this new group was a reaction against the original group which spawned it.

A second group was also created as a reaction to the grove, this time by Leon and Suni. Joining forces with a third person, Keri, who was also following the correspondence course, they formed what they called an 'independent conclave'. This group did not associate itself with the national organisation, and eventually all three members stopped following the course due to their dissatisfaction with it. Initially they advertised for new members, and at each meeting between five and ten new people would attend. These were never the same five to ten people, however, and sometimes no new people would attend. After about six months, Suni, Leon and Keri decided to stop advertising for members and work alone as a threesome for a while.

The original grove, meanwhile, continued to experience change, and in 1994 eight new members started attending regularly over a period of two months. The group now consisted of Kent, Beth, Sue and Rae (who attended sporadically), and eight new members. At this stage the structure was tightened somewhat so that meetings had a more business-like feel to them. A fee was introduced to cover mailing costs for the newsletter, and a formal mailing list was produced. All meetings took place at Beth's house, and she was clearly the organising force behind the group, although the older member, Kent, continued to behave as a group leader.

In mid-1994 I stopped receiving newsletters about forthcoming group activities, and it became clear that the group was 'closing' to outsiders. I kept in touch with Kent, however, through his participation in other Pagan activities. In late 1994 he also left the grove. He told me that he was not happy with the direction the national organisation was taking, and that he felt that it was time to work on his own for a while. There was also a clear indication that some sort of personality clash had taken place with Beth, although he did not discuss this.

So in a period covering little more than two years, this group and its off-shoots experienced a considerable amount of change with regard to membership, status and size. The grove, which began as an open group with five original members, lost four of those original members, gained 14 new members and lost four of those. It gradually changed it status from open to closed without making any formal announcement to this effect. It spawned two new groups, and several members left to become solitary practitioners. The new groups also experienced changes in size and status.

Rapid and radical change is typical of Pagan groups and of those who join them. A longer study than this one would probably indicate that change is almost essential to the long-term smooth functioning of

Paganism. Very few Pagan groups of which I am aware escape some degree of change. Even tightly structured covens sometimes experience unexpected alterations which affect group size. The Gardnerian coven in my study area recently lost two long-standing members over a personal disagreement. The change was sudden and, from the perspective of the High Priest, quite distressing. Yet shortly afterwards he was able to speak philosophically about it, allowing for the fact that such things do occasionally occur for a reason, and perhaps in time everyone would come to see the change as being for the best. He was not at all worried about losing members (he considered his coven to still be a 'healthy' size), and he was even hopeful that the departing members would be successful in starting a coven of their own. He was disturbed that the change had occurred beyond his control. Normally coven members only 'hive off' from a coven upon receiving permission from the High Priest and High Priestess. He did admit, however, that sometimes even sudden and radical change must occur in order to keep things in balance overall.

Although groups may change size frequently in order to maintain group harmony, the size is more likely to decrease rather than increase. In general, Pagan groups tend to be small, usually ranging in size from two to twenty members. Even large national organisations, such as the Pagan Federation, OBOD and the Fellowship of Isis, have smaller, regional branches across the country. In some Wiccan covens there is a tradition of limiting group size to 13 members, although this rule is not always observed. However, the size of a group often determines to some degree how well it will function over time. Of the five groups I observed closely over 2½ years, only one ever rose in size above 20 members, and this was also the only group which did not function as a 'working' group. Its members met only to hold discussions and to hear speakers. It currently has a mailing list of over 60 members, but usually less than a third of those members attend meetings regularly.

Size is important for several reasons. One reason is a practical consideration. Most Pagan groups meet in private homes, when not meeting outside, so size must be limited, as one Witch put it, in proportion to the number of available coffee mugs. Secondly there are fewer complications involved when fewer people are meeting. Many Pagans have small children, or live long distances from each other, or have no transport available much of the time, or work in shifts–all of which tend to make getting together difficult. Festival sabbats and lunar rituals are meant to be celebrated on fairly specific dates, but it often becomes impossible in the light of the above considerations, and more so when greater numbers are involved. In addition, Pagans are still few in number. Groups sometimes remain small simply because the local Pagan population is small.

Thirdly, and more importantly, is the issue of intimacy. Meeting to hold discussions or to socialise is one thing, but people who meet to hold rituals together must be able to trust one another and to feel relatively comfortable around each other. The larger the group, the less likely that this will be the case. Groups which seem to dissolve the quickest are often large, open ritual groups where a high number of people who have not met before suddenly find themselves conducting a very personal rite together. For some, this might be an introduction to group work. It can be quite frightening or disillusioning, leaving the novice feeling alienated and exposed.

However, this may now be changing as more Pagans begin participating more often in open group work. Paganism may, in fact, be experiencing a form of religious polarisation resulting in two distinctive forms of ritual groups. On the one hand, taking part in one of the eight seasonal sabbats is becoming more commonly practised by Pagans across all traditions as more information about these festivals is made available and as there is greater interaction between Pagans from different traditions. On the other hand, rituals involving magical 'workings' continue to be reserved primarily for either solitary rites or rites involving a closed group or a close circle of intimate friends.

Another characteristic feature of Pagan groups, which may also serve as a fourth reason for small group size, is that they frequently consist of an unusually diverse collection of individuals. Crowley notes that, 'Often Pagan groups are very mixed in terms of age, education, occupation and interests' (1994, p243). Because Pagans are scarce on the ground, groups will often be composed of people who would otherwise never interact. Sometimes this becomes problematic, as with the case of Leon above, but usually I have observed tremendous tolerance of differences amongst Pagans, even when those differences were strongly felt.

Small religious groups have not often been the subject of religious or sociological study in Britain, and this is reflected in the available literature. Additionally, a survey of small group research conducted by McGrath and Altman (1966) indicates that most of the material collected was concerned with managerial and psychological studies, not religious studies. When religious groups have been the subject of studies, this research has often taken the form of either studies of small mainstream religious groups (Phillips, 1965), or of large and often controversial sects or cults (Wilson, 1973; Barker, 1982; Wallis,

1984; Beckford, 1985).

One possible reason for this, as Wilson notes in a footnote to Phillips' study, is that until recently in Britain small groups, particularly religious groups, were infrequently found. Outside of belonging to families, clans and possibly clubs or societies, the British population did not characteristically join groups in order to pursue personal issues. For the majority of the population, the parish church provided any small group needs which extended beyond family and club. But with the increasing secularisation of British society, which Wilson sees taking place since the Second World War, social stratification and individual identity became 'unclearly articulated' (1965, p294), thus necessitating the emergence of a greater number of artificially formed small groups. In America, where psychology and encounter group techniques have become popular therapeutic tools during the last 30 years, such groups have primarily taken the form of New Age or human potential groups. But in Britain intimate interactive groups have been slow to catch on.

One reason why this may be so is to do with the difference between the British and American approach to self-analysis, self-development and individual forms of therapy. During the 1960s and 1970s, America appeared to welcome a variety of psychological therapies into its national make up. Gestalt therapy, *est* group therapy, primal scream therapy, and many others became popular and acceptable alternatives to traditional psychiatry for coping with psychological stress or social dysfunction. These early therapies spawned many others, which sometimes combined Western psychological techniques with Eastern philosophical approaches (Transcendental Meditation, Rajneesh cathartic meditations), thus introducing a spiritual element into the equation. Eventually political issues, such as feminism and environmentalism, were introduced into the mixture, as well as a growing fascination with European cultural roots, eventually producing a variety of New Age and Pagan groups. Throughout this entire developing process, the American fascination with what Heelas (1988) calls 'self-religions' continued to be encouraged and accepted by much of mainstream American society.

In Britain, self-development through the use of psychological therapies, especially group therapies, has not been popular. The British attitude continues to encourage inner strength and private suffering. British reserve is considered to be a positive personality characteristic, and the need to consult an outside therapist for personal or family difficulties is usually viewed as a last resort. It has only been very recently that New Age forms of therapy and healing have begun to gain acceptance in mainstream British society.[5] For the most part, Britain appears to have remained somewhat resolutely disassociated from the developments of the rest of Western society (reluctantly agreeing to join the EC, rejecting American-style cable television) until the 1980s and the Thatcher Era. During that decade much of British society began to drastically change, in many more ways than it is possible to go into in the space of this discussion. Most notably, certain ideas which had previously been foreign to British thinking began to become accepted and pursued. Privatisation was probably one of the most significant of these ideas, creating in Britain a new approach to ownership and, to some degree, a new class of owners. One of the far-reaching effects of this era, for example, was the ability to purchase council houses. Tenants became homeowners for the first time. Another related change had to do with credit purchases. People who previously could not afford expensive items such as cars, stereos and washing machines, could now buy them on credit. Consumerist society caught on rapidly and flourished. Such changes were felt deeply in the British psyche, and one reaction to them was a radical rejection of them.

Consumerist 'yuppies' found their counterparts in New Age travellers, as the media referred to them, who began to develop lifestyles which rejected everything postmodern society stood for. In some respects, New Age travellers became the 'new Romantics' of postmodern Britain, embracing a nomadic, individualistic lifestyle which featured living close to the land, rejecting the idea of conventional employment and, sometimes, incorporating a form of contemporary Paganism into that lifestyle. Paganism was, of course, already being practised in Britain long before the emergence of the travellers, but the media's sensationalising of the travellers probably boosted the public's awareness of modern Paganism. Membership numbers in national Pagan organisations certainly appear to reflect a sudden acceleration of interest towards the end of the last decade.[6]

Thus, in Britain, the development of small groups appears to be more of a sociopolitical reaction against social changes rather than a pursuit of self-development techniques and philosophies. This is not to suggest that contemporary Paganism does not employ and encourage techniques of self-development as well, for it does. But, unlike American groups, British groups more often reflect a growing spiritual rejection of established social attitudes, and a decidedly more religious focus which emphasises a connection to nature, native Celtic traditions and surviving forms of ancient folklore. Although none of the Pagans in my own study are New Age travellers, many are supportive of the travellers and admire their commitment to their choice of lifestyle.

Why do Some Pagans Join Groups Whilst Others do Not?

British Paganism in the 1990s has produced two sorts of Pagans: those who are known as 'solitaries', who prefer working alone; and those who prefer working with groups, who I shall refer to as 'groupies'. Not only is it interesting to examine the different characteristics of these two generalised types, but it is also worth exploring how they come to prefer one practice over the other, and what specific aspects of group or solitary work are particularly attractive to them. It is important to state at the outset that most Pagans I have encountered actually participate in both group and solitary rituals, but tend to *prefer* one over the other.

First of all, what denotes a 'groupie' and how do Pagans come to prefer working with groups? One point which should be made initially is that very few Pagans begin their practice by working with groups. Most Pagans start out alone through necessity–groups are often difficult to locate–and so must work as 'solitaries' until a group is located. This trend is currently undergoing some change, however, and this change will be further explored in the final section of this paper.

Many Pagans subscribe to Pagan journals, or read books on the modern British Pagan movement (or at least patronise bookstores where Pagan books are sold), and usually find out about a local or national Pagan group through their reading. Less frequently they may hear of a local group by word of mouth, or via participation in a new age or metaphysical group or society. Once a group is located, it is normally either approached for purposes of membership, or it is used as a contact point for locating other groups and individuals who might be interested in forming groups. Over half of modern British Pagans are thought to be Wiccan, and other surveys support this estimate,[7] so it is not surprising that the first group many new Pagans locate is either a Wicca-orientated open group, or a closed Wiccan coven. Sometimes this fact determines the tradition a Pagan will choose. Sean, the Gardnerian High Priest, told me that when he began looking for a Pagan group to join 14 years ago, the only group available at that time was a Wiccan coven. Many Pagans begin by joining a national organisation such as the Pagan Federation.

However, 14 years ago the Pagan Federation was also primarily Wiccan. Today the situation has changed considerably.

So quite often groups are sought out by Pagans simply in order to meet other Pagans. Groups also tend to provide a means of socialising with others who have chosen a similar path, and group work often provides people with a feeling of fellowship. Some Pagans have indicated that they initially sought out a group when they reached a point in their studies where they felt they could go no further without a teacher or guide of some sort. Certain types of people seem to work better when work is presented to them in gradual levels, one step at a time, as in a correspondence course. This is often why 'groupies' prefer the formal structure of a working group. Such a group will often have different levels of initiation, clear roles for all members, specific lessons, ritual scripts and membership requirements, and often group secrets which must never be revealed to outsiders. Furthermore, there are usually group leaders who are seen to be more experienced and knowledgeable in most subjects and, therefore, properly qualified to act as guides or teachers. The leaders often do the majority of organising as well, which relieves the other group members of this responsibility. In return, the group member is expected to make a considerable commitment of time and energy to the group, and to remain loyal to the group members.

One other consideration which differentiates 'groupies' from 'solitaries' is that often Pagans who belong to working groups hold the belief that magic works better or is more effective when performed by a group of people rather than one person alone. Crowley speaks of a 'group mind' which produces symbols that are 'not the product of any one individual in the circle but are the product of the group itself which, by the workings of the ritual, has become a separate entity; the whole but more than the sum of the parts' (1989 p121). These symbols are then used to carry out magical 'workings'. Sean echoed this theory when he stated that, 'provided a group is in good harmony, the total magical power that can be raised is greater than the sum of the parts. You can achieve more'.

Other Pagans disagree. Cunningham reviews several systems of magic, but notes that none of these systems are necessary to a successful practice of magic. 'In Wiccan magic, personal power is recognised as our direct link with the Goddess and God. Magic, therefore, is a religious act in which the Wiccans unite with their deities ... Anyone can practice [sic] magic–within a religious context or not' (1990 p23). For Cunningham, as for many 'solitaries', it is more important that a connection is made with the divine rather than with other Pagans. The emphasis is upon direct experience.

Many Pagans choose not to join groups, and this appears to be a growing trend, as will be discussed further. For many Pagans there are practical considerations which determine the necessity for a solitary practice. As mentioned earlier, other Pagans may not live locally. Groups may not exist in the area. Perhaps the individual's specific tradition is not represented by local groups. I found that, whereas Druid and Wiccan groups were fairly well represented in my study area, there was a discernible lack of Odinist regional groups. Other factors must be considered as well. 'For if you lack money or have children to consider, or if you have a demanding job ... then it is really not feasible to celebrate the Sabbats and Full Moons regularly, at someone else's choice of hour in someone else's house, some distance from your home' (Beth, 1990 p18).

Many who are new to Paganism lack personal confidence to work with others, and therefore prefer to spend a period of time working alone, practising certain techniques until they feel comfortable enough to perform them in front of others. Some Pagans who have been practising alone for a number of years find it difficult to adjust to the styles of others, and so choose to continue practising alone. Sometimes personality differences enter into the equation. 'I think a lot of it comes down to personalities. And so if you're working in a tradition, but you can't stand the people you're working with, either you have to change your group or decide to work on your own ...' (Keri). Complications are inevitable as more people are added to a group. Working alone avoids such complications altogether.

Many 'solitaries' dislike formal group structures, and are especially loathe to become involved in hierarchies in which it is often felt that those in authority abuse their positions of power. With regard to hierarchies, Keri replied, 'I have an innate distrust of them. I think it creates a division which shouldn't exist'. Many solitary practitioners acknowledge that within group structures it is usually necessary for someone to emerge as an organiser or leader. This is seen to be a natural part of group formation. However, most 'solitaries' choose to avoid anyone else's authority altogether, and this can only be accomplished by not joining a group.

One final reason for practising alone was first suggested to me by a 'hedgewitch' (a term used to denote a Witch who is not part of the coven structure). He believed covens to be a relatively modern invention, probably of Gerald Gardner (after whom Gardnerian covens are named), having no historical precedent in Britain prior to the 1930s. Beth echoes this idea, claiming that, unlike the coven witch, hedgewitches, or 'modern wisemen or wisewomen, ... have always existed ... as midwives and healers for the community' (1990 p18). In 1990s Britain, the solitary practitioner is becoming an increasingly popular concept, and is now being linked with the idea of the shaman. The term 'Celtic shaman' has been used by John Matthews (1991), and more recently I have heard various Pagans refer to themselves as 'shamanic Witches' or 'shamanic Druids'. The shamanic Pagan is perhaps the most emphatic statement of individualism within this highly individualistic religion. Such Pagans are under no one's authority, are usually self-initiated if they feel that initiation is necessary, and often have created a religious and magical practice which is uniquely their own. They may also design personal symbols and liturgies which may be based upon or borrowed from others, but are altered to suit their own preferences. Shamanic Pagans, in short, seem to be making strong statements about individual religious practice, whilst living in a modern society which encourages conformity and homogeneity.

Owen is a hedgewitch as well as what I would describe as a shamanic Pagan. In many respects he is very similar to Sean, the High Priest of the Gardnerian coven. Like Sean, he is in his late forties, married with children. He has lived in the same area most of his life, and, also like Sean, he works for the health service as a nurse. He began practising as a Pagan at approximately the same time as Sean did, and read many of the same books on Wicca which were available at the time. But unlike Sean, he did not join a group. Only now, some ten years later, he is beginning to participate with a few open groups, and then only sporadically. This may have, in part, been due to the fact that, unlike Sean, ten years ago Owen had young children to think about (Sean has only recently become a father). As Beth has suggested, people sometimes choose hedgewitchcraft due to practical concerns, such as children.

Owen is part of an older generation of Pagans who became 'solitaries' through necessity. When Owen first began practising as a Witch, he was unable to locate any local groups to suit his needs. Now, whether groups are available or not, there appears to be a growing trend amongst Pagans to work alone more often.[8] Other trends may also be starting to emerge in Paganism, and this is the subject of the next section.

Is it Possible to Determine Trends or Patterns of Group Formation and Transformation in Paganism?

There are two answers to this question. The first answer is that it is not possible *at this stage* to talk about patterns of group formation and change because modern Paganism has only begun to emerge as a new religion, and few studies of Paganism have been done so far. Most of the available literature on modern British Paganism has been produced by Pagans themselves, some of whom are academically trained (Crowley, 1994; Carr-Gomm, 1993; Jones and Matthews, 1990; Kelly, 1991), some of whom are not (Farrar and Farrar, 1981; Crowther, 1981; Valiente, 1989). In either case, such books are not written as academic research, but as informative texts to be used primarily by Pagans.

Academic research has been carried out over the last decade, but published works are still quite thin on the ground (Luhrmann, 1989; Hutton, 1991; Harvey, 1993a, 1993b, 1994). Unpublished research, or soon-to-be-published research, has taken the form of postgraduate or undergraduate dissertations (York, 1991; Quester, 1992; Greenwood, n.d.; Dudley Edwards, n.d.; Simes, n.d.), and surveys, both academic (Harvey, n.d.) and non-academic (Vayne, 1993; Shan, 1994). Current and recent academic research has taken place in the fields of social anthropology, history, folklore, religious studies, sociology and theology. There has been no research done yet in the field of psychology, which would inevitably shed new light on group formation and behaviour.

Another consideration is that Pagan groups are difficult to locate (even for Pagans, as was noted earlier), often difficult to keep track of, and sometimes difficult to observe and participate in. Most academic studies, limited by time considerations, have had to focus on a small collection of groups in a small area. From such specific information it becomes difficult to draw general conclusions about Pagan groups.

The other answer to this question, however, is that it is possible to discuss patterns of behaviour, not of groups, but of *individuals* who choose to join or not join groups. Even in my own brief study I have begun to notice clear patterns of behaviour which have led me to be able to suggest a general trend amongst modern Pagans who have been practising for some time. The trend can be diagrammed as follows:

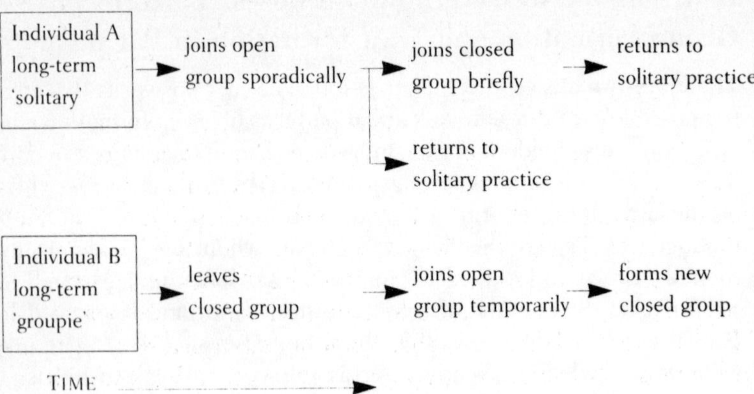

What this diagram quite clearly suggests is that, amongst Pagans who have been practising for a significant period of time, there is a tendency to briefly test different ways of practising before returning to the original style of practice. In other words, once a 'solitary', always a 'solitary', and once a 'groupie', always a 'groupie'. It is probably dangerous to make such a broad generalisation as this one, and there are undoubtedly many exceptions to be found. However in my own study, the data seems to support such a trend.

Pagans who are relatively new to Paganism–those who have only begun practising in the last two years or so–suggest that a new trend may be emerging. As was noted earlier, Paganism in the 1990s in Britain is very different from Paganism of ten or twenty years ago. For one thing there are significantly more Pagans than before. Pagan Federation membership figures suggest that in the five years leading up to 1992, the number of Pagans had quadrupled.[9] My own research data indicates a significant rise in numbers over the last 2½ years, and this data is supported by the regional representatives of both Paganlink and the Pagan Federation who oversee mailing lists for the East Midlands region. It may be that the actual number of Pagans has not risen so dramatically, but that more Pagans are contacting national organisations and becoming involved in local activities than in previous years. It would be difficult to determine which was the case.

Pagans who are currently looking for groups to join are finding greater options available to them than in years past. In the Nottingham area there are several open working groups, a discussion group, a Druid grove, a newly-forming Wiccan coven, a representative of the Hedgewitch Association, a representative of Dragon, and three regularly scheduled pub moots. Ten years ago this was not the case. In fact the majority of these groups have formed since 1992 when I began my study.

One outcome of multiple options is that a new type of Pagan is emerging, one which I have come to call a 'multi-traditional' Pagan. This is a Pagan who belongs to more than one tradition. In past years this would have been very unusual, if not unacceptable. Pagan traditions, such as Wicca, Druidry and Odinism, were very distinctive and required exclusive loyalty. It was uncommon for seasonal festivals to be celebrated cross-traditionally, as is commonly done today. Some Pagans even took the view that Druidry and Wicca were opposing traditions. One could belong to one or the other, but certainly not both.

With the popularisation of shamanism this has all changed. As noted earlier, the shaman is independent of any group authority and, as such, is free to follow any tradition, or no tradition at all. As a result, some people who are new to Paganism never actually join one specific tradition, but may instead claim to belong to several traditions simultaneously. Or sometimes established traditions are rejected for a newly-created, personal tradition, such as Leon's creation of the 'shamanic Celtic Druid' tradition. There is no central Pagan authority who can approve or disapprove of such creations, and so it continues to manifest. In some cases it manifests under the title of an established tradition, such as the recently-created Gorsedd of Caer Abiri in Avebury. This is an organisation which owes its name to the tradition of Druidry, but the group members are comprised not only of Druids, but of Wiccans, Odinists and Christians as well, amongst others.

Perhaps it is safer, for now, to stay with the earlier answer to this question, that is, that it is still too early to generalise about trends of group behaviours. Academic studies are still breaking ground, and only in small sections of Britain. Very little work, for example, has taken place outside of cities. To my knowledge, almost no work has been done on current Pagan activities in Wales or Scotland. There are certain traditions in Paganism which need greater study as they become more integrated into the religion. Vayne notes in his survey that a polarisation of practice and belief is becoming more pronounced recently in Paganism, indicating a newly forming opposition between magical and religious traditions (1993 pp9–10). This trend, if researched in greater depth, might alter much of the current thinking in Pagan studies. It undoubtedly would shed greater light on the subject of this paper.

The study of Paganism and Pagan groups is in its infancy, but progress is being made rapidly as Paganism expands and evolves. As a religion of paradox it is reflective of the modern era, encouraging social behaviour alongside individual creativity. It is a religion of unusual combinations, influenced by the society around it, but selective and self-authoritative of what it deems acceptable. As a new religious movement it is indicative of a modern spiritual trend which supports and encourages individuality without denying a need for communities within society. It is a religion for a modern world in transition.

Notes

1 The interview is partially open-ended, consisting of 55 questions, and concerned with personal background, beliefs, ritual practice, symbols and lifestyles. Twenty-five separate interviews were conducted during 1994–5 with individuals who represented the Pagan traditions of Wicca, Druidry, Odinism, hedgewitchraft, as well as with individuals who described themselves as 'non-aligned' Pagans.

2 Birmingham University, Manchester University, Leeds University and DeMontfort University all have established Pagan Societies which meet regularly.

3 With the exception of a Druid grove which was clearly organised under the authority of the Order of Bards, Ovates and Druids.

4 All names have been changed.

5 The Mind, Body and Spirit Festival held every year in London has currently been in existence since the late 1970s, and only recently expanded its format to cover ten days instead of the original five.

6 Membership numbers, although not publicly available, have been discussed at various meetings and events by representatives of the Pagan Federation, the Fellowship of Isis, and the Order of Bards, Ovates and Druids. All three groups have experienced significant growth over the past five to six years.

7 Bray, 1989; Vayne, 1993; figures produced by the House of the Goddess, the Pagan Federation and Paganlink, 1994.

8 Vayne's survey supports this notion. The majority of his respondents described themselves using the term 'hedgewitch' (1993, p8).

9 Figures noted during the Presidential Address, Pagan Federation Annual Conference, Conway Hall, London, 28 November, 1992.

Bibliography

Barker, Eileen, ed. 1982 *New Religious Movements: A Perspective for Understanding Society*, The Edwin Mellen Press, New York.

Beckford, James, 1985 *Cult Controversies*, Tavistock Publishers, London.

Beth, Rae, 1990 *Hedgewitch*, Robert Hale, London.

Bray, Chris, 1989 *The Occult Census: 1989–Statistical Analysis and Results*, The Sorcerer's Apprentice Press, Leeds.

Carr-Gomm, Philip, 1993 *The Druid Way*, Element, Shaftesbury.

Crowley, Vivianne, 1989 *Wicca: The Old Religion in the New Age*, The Aquarian Press, London.

Crowley, Vivianne, 1994 *Phoenix From the Flame: Pagan Spirituality in the Western World*, The Aquarian Press, London.

Crowther, Patricia 1992 (1981) *Lid Off the Cauldron*, Samuel Weiser, Inc., York Beach, Maine.

Cunningham, Scott 1990 *Wicca: A Guide for the Solitary Practitioner*, Llewellyn Publications St Paul, Minnesota.

Farrar, Janet and Stewart Farrar 1992 (1981) *Eight Sabbats for Witches*, Robert Hale, London.

Harvey, Graham, 1993a 'Avalon from the Mists: the contemporary teaching of the Goddess Spirituality', *Religion Today* 8 (2) pp10–13.

Harvey, Graham, 1993b 'Gods and hedgehogs in the Greenwood: the cosmology of contemporary Paganism', *Mapping Invisible Worlds* Cosmos 9. G Flood, ed. pp89–94.

Harvey, Graham, 1994 'Pagan ways of death and remembrance', *Ritual and Remembrance: responses to death in human societies* J. Davies, ed. Sheffield University Press.

Heelas, Paul, 1988 'Western Europe: Self-Religions' in *The Study of Religion, Traditional and New Religion*, S. Sutherland and P. Clarke, eds., Routledge, London.

Hutton, Ronald, 1991 *The Pagan Religions of the Ancient British Isles*, Blackwell, London.

Jones, Prudence and Caitlin Matthews, eds. 1990 *Voices From the Circle*, Aquarian, London.

Kelly, Aidan, 1991 *Crafting the Art of Magic* Book I: *a history of modern witchcraft 1939–1964*, Llewellyn Publications, St Paul, Minnesota.

Luhrmann, Tanya, 1989 *Persuasions of the Witch's Craft*, Blackwell, Oxford.

Matthews, John, 1991 *The Celtic Shaman*, Element, Shaftesbury.

McGrath, Joseph E. and Irwin Altman, 1966 *Small Group Research*, Holt, Rinehart and Winston, Inc., New York.

Phillips, Margaret, 1965 *Small Social Groups in England*, Cox & Wyman Ltd, London.

Quester, Art, 1992 *Wicca: the 'Craft of the Wise'*. Unpublished undergraduate dissertation, Cartmel College, Department of Religious Studies, Lancaster University.

Shan, 1994 *Pagan Index*, House of the Goddess, London.

Valiente, Doreen, 1989 *The Rebirth of Witchcraft*, Robert Hale, London.

Vayne, Julian, 1993 *Paganism–Spirituality of the Earth: Research Data*. Unpublished research material from 1992–3 survey.

Wallis, Roy, 1984 *The Elementary Forms of the New Religious Life*, Routledge & Kegan Paul, London.

Wilson, Bryan, 1973 *Magic and the Millennium*, Heinemann, London.

York, Michael, 1991 *A sociological profile on the New Age and Neo-Pagan movements*, PhD thesis presented to Dept of Theology and Religious Studies, King's College London.

Susan Greenwood

THE MAGICAL WILL, GENDER AND POWER IN MAGICAL PRACTICES

Introduction

> *Paganism has its roots in the ancient nature religions of Europe. Its adherents celebrate the sanctity of Nature's infinite variety, revere the divine Feminine in all her aspects, and the divine Masculine in his. Pagans respect all people and all life forms as part of a sacred whole...*

Pagans do not follow the dictates of 'gurus', 'masters' or a particular book. We believe that since we are all part of Nature, we can each tap into the sacred which is found around us and within us.

The above quote is from a recent Pagan Federation handout called 'Paganism Introduced' and claims that each magician[1] has direct access to her or his own spirituality without the intercession of religious expert, official or priest. Magical practices are monistic and inherently self-legitimating; there are said to be no masters or guru figures. Magicians say that the 'truth within' can be revealed by magical practices. Many magical practices are often initially psychotherapeutic techniques which aim to balance the forces or energies within to bring the magician to an awareness of her/himself in relation to divinity (however that is experienced). This process is often synchronous with a magician realising that the microcosm (the individual) is part of the macrocosm and that all is part of the sacred whole. This is often seen as a spiritual journey which is said to bring individual empowerment. This empowerment is based on an internal balancing of the forces within and this is the locus of the magician's power and is developed into what is called the 'magical will'. Drawing on psychoanalytically-orientated theories, I will argue that the magical will may be gendered and that this has important implications for the way that power is used in magical groups. Magicians work magic in groups which are hierarchical or democratic depending on a particular tradition or philosophy. I will examine the phenomenon of charisma and how it relates to gender in contemporary magical practice.

The Magical Will

Modern magic was developed into a coherent magical system from elements of the Kabbalah, the Tarot, alchemy, astrology, numerology, divination, Masonic symbolism, visionary experience and ritual magic by Samuel Liddell Mathers (1854–1918) who founded (with William Wynn Westcott, William Robert Woodman and the Rev. A.F.A. Woodford) the Hermetic Order of the Golden Dawn in 1888. (King 1989, Cavendish 1990). Mathers based his magical working on Eliphas Lévi's system of magic which itself drew on Mesmer's theories that planets influenced human beings through the 'fluid of animal magnetism' (ibid, p130). Mesmer had discovered that animal magnetism, as a universal medium, could be directly controlled by the human will. This became a 'bastion of modern magical theory' (ibid, p131). Lévi identified animal magnetism as the 'astral light', which like a magnet had opposite poles which carried good and evil and responded to the human will. 'To direct the magnetic forces is then to destroy or create forms; to produce all appearance, or to destroy bodies; it is to exercise the almighty powers of Nature' (Lévi 1959 quoted in Cavendish 1990, p136).

In 1875 Lévi died and Aleister Crowley was born. Crowley believed that he was Lévi's reincarnation (ibid, p148). Crowley's brand of magic was based on Lévi's theories and made the human being the centre of the universe. It emphasised finding the 'True Will', which is the magician's magical identity–his or her 'true self'. For Aleister Crowley each individual is the centre of his/her own universe–'his essential nature determining his relations with similar beings and his proper course of action (1989, p796). Crowley's maxim 'Every man and woman is a star' was a restatement of Paracelsus' theory that the mysterious power of the magnet was a force emanating from the stars and was possessed by all living things (Cavendish 1990, p130).

Gender and the Magical Will

I shall argue that the magical will may be seen in different ways by male and female magicians and that this may have important implications. Carol Gilligan argues in *In a Different Voice* that there is a disparity between women's experience and the representation of human development–women do not seem to fit into existing models which take the male as the norm (1993). Gilligan says that the different experience of women is characterised by Nancy Chodorow's theory (1978) that differential development in boys and girls is due to women's universal responsibility for mothering which creates asymmetrical relation capacities in girls and boys. Because girls are mothered by someone of the same gender they develop fluid ego boundaries, whereas boys develop their sense of self in opposition to their mothers and develop more rigid ego boundaries.[2] Gilligan concludes that relationships experienced by women and men are different: boys experience separation and individuation tied to their gender identity, which is threatened by intimacy; while a girl's identity does not depend on the progress of individuation but is defined through attachment and is threatened by separation. Women come to define themselves in the context of human relationships which, when compared to the human developmental model (based on the male experience), is seen as a weakness in comparison with individuation and individual achievement. Much feminist writing has described female identity as 'Other' or as a lack against which masculine identity differentiates itself (for example de Beauvoir 1973).

It appears that the concept of the magical will and the way it has been developed in magical practices may be on the lines of a specifically masculine model. I will contrast Crowley's magical ideas with feminist witchcraft, which has developed as a movement in response to what is viewed as the suppression of women's experience in orthodox religions.

Aleister Crowley and Thelema

Every superior human being will instinctively aspire after a secret citadel where he is set free from the crowd, the many, the majority ...

FRIEDRICH NIETZSCHE BEYOND GOOD AND EVIL (1978, P39).

Aleister Crowley, whose writing on magic bears a resemblance to Friedrich Nietzsche's philosophy, is one of the most influential figures in the modern magical revival. Crowley was brought up as a strict Plymouth Brethren and in his autohagiography he describes how he accepted the theology of the Brethren, but 'simply went over to Satan's side' (Symonds and Grant, 1989, pp66–7). He recounts his uneasiness about the fact that supernaturalism 'might not be true' and describes how this feeling was eased by his resolve to 'reach the spiritual causes of phenomena, and to dominate the material world, which I detested, by their means' (ibid, p67). In 1904 *The Book of the Law* was revealed to Crowley by a discarnate intelligence named Aiwass. The aim was the emancipation of mankind (sic) by the announcement of an 'unconditional truth' which was 'appropriate for the present evolutionary stage'. This truth was to 'reconcile an impersonal and infinite interpretation of the cosmos with an egocentric and practical viewpoint, so it makes 'infinite space' speak in the language of a goddess ...' (ibid, p398). *Thelema*[3] was a new cosmology, philosophy and ethics for the new aeon of Horus and marked the collapse of humanitarianism. The aeon of Horus marked a new stage evolving from the previous stage of the worship of the Father, which had been preceded by the worship of the Mother. The aeon of Horus would 'destroy the formula of the "Dying God" ' (ibid, p399), and by offering 'complete moral independence', would release humankind from altruism, fear and the consequences of sin. Humankind was to govern itself. Self-sacrifice was 'romantic folly' (ibid, p796) and the sacrifice of the strong to the weak was 'against the principles of evolution' (ibid, p401). Thelemic ethics were, 'There is no law beyond Do what thou wilt', and 'Thou hast no right but to do thy will' (ibid, p400). Further:

> *In a galaxy each star has its own magnitude, characteristics and direction, and the celestial harmony is best maintained by its attending to its own business. Nothing could be more subversive of that harmony than if a number of stars set up in a uniform standard of conduct insisted on everyone aiming at the same goal, going at the same pace, and so on (ibid, p401).*

Crowley's view of the true will is Nietzschian in the sense that Nietzsche saw the will as a cosmological force, an innermost essence striving to power (Clark 1990). For Nietzsche 'truth' is a concept belonging to the human mind and will. Truth is individual and something that is created by will. Zarathustra, Nietzsche's prophet of individuality, declares, 'And you too, enlightened man, are only a path and footstep of my will: truly, my will to power walks with the feet of your will to truth', and 'Only where life is, there is also will: not will to life, but–so I teach you–will to power!' (1969, p138).

The knowledge of the will is the basis of a magician's empowerment. Crowley describes his initial meeting with the Masters of the Temple, who were 'veiled in motionless majesty, shrouded in silence' (Symonds and Grant, 1989, p621). His guardian angel (his 'higher self'):

> *... had me understand whereto my aspiration led: all powers, all ecstasies, ended in this–I understood. He then told me that now my name was Nemo, seated among the other silent shapes in the City of The Pyramids under the Night of Pan; those other parts of me that I had left for ever below the Abyss must serve as a vehicle for the energies which had been created by my act. My mind and body, deprived of the ego which they had hitherto obeyed, were now free to manifest according to their nature in the world, to devote themselves to aid mankind in its evolution (ibid, pp621–2).*

This is the evolution of the aeon of Horus–the aeon of individualism and the will to power.

Feminist Witchcraft–Finding Power Within

Crowley's emphasis on the true self requires the annihilation of a particularly male ego. By contrast, feminist witchcraft covens focus on finding the magical self from an essence of less-bounded ego. This is clearly different from Crowley's male 'norm'. Feminist witches say that they have to strip away layers of patriarchal conditioning to reveal their true selves.

At a feminist witchcraft Winter Solstice ritual we purified ourselves in the darkness–each shouted out her anger. One woman was angry with the Goddess because she had fallen for the wrong person again. She was feeling unhappy about the way a relationship had worked out and this was making her feel bad about herself, she felt there must be something wrong with her. Space was given for everyone to express their negativity. We imagined opening the circle in the dark. The women spoke about how they were imagining the circle. At one moment it was a web, at another a cocoon, spinning around and around past the north over our heads and under our feet. We held hands and spoke about our feelings for the dark and what we wanted from the light. The emphasis was on the changing seasons–the moving from the dark into the light. We then lit the candles of the four quarters. We shifted around to sit where we felt most comfortable, or to where we felt we needed a particular energy. The next part of the ritual was concerned with sending healing. We sent healing energy to an absent member's son who was unwell. He had trouble with his eyes, perhaps he did not want to see the difficulties his parents were having, someone suggested. Then we sent healing to ourselves. Each took a turn in the centre of the circle while the others shouted and chanted her name as she first stood and then lay on the floor. When she was lying down the chanting changed to a crooning which became an eerie wail. It was quite a strange experience opening my eyes to everyone leaning over me moaning Sssssuuuuuussssssssaaaaaannnnnnnn. When the ritual was over we all shared a meal, which had been contributed by group members and was passed around using a common plate.

The emphasis here is on the communal elimination of negativity (due to living in a patriarchal society) and the creation of connection, via web and cocoon imagery, to establish a healing space. In contrast much magic based on the Crowleyian male model relies on solitary practice. This is illustrated by the fact that when Crowley assumed leadership of the Hermetic Order of the Golden Dawn he restored the original rule that members 'should not know each other officially' and 'have as little to do with each other as possible' (ibid, p562). Crowley's magical view is based on the dissolution of the specifically masculine ego. The development of a magical will is specifically masculine. It is Nietzschian in the sense of meaning autonomy, anarchy, control of the universe and explicit power. Crowley founded the Abbey of Thelema in Sicily on the principles of enabling each individual to fulfil their own function. However, this was too much for some: 'We found that life in the abbey with its absolute freedom was too severe a strain on those who were accustomed to depend on others. The responsibility of being truly themselves was too much for them ...' (ibid, p854). *The Book of the Law* anticipates this: 'The bulk of humanity, having no true will, will find themselves powerless. It will be for us to rule them wisely. We must secure their happiness and train them for ultimate freedom ...' (ibid, p854).

On the other hand, the feminist conception of the magical will firstly concerns 'finding' the self from a starting point of no bounded self. Having found this self it is said the witch's immanent power is realised. Feminist magic is concerned with what Starhawk has termed 'liberation psychology' (1990)–a connection with the earth, egalitarianism and feminist politics. The magical will is realised through the feminist witch's empowerment and resistance to 'power over':

> *In resistance, we violate the taboos and reclaim responsibility for our own truths and actions, finding safety through solidarity with each other. And effective resistance is sustainable, for we know that transforming culture and reshaping the world is a long project, a lifetime term of service (ibid, 1990, p313).*

At the heart of all magical practices lies the ideology that the microcosm is a reflection of the macrocosm and *vice versa*. However, as the magical will is gendered there are differences in emphasis. For Crowley the emphasis is on the microcosm, the individual–Nietzsche's superman. For feminist witches the macrocosm, the patriarchal social world, must be changed. By using magical means a more egalitarian society can be achieved. Democracy thus becomes the basis of feminist practice. I will now turn to an examination of wicca. In contrast to feminist democracy, it is a hierarchical practice which, through ritual, gives the High Priestess explicit power within her coven as representative of the feminine force in the world–the Goddess.

Explicit Power and the Role of Charisma

In feminist witchcraft there is usually no explicit hierarchy and therefore no overt role for a charismatic leader. Margot Adler writes that 'Most feminists have had strong experiences in collective decision-making without leaders or stringent rules beginning in their consciousness-raising seminars and continuing in their feminist organisations and other groups' (1986, p220). She says that most women who come to witchcraft from feminist movements favour a nonhierarchical, informal structure, preferring loose types of decision-making including the rotation of responsibility and leadership (ibid, p221). By contrast, wicca is based on a hierarchical structure of three initiatory degrees, and although everyone is seen to be equal the High Priestess is 'first among equals' (Farrars 1991, p17). The High Priestess of wiccan witchcraft, in partnership with her magical working partner the High Priest, is overall leader of her coven, she is the 'channel and representative of the Goddess' and can 'identify directly with the Earth Mother' (ibid, p18).

Vivianne Crowley writes that 'The world of the circle is a mirror image of that of the outer world which is still largely patriarchal' (1989, p94). The Goddess is not superior to the God, and the female is not superior to the male but the feminine is valued because 'it is the feminine energy which is considered to be the impregnator on the magical and spiritual planes; just as the male is on the material plane' (ibid, p94). The unconscious is the realm of the feminine:

> *In the circle between the worlds, the God subordinates his intellectual world to the spiritual and intuitive world of the Goddess and in Wicca both sexes must learn to use not the world of the*

intellect, the world of the conscious mind, but the world of the unconscious, of intuition, the world of the feminine (*ibid, p95*).

In the Wiccan circle the High Priestess represents the feminine–the Goddess is drawn down into her during the invocation of 'Drawing Down the Moon'. This is a central element of Wiccan ritual. The God is drawn down into the High Priest in the 'Drawing Down the Sun' invocation, but, in comparison, it is more peripheral. The High Priest invokes the Goddess into the High Priestess:

I invoke Thee and beseech Thee, O Mighty Mother of all life and fertility. By seed and root, by stem and bud, by leaf and flower and fruit, by life and Love do I invoke Thee to descend into the body of this thy servant and High Priestess (*Kelly, 1991, p52*).

Offering a direct channel to the Goddess, Wiccan practices open up new perspectives of power for women. The High Priestess is given authority and power–the Goddess speaks through her. I shall suggest that:

a) as women develop their magical will through relatedness this becomes a specific model of female power which can be utilised by the High Priestess in her relationships with her coven.
b) the 'Drawing Down the Moon' invocation is the vehicle by which the High Priestess may become charismatic.
c) the Wiccan High Priestess is in a privileged powerful position.

According to magical ideology, legitimacy is self-referential and internal and is not located in any spiritual leader as such. The High Priestess may be seen as a teacher, a pointer of the way, but she is specifically not a guru-figure in whom spiritual power is located. The Goddess may be drawn down into her as representative, but she is no more the goddess than any other woman. In short divinity is immanent within anyone, the difference is that magicians are attuned to it. However, some individuals are seen to be more magically developed than others and the initiatory system of three degrees is a spiritual hierarchy. How then do we explain the phenomenon of charisma within magical practice, or, in other words, is the phenomenon of charisma relevant to a study of magical practice?

For Max Weber a charismatic leader is one possessed with specific physical and spiritual gifts which are regarded as magical ([1922, pp662–79] 1978, p226). He says that charisma has no form and no organisation and only recognises 'those stipulations and limitations which come from within itself' (ibid, p227). It is *internal*, a force which is 'essentially outside the everyday' (ibid, p235). Charles Lindholm says that charisma is 'a way of talking about certain emotionally charged aspects of social interaction' (1990, p6). It is 'above all, *a relationship*, a mutual mingling of the inner selves of leader and follower' (ibid, p7). Those attracted 'feel their personal identities lost in their worship of the charismatic other' (ibid). Wiccan covens do not explicitly worship a charismatic other and Durkheim's meaning of charisma as the creative principle of shared participation of the group, in contrast to Weber is, on the surface of it, more relevant to a discussion of a self-referential magical self-development. If a person does become a sacred symbol, then for Durkheim, he or she is 'less a person than the group incarnate and personified' ([1965, p241] ibid, p32). However, both Weber and Durkheim agree that charismatic attraction implies a *loss of personal will and identity* (Lindholm 1990, p35). Accordingly it could thus be said that charisma, the antithesis of a search for individual magical identity, has no place within magical practice as a whole.

One Wiccan High Priestess, whom I shall call Una, told me that 'the Craft is a family' in which everyone knows their place. She was a powerful woman in her late fifties and ruled her coven with a rod of iron. Her High Priest told me that Una was a 'wonderful lady, but she has too much power–she rules the roost when she should be bringing others along–handing over ritual power and becoming an elder'. My fieldwork notes reveal an extremely ambivalent entry about a different Wiccan coven of which I was a member at the time:

> *The absolute power of the High Priestess is amazing–she has the ability to paralyse individual thought, creativity and enthusiasm; her control is absolute, stifling alternative views and ideas.*

This High Priestess gained power through the ritual process and charisma of the Drawing Down the Moon invocation. I felt, as a member of her circle, that the rituals were essentially about her empowerment and that she was using the psychic energies of the group. She frequently made comments about her psychic abilities. The claim to be psychic greatly enhances a magician's power and negative sanctions, or the threat of them, can cause much distress. Dion Fortune, herself a victim of what she calls 'psychic attack', explains that some people misuse the laws of the universe. I am not suggesting that Wiccan High Priestesses generally misuse their authority, or that they are the only magicians who would abuse their power, but the Wiccan coven and ritual structure gives the High Priestess an unusually powerful position. This is because Wiccan covens are autonomous small units which are often run like a 'family'. People are attracted to the closeness of the group which may be a surrogate for an individual's kin group. The High Priestess is overall leader of the coven and through her position she has explicit power and authority. This authority is symbolically enacted in the Drawing Down the Moon invocation when the Goddess is believed to descend into her. This ritual often transforms a High Priestess and may make her charismatic. Charismatic leadership, defined as spiritual authority located within an individual, stands in opposition to the notion that magic is a spiritual path leading to a magician finding her or his true identity within. Group dynamics and the individual High Priestess will determine whether the group fosters and encourages individual growth or dependency–I suggest that the potential is there for both.

By contrast feminist witchcraft is based on democracy and there is no ritual structure for individual authority and overt power. There are no ritual elements which could specifically induce charismatic power. Starhawk uses the magic circle and the four elements as a framework for 'thinking about the roles and tasks of leadership'(ibid, p277):

> *For the East, the direction of air, of the mind and vision, we have the Crows, who keep an overview of the group's tasks and progress. For the South, the direction of fire, of energy, we have the Graces, who help the group expand. For the West, the direction of water, of emotion, we have the Snakes, who keep an underview of the group's feelings and emotions. For the North, the direction of earth, of the body and finitude, we have the Dragons, who establish and guard the group's boundaries, who keep the group grounded. In the center, the place of spirit, we have the Spider, who weaves the group's connections (ibid, p277).*

For feminist witches the issues of power and politics–of resistance to patriarchy–are central and this has a direct effect on group working. This is not to say that power is not misused. It could be argued that the misuse of power may thus be correspondingly greater whereby an individual may say one thing and do another and not be held accountable for their actions–at least power that is visible can be identified and resisted.

Conclusion

I have argued that the development of a magical will is gendered and takes different forms in male and female magicians, leading to different conceptions of its use. For Aleister Crowley power is directed to the microcosm (the individual). The aeon of Horus represents humanity's evolution to individuality and power. This, in effect, is an elaboration of the male ego, which may not be transcended, while feminist magical power originates from the microcosm (power within) but is directed to the transformation of the macrocosm. Equality forms the basis of the feminist ethic. I have argued that women's development is based on relatedness. This may have important implications in the way that power is used within hierarchical magical practices. In Wiccan coven ritual, the High Priestess has explicit power and I have argued that this may become a model for a specifically female power based on relatedness which depends on the integrity of the individual High Priestess.

Magical practices attract people for various reasons. Some involvement may stem from a sense of connection with the magical cosmos and/or a desire to change political or social structures. Some may see magical practice as a means to gain power, while others may be attracted to a charismatic individual and the role of disciple. A disciple gives up responsibility for their own spiritual development and hands it over to the spiritual leader or guru. Eileen Barker writes that practices leading to dependency are not found only in obviously authoritarian groups but also in groups which claim to offer freedom within:

> *It is, indeed, possible to observe individuals who have joined such groups becoming more independent; but it is also possible to observe their becoming more dependent upon the guru or the group. Stripped of their erstwhile benchmarks, followers may find themselves as helpless as children who have not yet learned the ways of the world and are at the mercy of whatever situation they find themselves in. An assumption of many of the so-called 'self religions' which celebrate the quest for 'the God within' is that, by removing layers of socialisation from individuals, the true kernel of the individual will be revealed. This assumption needs to be carefully balanced against the alternative metaphor of an onion. Or, to make the point another way, individuals without social conditioning of one sort or another find it difficult, if not impossible, to function effectively as individuals (1992, p251).*

Magical practices draw on ancient Mystery Traditions–finding the sacred within. Part of the process is an understanding of self. This understanding may be deeply affected by issues of magical will, gender and the way that power is handled in groups.

Notes

1 I will use the term 'magician' broadly to refer to an individual, regardless of tradition, who practises magic.
2 I am aware of the eurocentric assumptions of this theory, however it remains a useful analytical tool for western societies.
3 *Thelema* means 'the will' in Greek.

Acknowledgements

Thanks are due to Olivia Harris for constructive criticisms and comments on earlier drafts of this paper. I also wish to thank the practitioners of magic who shared their experiences with me. The research on which this work is based has been funded by the University of London Central Research Fund and The Economic and Social Research Council, Great Britain.

Bibliography

Adler, M. 1986 *Drawing Down the Moon* Boston, Beacon.
Baring, A. and J. Cashford 1993 *The Myth of the Goddess* London, Penguin.
Barker, E. 1992 'Authority and Dependence in New Religious Movements' in *Religion: Contemporary Issues* ed. Bryan Wilson, the All Souls Seminars in the Sociology of Religion. London, Bellew Publications.
Butler, J. 1990 *Gender Trouble* London, Routledge.
Cavendish, R. 1990 *A History of Magic* London, Penguin.
Chodorow, N. 1978 *The Reproduction of Mothering* Berkley, University of California Press.
Clark, M. 1990 *Nietzsche on Truth and Philosophy* Cambridge, Cambridge University Press.
Crowley, A. 1991 *Magick in Theory and Practice* New Jersey, Castle.
Crowley, V. 1989 *Wicca: The Old Religion in the New Age* London, Aquarian.
de Beauvoir, S. 1973 *The Second Sex* Harmondsworth, Penguin.
Farrar, J. and S. Farrar 1991 *A Witches Bible Compleat* (sic) New York, Magickal Childe.
Fortune, D. 1988 *Psychic Self-Defence* London, Aquarian.
Gilligan, C. (1982) 1993 *In a Different Voice* Massachusetts, Harvard

University Press.

Hewitson-May, G. 1992 *The Dark Doorway of the Beast* Yorkshire, New World Publishing.

Hutton, R. 1991 *The Pagan Religions of the Ancient British Isles* London, BCA.

Judge, W. (1893) 1969 *The Ocean of Theosophy* Bombay, Bhargava and Bhargava.

Jung, C. (1953) 1993 *Psychology and Alchemy* London, Routledge.

Kelly A. 1991 *Crafting the Art of Magic* Minnesota, Llewellyn.

King, F. 1989 *Modern Ritual Magic: The Rise of Western Occultism* Dorset, Prism.

Klaniczay G. 1990 *The Uses of Supernatural Power* Cambridge, Polity.

Lindholm, C. 1990 *Charisma* Massachusetts, Blackwell.

Melton, J. Gordon 1993 'Another Look at New Religions' in *Annals* AAPSS, p527.

Morris, B. 1991 *Western Conceptions of the Individual* Oxford, Berg.

Nietzsche, F. 1978 *Beyond Good and Evil* Harmondsworth, Penguin.

Nietzsche, F. 1968 *The Will to Power* ed. Walter Kaufman, London, Weidenfeld and Nicholson.

Nietzsche, F. 1969 *Thus Spoke Zarathustra* London, Penguin.

Puttick, E. and P. Clarke 1993 *Women as Teachers and Disciples in Traditional and New Religions* Lewiston, The Edwin Mellen Press.

Ransom, J. 1938 *A Short History of the Theosophical Society 1875–1937* Madras, Theosophical Publishing House.

Runciman, W. G. 1978 *Max Weber–Selections* Cambridge, Cambridge University Press.

Starhawk 1990 *Truth or Dare* San Francisco, Harper and Row.

Symonds, J. and K. Grant 1989 *The Confessions of Aleister Crowley. An Autohagiography* London, Arkana.

Valiente, D. 1986 *An ABC of Witchcraft Past and Present* London, Hale.

Webb, J. 1976 *The Occult Establishment* Illinois, Open Court.

Shan Jayran

DARKLIGHT PHILOSOPHY:

A Ritual Praxis[1]

Preparation: The Things of this World

Before beginning to speak, she selects a large table, and sets out four coloured candles at the cardinal directions on it, with a staff (wand) and cauldron at the centre. At the back (North) she sets a green candle, a small clay goddess figure, with bread and salt. In the East she lights incense beside a yellow candle. In the West she puts a blue candle and a large cup of fruit juice. She sits in the middle of it all, with her drum in front of her (South) with a red candle.

Just like any other important task, a ritual circle begins as I decide what I want to do and then put together all the things I need to do it. In laying out these things I am working with my outward reality, unlike the many teachings that tell me to focus on another, inward world. Some people are fascinated by wands, drums, incenses, and paraphernalia, but many others are embarrassed and put off by them, feeling it is far superior and more spiritual to look away from mere things, and concentrate on something higher and better.

Our Western culture has demonstrated centuries of affinity for material skills, taking technology further than any that has existed before, yet always with the accompanying fear and guilt about the Frankensteinian monster. Today the fear and guilt are very much uppermost, as the ecological movement shows us the grim results of our skill. Yet this urgent modern spirituality does not, and by its nature, cannot, demand that we turn away from the things of this world. In order to solve the problem, we must actually pay them more attention, not less. For we are beginning to understand that by despising material reality and treating it as a mindless mechanism, we have brought about disaster.

The roots of this mechanistic attitude go far back to the split spirit of Light and Dark, Good and Evil, God and Devil, which we can trace to the Aryan theology of about 3,000 years ago, both in the early Brahmanic traditions of India and in the Zoroastrianism of Iran. In the West, this developed into the Gnostic cults of the early Christian era.

The basic key to Gnosticism is that God, or Spirit, is utterly remote, immeasurably beyond the material universe, unknown and unknowable, named as Light, Life, Father–but never Creator. The Creator of the world is instead a lesser being, the demiurge, in fact the Devil. Material life on earth is perceived as suffering, so it must come from evil, not goodness, and it is ruled by the Devil, Dominus Mundi, Lord of the World.

Many forms of Gnosticism refer to the original cosmic split as arising through Sophia, feminine wisdom, whose arrogance or excessive desire to know God led to the first fall. Her sphere of being remains a bridge back to the divine (cf. the Judaic Sophia/Christian Mary) but she is also identified as the mother of the demiurge, the Devil himself. This theology developed at a time when the Goddess religions were beginning a long slow stripping of their honours while patriarchal systems were emerging (See Stone 1979).

While catholic Christianity condemned the Gnostic teachings as heretical, the latter still made a huge impact on the emerging new Christian religion. Augustine, for example, spent years involved in Manicheeism, which was one type of Gnosticism, before he joined the catholic Church. According to Hans Jonas, a foremost modern scholar of the Gnostic view, a central Gnostic tenet held:

> *The material universe ... is like a vast prison whose innermost dungeon is the earth, the scene of man's life* (Jonas 1972, p339).

It is immediately obvious how close this is to the dominant theology of Christianity.

By contrast, with some relief, we can look to the loveliness of Zen Buddhism, which assures us that 'nature is replete with spiritual meaning', and emphasises 'the rapport between individual and nature' (Smart 1972b, p367). Back home in the West, Martin Buber speaks of even the miraculous as immanent.

> *The miracle–is not the setting aside of the laws of nature but an event of wonder that shines through nature without displacing it (Buber 1946).*

Lovelock's Gaia hypothesis, courtesy of NASA research, argues that:

> *The chemical composition of the atmosphere bears no relation to the expectations of steady state chemical equilibrium ... The climate and the chemical properties of the Earth now and throughout its history seem always to have been optimal for life. For this to have happened by chance is as unlikely as to survive unscathed a drive blindfold through rush hour traffic* (Lovelock 1979, p12).

which has provided even sceptics with

> *an alternative to that pessimistic view which sees nature as a primitive force to be subdued and conquered* (Lovelock 1979, p10).

The Earth Mother has returned to us dressed in the latest fashion.

For us, as Pagans, perhaps there is no need to spell out the controversy, except that we too are part of this civilisation which presents material things as more or less pornographic. We too have all had to work at it to clean away the grubby Puritanism laid on us. But at least as Pagans we can consult our own classics such as the Goddess assuring us:

> *I am the Mother of all living and my love is poured out on the earth ... I am the beauty of the green Earth Charge*

while teachings of sacred tree, sacred animal, sacred plant, sacred stone are a Pagan commonplace.

In my own tradition as well as in many others, the crafting of our magical tools is a first step for any apprentice to the Craft.

> *The practical ... crafts actually teach us how to tackle the big ones like sex, leadership, parenthood, and politics* (Shan 1994, p102)

and the Craft of life itself.

Purification: Blood and Dirt

> *She takes the silver bowl, puts three generous pinches of salt in it, stirs it. She looks into the bowl and says 'I want to put into this bowl the enormous fear I feel about facing you all and doing this.' (There is a ripple of sympathetic, slightly nervous laughter) 'I put into this bowl the long car journey to get here, and the tummy bug that had me throwing up so we got here late. I put in weeks of work of preparation ... my worry about caring for our little boy here at the conference ...' She continues until her face relaxes and brightens,*

> *ending solemnly 'and I undertake to put all this down the lavatory when my Circle is finished.' More laughter.*

Before going into the Circle, it is necessary to Purify. Purification has a sonorous ring to it, as befits a ritual mode with such profound power, for it is this second stage, done carefully, which can ensure excellent results even if a complete John Cleese comedy of errors follows it!

Yet unfortunately the name itself is suggestive of just that grubby Puritanism which we have rejected–a cleansing of the sinful self to be fit to enter sacred space. Gnostic dualism taught that:

> *In its unredeemed state the spirit, ... immersed in soul and flesh, is ... intoxicated by the poison of the world (Jonas 1972, p340).*

To call the Gnostic view hostile to the world almost understates the case. That it led to asceticism to avoid contamination is unsurprising. Its emphasis on celibacy however makes even the horrors of sexual guilt a symptom, not a cause. The real aim was to avoid procreation, to rob the Devil of more vehicles to entrap spirit.

Liberation was through the illumination of knowledge, firstly, knowledge of the demonic nature of the created world. The Vedic teachings of Aryan India tell us in the same vein:

> *The soul can gain release [moksa] by discriminatory knowledge (viveka) realising the distinction between itself and nature (Smart 1972a, p157).*

(In a delightfully neat opposition Rinzai Zen Buddhism points out that:

> *If all discriminations, perceptual and otherwise, are illusory, so likewise is the distinction between the Absolute and phenomena (Smart 1972b, p367).*

However, until recently Zen couldn't help us Westerners, to whom Gnosticism recommended training in:

> *sacramental and magical preparations for [the soul's] future ascent and the secret names and formulas that force passage (Jonas 1972, p340)*

... upward after death, to reunite with divine substance.

The description of this ascent is found in 'Poimandres' the first treatise of the Hermetic corpus. These Hermetic teachings are even today taught by occultists, a clear example of the crucial difference between the occult and Paganism. The occult is Gnostic, aimed at transcendence, and hostile to the Earth.

While the asceticism of the Gnostics is to be expected, it can be a shock to realise that to a Gnostic initiate all acts are neutral, however vile. For moral law is only a part of this world's grip on us, and 'retribution can affect only the body and the psyche' (Jonas 1972, p339) which don't matter anyway.

It is time to look at a healthier alternative than this.

> *'Sabbatu' was the sabbath or menstruation of the Babylonian goddesses: a taboo time at which no work was done. (Shuttle, Redgrove 1978, p218)*
>
> *In Arabic the source of the concept 'pure and impure' is menstruation. 'Taboo' or 'sacred' in Polynesian is the same word as 'menstruating'. In Dakotan 'Wakan' means 'spiritual, wonderful, menstrual' (Shuttle, Redgrove 1978, p62).*

Menstruation, in recent history named 'the curse' is now being reclaimed as one of the deep magics of the female body, when her increased sexuality is:

> *not just a heightened ability to 'have it off' [but] when the perceptions of one's own self, the world, and of course any partners that might be involved, becomes heightened and, it may be, more meaningful. The range of sexual experience goes from a simple discharge of tension to a complex act of sensuous relationship to people and things in the outer world. (Shuttle, Redgrove 1978, p63)*
>
> *If a woman becomes a shaman or priestess in a culture that recognises such functionaries, she is able to do so because she has developed a special relationship to the 'spirits' of her menstruation (Van Waters 1913, p400).*

As Shuttle and Redgrove show, sacred dreaming as guidance is particularly clear around the menstrual peak (Shuttle, Redgrove, 1978, pp96–118). My own view arising from fifteen years' practice as a humanistic therapist is that our famous menstrual temper and irritability is the suppressed resentment of other times speaking out. The veil of the inner temple is torn away, and so too is the veil of pretence. Menstruation is an oracle, but she has her gentle voice if her harsh one is not ignored.

Obviously this owes a debt to Jung's Shadow concept, the feared, rejected part of the Self which can be transformed into strength and wisdom by being accepted. Starhawk, who is internationally respected as the pioneer of our contemporary Craft movement, named her first coven 'Compost' to invoke the immense value of the rejected as that which fertilises renewal (Starhawk, 1981).

And finally, speaking of dirt, Mary Douglas' analysis of taboo is not only helpful, but Paganly pragmatic: she points out that shoes on the floor are fine, shoes on the dinner table are not (Douglas 1970). To be impure, or taboo, is to be simply in the wrong place.

It is in this sense that Circlework teaches Purification. It asks for attention to each item which may distract me from being here now completely; that is, things both nice and nasty that are in the wrong place. If something is painful, then its recognition and release will be especially important, towards creating 'perfect love and perfect trust' (Charge) according to the Craft tradition. Movement (stirring the water, passing the bowl, and the meditational walk) is *widdershins* (anticlockwise), the ancient direction of the negative, as a deliberate honouring of the dark to balance the *deosil* (clockwise) casting that follows.

In its sometimes frustrating negativity, thoroughness and slowness Purification releases our passage into the place beyond time.

Casting the Circle: Pieces of the Whole

> *She faces East, saying 'I call the power of Air, and intelligence', lighting the yellow candle. She then faces front and South, saying 'I call the power of Fire, and of the will', lighting the red candle. She then faces West, saying 'I call the power of Water, and of emotions', lighting the blue candle. She then turns behind her to the North, saying 'I call the power of Earth, and of the body', lighting the green candle. She raises her wand to point upwards saying 'The circle is cast. I am between the worlds, beyond the bounds of time, where night and day, birth and death, joy and sorrow, meet as one.'*
>
> *Mandala, meaning an orb or circle, symbolises wholeness and the outer visualisation of cosmic energy. Whether drawn on earth, on walls, on paper, on cloth or engraved on metal, as a symbol of mysterious power, mandalas were man's earliest attempt to communicate concentrated, non verbal meaning (Jayakar 1989, p109).*

It is ridiculously nonsensical for me to attempt to put the Circle into words, but naturally, nonsense has its place.

It was Jung of course who won widespread recognition for the four-quartered mandala, bringing the 'superstition' of shamanism into the halls of academe, and winning respect for it. Linda Jean Shepherd MD (USA), writing on the feminine face of science tells us:

Today, the Myers-Briggs Type Indicator (MBTI) is an extensively used measure of personality dispositions and preferences based on Jung's theory of types. Every year over 1.5 million people take the MBTI in business organisations, educational institutions, personal and vocational counselling, and governmental agencies (Shepherd 1993, p54).

Jung's theory of types was developed from the immeasurably ancient philosophy of the four Elements, Air, Fire, Water and Earth. This four-quartered Circle is found everywhere in the world, with only slight variations, in all our oldest forms of faith. In India, Tibet, Siberia, China, the Pacific, Australia, North and South America, Africa, and Europe, the ubiquitous cross-quartered circle symbol can be seen in prehistoric carved stone or bone, and survives in aboriginal art, myth and custom.

Jung specifically adopted the term 'mandala' from India, where the Vrata mandalas predate the Aryan conquest. They have:

through the centuries ... maintain[ed] their integrity and existence, independent and parallel to the orthodox Brahmin dominated culture (Jayakar 1989, p35).

The Circled space is understood by some magical practitioners to be a defensive walled place where impure and unclean spirits have been cast out or exorcised. Circlework instead emphasises the Circle as:

The Pot ... a container, in terms of the positive nature of what it holds within, rather than what it keeps out ... a kind of pressure cooker which speeds up natural processes, and 'cooks' ingredients put in it (Shan 1994, p32).

There is also a caution given about:

what is shut in with you–you yourself ... inside this container, full of your natural equipment of fears, aggression, sadness and so on (Shan 1994, p132).

which goes to show yet again how crucial Purification is in order to recognise and work with those forces in each one of us.

Our need as humanity to accept our fears and aggressions, and work with them, rather than the way we tend to contemptuously condemn our nature and try to escape it, is horribly emphasised when we look at the peculiar history lesson of Europe. We bear here a unique heritage of a destroyed religious leadership across much of a continent. What the Romans began, the Christians virtually completed.

From the Circlework view Druidry may possibly have been too dualistic, too like the Brahmins (Rutherford 1985, 1987). Nevertheless, it was a profound, sustaining and vigorous faith that sustained ancestral traditions, united tribes, inspired repeated rebellions against the might of Roman standardisation, and generated a life-loving Celtic Christianity which challenged orthodoxy with immense passion and tenacity through many succeeding centuries.

Pelagius of 5th century Britain (360–431 BCE) taught that we achieve redemption by our own efforts for our nature is inherently good, and that the divine itself is met through nature. (Mourani 1972, p78) He was bitterly condemned by Augustine. John Scotus Erigena, 9th century (810–877 BCE) taught a fourfold basis of being, and that everything is 'theophania', that is, a manifestation of God. His teaching was condemned as 'pullulating with worms of heretical perversity' and as 'Irish porridge' (MacIntyre 1972, p34).

So resourceful was the Celtic faith that the Goddess Brigit's tradition, for example, once it was delicately repackaged as St Brigit, survived intact right up to the wholesale destruction of Cromwell only 400 years ago (McCrickard 1990, 1985). I have spoken to those who still practise her festival customs today as an inherited folk tradition both in the Hebrides and in western Eire.

The quartered Circle survived as the 'Celtic Cross' but it is significant that by that name the cross is emphasised and the circle discreetly discounted.

In spite of the undoubted wisdom and persistence of such Celtic traditions, (and of the Nordic and Saxon ones of which I know far less), the broken circle of our religious traditions as a continent is a tragedy of persecution and great suffering. The vacuum left by the loss of most of our own formal religious network was filled by an impoverished variety of a foreign faith which concentrated on status, power and property. Lacking spiritual depth during centuries of continual wars and plagues, its priests fell victim to real despair, teaching that 'God has turned away from us'. And the reason appeared so logical–because we are bad.

The Problem of Evil, as the philosophers debated it for centuries is this:

If God is all-powerful he must be able to prevent Evil.
If God is all-good, he must want to prevent it.
Evil exists.
Therefore God is either not all-powerful or not all-good (Hicks 1972, p136).

The genuine dilemma here has created numerous scholarly headaches, requiring copious willow bark remedies, modern aspirins, and lifetimes of painstaking theological analysis.

What is not open to a dualistic theology, as it is to ours, is to relinquish the all-good God. We do not need, contrary to the dying popular stereotype, to replace this with the Gnostic Devil. Instead we can return to a wholeness neither good nor evil, but natural. The 'Force' or 'Source' is not good or evil, just utterly complete.

Yet there still remains a more limited problem of evil, located for example in my sense of outrage at certain cruelties and injustice, especially the hurt of children.

One way to an answer comes from Plotinus, 3rd century (205–270 CE) who says that what appears to be evil, when seen in isolation or a too limited context, is a necessary element in a universe when viewed as a totality (Hicks 1972, p137).

Personally when I am feeling particularly detached and intellectual I can just about comprehend this neutral reality–after all war stimulates invention, and refugees carry cultural cross-fertilisation. But Plotinus goes too far when he claims that this totality that includes all is wholly good. (For one thing, logically, if all is good, nothing is good, for good is meaningless without its opposite, bad.)

Far, far more importantly than any logic, as a mother I cannot ever encompass napalmed children in a good universe. Yet with enormous difficulty, I can see that to the tree rooted nearby the appallingly hurt child is not the same atrocity as it is to me.

Thomas Traherne, a 17th-century Celtic mystic, expresses it:

> *You can never enjoy the world aright, till the Sea itself flows in your veins, till you are clothed with the heavens, and crowned with the stars; and perceive yourself to be the sole heir of the whole world, and more than so, because men are in it who are every one sole heirs as well as you (Traherne, 1668–71, but see 1991, p197).*

My simple rage at our hurt children is quite sufficient to put their suffering on the agenda as bad and unjust. Yet my champion spirit may, and actually does, have to contend with those who feel differently–all the more reason to 'perceive (myself) as the heir of the world' or, I should say, to see the child as the heir.

What pattern in the whole, then, can possibly put meaning in this long ugly wounding of the European spirit? Victor Frankl, on considering the 20th-century holocaust he himself survived, points at the few who did not become completely debased.

> *The way in which a man accepts his fate ... gives him ample opportunity–even under the most difficult circumstances–to add a deeper meaning to his life (Friedman 1992, p15).*

This is a modern restatement of Irenaeus' 2nd-century description of the world as soul maker, giving opportunities for heroic virtue (Hicks 1972, p138). Maurice Friedman reproaches Frankl that this heroic view has:

> *not very much compassion for those whose lack of confirmation in their past lives left them unequipped (Friedman 1992, p113)*

for such heroism.

So if the individual view is bleak, what of the wider, though not greater, perspective? Well, in tracing the shape of a truly Pagan tradition, I have significantly not been calling on a list of accredited Western Pagan teachers. Our heritage is too fractured for that. I speak to you from modern psychology, the physical sciences, anthropology, Judaism, Zen, and Taoism. Of course, it is not that we do not have our own Pagan teachings, but that they are fragmented survivals, often embedded in myth and folk culture. Our sources are not found in the formal records of our socially respected institutions. Forced by splintered sources to look outward to compare, check and amplify them, I join the current dynamic, world movement of interfaith and eclectic philosophy, which I would argue actually has its roots in the deprived needs of Europe, and so becomes a gift forged of suffering.

Impoverished by our ancestral loss we may be, yet we are not just spiritual beggars. By learning from faraway teachings we can darn the lacunae in our own native sources: discovering that the stoics were Zen teachers, that the Craft parallels archaic pre-Aryan India, that heretics and mystics such as our own Pelagius, Erigen and Traherne taught the Tao under other names.

Meeting the gods in my own country is not an encounter with the remote, or the dizzyingly virtuous. These are certainly awesome, powerful beings, yet the teachings that can still be picked out of myth and folklore give excellent and specific guidance on how to manage these meetings–do not eat their food if offered as Thomas the Rhymer learned to his cost and do not make love with them if you wish to return to your ordinary life–Thomas the Rhymer again and Pwyll Pen Defig Dyfed (Gantz 1976, p46). There is a craft to these things.

Raising Energy: Sex

She raises the drum, a Celtic patterned double bodhran, and beats a resonant sound from it that soothes as it startles. Suddenly she shrieks, a harsh, atonal voice with primitive power. She sings a little of Goddess and God, then sets aside the drum.

When I first started studying all this, I was training in Tai Chi. Over and over again my teacher told me I must learn to move from my 'tan tien' if I was to move in power. Asked what or where this was, she said it was 'about six inches down from the navel on a diagonal line aimed at the anus'. None the wiser I trotted off and asked my best friend, a medical artist, where that would be. 'Oh', she said casually, 'That's your cervix'.

Around then I stumbled on the strange contradictory nature of certain goddesses. Anat, the Great Goddess of Ugarit/Syria:

slew everyone in sight, wading maniacally in knee deep blood and strapping dismembered bodies to her waist ... She also sought her lover Baal while he was hunting, whereupon they copulated 77 times in the wilderness (Monaghan 1981, pp16, 17).

Sekhmet of Egypt 'became so disgusted with humanity that she commenced a wholesale slaughter of the race', (Monaghan 1981, p264) yet as gentle Bast she 'ruled pleasure and dancing, music and joy'. (Monaghan 1981, p42)

A seal from the Indus valley shows:

The earth is the great yoni [vagina] ... the fecundating source ... On the reverse ... is a figure who sits with streaming hair and arms upraised while [another] holding a knife and a cup approaches ... Significantly the identical script appears on both sides of the seal, connecting the two rituals of death and birth (Jayakar 1989, p67).

After a good deal of pondering I came to understand that it is desire, or passion, which unites opposites.

Releasing passion in the circle certainly proved itself a healthy and enjoyable practice for me. But after several years I actually got heartily fed up of being typecast as the 'Pagan Jane Fonda' because my meetings usually included vigorous shamanic chanting, drumming and dancing, which sometimes reached a level of real catharsis.

The Craft celebration of sexuality was to me personally, as to many others, a welcome antidote to a sexually crushed and unbalanced society. Sukie Colegrave observes that excessive reliance on the masculine discriminating principle leads away from relatedness to despair and a loss of meaning. Excessive reliance on the feminine principle submerges us in a sea of sameness, and we lose the will to act and think as an individual (Colegrave 1979).

But I found confirmation of the power of sex as profound renewal in a totally unexpected place.

> *Sex is a kind of redemption by which each generation reverses biological decay. In some ways sex is the key to immortality. It is the fountain of eternal youth, not for the individuals who indulge in it but for the genes they carry (Jones 1993, p101).*

Just like making a series of photocopies, a little information is lost as our cells replace themselves through our individual lifetime. Parts of our genetic message disappear with time; our cellular DNA halves its length over a 60-year life. Death happens when the genetic message has become so degenerate that its instructions no longer make sense (Jones 1993, p93).

Egg and sperm start with a double set of chromosomes each. As they lie in ovary or testis these pairs literally exchange and shuffle their cards to produce a new pattern of play. Once reshuffled, each sheds one set, and goes to meet the opposite sex partner with a 'recombined', completely new mixture of genes. The less successful patterns of previous generations fail to be passed on by breeding, while new possibilities of success endlessly develop (Jones 1993, p58–9).

Prakrti, the active female life force of archaic India:

> *ascends, she transforms, she permeates, she fills ... she strides four fold ... They each kill her in turn, and she in turn arises springing back into existence, for she is ... the indestructible energy principle (Jayakar 1989, p62) (cf. Tiamat of Babylon.).*

In archaic, pre-Aryan India again, I found one of the most beautiful and ancient images of the god. Kama is desire, Lord of love and procreation:

> *his fragrant face, his lotus eyes, his sensuous limbs, his unassuaging fires ... the cloud dark lover, the blue black thunderbolt of desire (Jayakar 1989, p86).*

The powerful arrows of Kama later became Krishna's sweet flute. Kama's fierce and tender, frankly phallic eroticism became watered down into an otherworldly allegory, similar to the biblical Song of Songs' love affair between soul and deity.

Inanna, Goddess of Sumer, gifted us with the earliest recorded love song ever, with a most unmodern delight in the male:

> *At the king's lap stood the rising cedar. My honey man sweetens me always ... let me caress you ... Now I will caress my high priest on the bed (Wolkstein, Kramer 1983).*

There is also Pasupati of Harappa, Lord of the Animals, phallic, masked, with wide buffalo horns. His body and arms are marked with bands while wild and virile animals surround his seated figure. In another seal he is guarded by two serpents. (Jayakar 1989, pp69–70) The comparison with the famous 'Cernunnos' on the reputedly Celtic Gundestrup cauldron is irresistible.

In 'The Myth of the Goddess'[2] we are offered a powerful synthesis between the two myths, female myth and male myth, going right back to Palaeolithic, cave-clan times. The female, Goddess myth, is:

> *concerned with fertility and the sacredness of life in all its aspects, and so with transformation and rebirth. By contrast, the myth of the hunter [centred on humanity, is] concerned above all with the drama of survival–the taking of life as a ritual act in order to live ... They seem, then, to tell different and even mutually exclusive stories: one where life and death are recognized as phases of an eternal process; the other, where the death ... becomes final, and our experience of life tragic ... the myth of the hunter is ultimately included in the myth of the goddess, along with all other aspects of life that are part of the whole ... but the hunter myth cannot contain the goddess myth (Baring, Cashford 1991, p39).*

Working: Me and You

> *She says 'Obviously I cannot show you the working part of a Circle, so all I can do is to show you a symbol.' She holds up her hands as if in prayer, but curved open as a vaginal gateway.*
>
> *On average two people differ in about one DNA per thousand–three million places in our inherited message differ person to person (Jones 1993, p28).*
>
> *What the human is, can be, and ought to become is continually changing, however, not only with each new culture and period of history, but also with each new individual (Friedman 1978, p18).*

'In the Circle you can't do it wrong' (Shan 1994) is the Great Guiding Principle of Circlework. Because however you do it is how THIS ritual is supposed to be.

> *To be in accord with Tao everything must nourish its own nature and follow its own destiny. Individual differences do not imply discrimination, neither should they be denied and ignored (Chuang Tzu).*
>
> *There is a way the individual person can discover one's unique path. That is by listening to the call of one's own heart ... that which we mean by the HEART is the wholeness of the person, and here too one can be mistaken. Human history is littered with ... mistaking intensity, logic, emotion, or inspiration for human wholeness. One of the reasons such a mistake is made is that we tend to trust one of our faculties more than another and wish to identify the I with that faculty (Friedman 1992, p67).*

'We are always in two minds about it all' (Shan 1994, p66). 'Welcome to the wondrous wedding and passionate bedding of Intelligence and Intuition' (Shan 1994, p69).

> *But it takes a great deal of listening to allow what happens to come forth spontaneously (Friedman 1992, p67).*
>
> *Many scientists feel they cannot compete if they slow down enough to be receptive. Being receptive looks like they are not doing anything ... goofing off. Ours is a 'doing' culture. There is an unrelenting pressure to produce ... stepping back and reflecting seems an admission of uncertainty–that you may not know what is going on or what to do next ... Receptivity depends on an implicit trust that there is something of value to be received (Shepherd 1993, p79–80).*

While acknowledging the great debt we as Westerners, and Pagans, owe Jung, who brought the Self, the Goddess, the Shadow and the dreaming, out of exile and into the centre of society, I have never felt the archetypes and the collective unconscious were enough. Jung, says Friedman, restricts the spiritual to the psychological (and this seems to me to be the widespread manner of understanding Jung today, even if it is not completely accurate):

> *There is no deity in the mandala, nor is there any submission or reconciliation to a deity. The place of the deity seems to be taken by the wholeness of man (Jung 1959 in Freidman 1992).*

In vivid contrast Martin Buber says:

Only when having become aware of the unincludable otherness of being, I renounced all claim to incorporating it in any way within me or making it part of my soul, does it truly become Thou for me. This holds good for God as for man (Buber 1988).

Friedman continues:

For all the numinous, guiding quality of Jung's collective unconscious, it is still an It, and not a Thou ... it can never be [just] identified with the conscious person or even with the personal unconscious. But there is no mutuality, no give and take, no sense that Jung's God needs us for the very purpose for which he created us (Friedman 1992, p91).

From Chuang Tzu we can receive this as:

The pure man abides in the great One, he becomes a 'companion of Nature' and does not substitute the way of man for the way of Nature (Chuang Tzu).

And from my own Way, the Goddess says 'I have been with thee from the beginning, and I await thee now.' (Charge)

Communion: ordinary matter

She takes up the cup on her right, raises it for a silent moment, then drinks. 'I give thanks that this seems to be going all right.' Laughter. She takes a tiny piece of bread and chews it. 'I give thanks for the reality of this Conference.'

I drink, and delight in what I drink, giving thanks. I eat, coming fully into the familiar, simple state of being my body.

The Hasidic Seer of Lublin says:

It is impossible to tell persons what way they should take. For one way is to serve God through teaching, another through prayer, another fasting, and still another through eating (Buber 1978, p313).

Around the agricultural communities [of India] the potter, the tailor, the printer, the barber, the blacksmith, the goldsmith, the washerman ... become the image makers, the carvers of icons and the magician priests at the shrines of the goddess (Jayakar 1989, p45).

Unlike the Brahmanic worship of mantra ... Vrata Puja and observances were open to the woman, to the non Brahmin, to the

> *Sudra and the tribal ... Vrata rites ... renewed through the worship of the earth, sun, water and ... the energy of growing things, of trees, plants and animals. The demands of sex and fertility, wealth and prosperity were translated into minutely detailed rituals (Jayakar 1989, p35).*

At first among the Stoics of the West there was a major emphasis on asceticism. Later such things as health, property and honour were considered advantages to be used, but not needed. Their opposites were disadvantages to be avoided–but not at all costs (Halllie 1972, p19).

Jean Pagels claims that catholic Christianity:

> *gradually developed rituals to sanction major events of biological existence: the sharing of food in the eucharist; sexuality in marriage; childbirth in baptism: sickness in anointment; and death in funerals (Pagels 1985, p85).*

However, some of these were a late development in Christianity, e.g. marriages were only celebrated in Church by the upper classes until the middle class emerged in the last 200 years.

Maslow has provided a useful approach to spirituality where:

> *the peak experience is felt as a self validating, self justifying moment which carries its own intrinsic value with it (Maslow 1970, Preface).*

But Maslow himself was concerned that:

> *out of the joy and wonder of his ecstasies and peak experiences he may be tempted to seek them, ad hoc, ... he may run the danger of turning away from the world and from other people in his search for triggers ... [losing how] the sacred is in the ordinary, that it is to be found in one's daily life, in one's neighbours, friends, and family; in one's backyard (Maslow 1970, Preface).*

According to Rinzai Zen:

> *There is no gap between the spiritual and the secular so one should not strive to gain illumination (Smart 1972, p366).*

'Eating earths us wonderfully', points out Circlework:

> *The spurting of saliva, the sensation of taste, the activity of chewing, the solid stuff sliding down to the stomach all demands and takes our attention. The blood supply moves to the digestion [sic] system ... away from the brain. We are therefore completely*

naturally and fairly quickly brought out of rarefied mental states (Shan 1994, p54).

An old friend of mine once remarked that people who refuse the pleasures of life were like rude guests at a garden party, given by the greatest hostess of all. Among feasting, dancing, playful children, music, lovemaking in the discreet shadows, and a variety of good company it is extraordinarily rude to sidle away and just say no.

Opening the Circle: Like Housework

She turns behind her saying 'Thank you, Earth'. She blows out the green candle, turns to her right, but can't reach. She asks Ronald Hutton to put out the blue one for her. She gives thanks to Fire in front of her, blows out the red candle, and does the same for Air and the yellow one.

And so to endings.

In a faith that centrally honours change, we come to accept that each thing has its beginning, its season, and its ending. We have comforting little sayings–'As one door closes another opens'. The two myths, the hunter's way of survival and the Goddess' way of cycle (Baring, Cashford 1991, p39) show us that thinking in straight lines leads to a bleak alienation. Mircea Eliade has taught us about archaic man's way of living in a continual present, following repeated cycles through the seasons that virtually obliterate unique events and much of personal history (Eliade 1959).

But we do not live in that timeless womb anymore. Facing death, we try to make a performance of it, like the rest of our anxious lives; we want 'a good death'. In *How We Die* Sherwin Nuland strips away this pathetic defence. Such an end, he tells us from years of doctorly experience, is only for some of us. The rest will go in discomfort and disintegration, because that's what it's about: death, disintegration.

Instead of insisting on a perfect tableau which is likely to lead to sadness and disappointment, he directs us to look at the whole of life for its meaning, accepting its end as only one part of it. Do not allow the shadow to obliterate the colours of life on the way.

It is so fatally easy to notice only the troublemakers in life, the obstacles, the crashes and disasters. All the while a constant busy petty housework is going on of small joys, tasks completed, all the overwhelming numbers of things which are NOT broken, dirty, and in a mess. Perhaps goodness is like that, like housework, and we mostly notice it when it's not done.

Many of us believe we will return and spin the wheel again, and it is not the Pagan who wants to get off the wheel. As the initiates of Isis said, 'In her service is perfect freedom'. Whatever we believe, I think the last word belongs to the mothers, who know well that the gate at one end, birth giving, is very messy, scored with pain, and so often not the scripted peak experience we tried to have. Yet however awful it is, mothers know it most certainly has its own meaning. The oldest teachings say death is like birth.

The circle is open, but unbroken.

Notes

1 *Gender language* It is of course a priority for me as a philosopher, and a veteran feminist, to respect the power of language. This means I do not use terms such as 'man' ambiguously. Where I refer to the male person (Latin: *vir*) I say 'man'. Where I mean the generic person or human being (Latin: *homo*) that is what I say. However, while sentences in my own words use 'he' to refer to one sex only, I have called on extensive quotation, and most of these derive from more or less masculinist cultures, which have distorted gender language into ambiguity. I consider that this is not accidental, but vicious. It actually illustrates one of the themes of this paper *viz* the pejorative equation of the female with lower, non spiritual, non central being. I therefore hold the writers responsible for it, and choose to leave their bias in plain view.

Christianity In this paper there are a number of references to Christianity which may appear unduly harsh. This is because it is the more political and aggressive sections of this faith which have unfortunately dominated Western history, and therefore come into the domain of my discourse. I wish to make clear my respect and indeed love for those other Christians whose political impact has been less in the past, but whose influence is an essential part of our future.

2 In the 'Myth of the Goddess' quote I have rearranged the order of the phrases a little, in order to give a brief but understandable excerpt.

Bibliography

Anon, *Ballad of True Thomas*–British folklore.

Baring, Anne and Jules Cashford, 1991 *The Myth of the Goddess: Evolution of an Image*, Penguin/Arkana.

Buber, Martin 1978 *Tales of the Hasidim*, Schocken, New York.

Buber, Martin 1952 *Eclipse of God: Studies in the Relation between Religion and Philosophy*, Harper & Brothers, New York.

Buber, Martin 1946 *Moses*, East and West Library, London.

Chuang Tzu *Chuang Tzu*, translated by Giles, Herbert 1961, Allen and Unwin, London.

Colegrave, Sukie 1979 *Uniting Heaven and Earth*, USA, Tarcher.

Douglas, Mary 1970 *Natural Symbols*, Barrie and Rocliffe, London.

Eliade, Mircea 1959 *Cosmos and History*, Harper and Row, New York.

Farrar J. and S. Farrar 1992 (1981) *Eight Sabbats for Witches*, Robert Hale, London.

Friedman, Maurice 1992 *Religion and Psychology*, Paragon House, New York.

Friedman, Maurice 1967 *To Deny our Nothingness*, University of Chicago.

Gantz, Jeffrey (trans.), 1976 *Mabinogion*, Penguin, Harmondsworth.

Hallie, Philip P., 1972 'Stoicism', *Encyclopedia of Philosophy* Vol 8, p19, Macmillan, New York.

Hicks, John 1972 'The Problem of Evil', *Encyclopedia of Philosophy* Vol 3, p136–7, Macmillan, New York.

Jayakar, Pupul 1989 *The Earth Mother* (previously *The Earthen Drum*), Penguin, Harmondsworth.

Jonas, Hans 1972 'Gnosticism' *Encyclopedia of Philosophy* vol 3, p337–42, Macmillan, New York.

Jones, Steve 1993 *Language of the Genes: Biological History and the Evolution of the Future*, HarperCollins, London.

Jung, C.G. 1958 *The Collected Works* Vol. 11: *Psychology and Religion: West and East*, Routledge and Kegan Paul, London.

Lovelock, James 1979 *Gaia, a New Look at Life on Earth*, OUP, Oxford.

MacIntyre, Alasdaire 1972, 'Pantheism', *Encyclopedia of Philosophy* vol 6, p34, Macmillan, New York.

Maslow, Abram 1970 *Religions Values and Peak Experience*, Viking, New York.

McCrickard, Janet (aka Sinead Sula Grian) 1990 *The Eclipse of the Sun: A New Look at Sun and Moon Myths*, Gothic Image, Glastonbury.

McCrickard, Janet 1985 *Brighde Goddess of the Fire*, Brighde's Fire, Glastonbury.

Monaghan, Patricia 1981 *Women of Myth and Legend*, Junction Books.

Mourani, John A. 1972 'Pelagius', *Encyclopedia of Philosophy* Vol 6, p78, Macmillan, New York.

Nuland, Sherwin 1994, *How We Die*, Chatto and Windus, London.

Pagels, Elaine 1985 *The Gnostic Gospels*, Penguin, Harmondsworth.

Rutherford, Ward 1985 *The Druids, Magicians of the West* Aquarian, Wellingborough.

Rutherford, Ward 1987 *Celtic Mythology* Aquarian, Wellingborough.

Shan 1994 *Circlework: A DIY Handbook of Ritual, Psychology and Magic*, House of the Goddess, London.

Shepherd, Linda Jean 1993 *Lifting the Veil: the Feminine Face of Science*, Shambhala.

Shuttle, Penelope and Redgrove, Peter 1978 *The Wise Wound: Menstruation and Everywoman*, Victor Gollancz, London.

Smart, Ninian 1972a 'Indian Philosophy', *Encyclopedia of Philosophy* vol 4, pp155–69, Macmillan, New York.

Smart, Ninian 1972b 'Zen', *Encyclopedia of Philosophy* vol 8, pp366–7, Macmillan, New York.

Starhawk 1981 *Dreaming the Dark*, Harper & Row, San Francisco.

Starhawk 1979 *The Spiral Dance: A Rebirth of the Ancient Religion of the Great Goddess*, Harper & Row, San Francisco.

Stone, Merlin 1979 *The Paradise Papers*, Virago, London. (Also published as *When God was a Woman*).

Traherne, Thomas, 'Centuries of Meditation', 1991 *Selected Poems and Prose*, Penguin, Harmondsworth.

Valiente, Doreen, 'Charge of the Goddess' in Farrar and Farrar 1992 and also, in a short version, in Starhawk 1979.

Van Waters, Miriam 1913, 'The adolescent girl among primitive peoples', *Journal of Religious Psychology* Vol 7 Part 1, Macmillan, New York.

Wolkstein, Nancy and Kramer, Noah, 1983 *Inanna: Queen of Heaven and Earth*, Harper & Row.

Leila Dudley Edwards

TRADITION AND RITUAL:

Halloween and Contemporary Paganism

Hey-ho for Halloween
All the witches to be seen
Some Black and some green
Hey-ho for Halloween.[1]

The festival of Halloween has been associated with witchcraft for many years in folklore. It is not surprising then that it should occupy a significant and symbolic position in the pagan festival calendar, and be celebrated with reverence and revels by modern pagans throughout Britain and beyond. Halloween occupies the point of the year where autumn is coming to an end and winter sets in, and is part of a yearly cycle of eight major days of celebration in the pagan calendar comprised of the solstices, equinoxes and the four Celtic quarter days. The latter are based on popular knowledge of the pre-Christian festivals of Imbolc or the feast of Bride, commonly observed on 1 or 2 February; Beltane or Mayday, Lughnasa or Lammas (1 August) and Samhain (1 November). It has been suggested that the celebration of these eight particular dates is one of three distinguishing traits which unify the various diverse aspects of paganism.[2]

For research into modern custom and belief surrounding Halloween it is necessary to examine briefly the historical and traditional background of the festival and to assess these influences on contemporary pagan philosophy and practice. As many pagans consciously emulate or refer to perceived pre-Christian ideals as expounded in myth and legend, Samhain as it is first encountered in Irish mythology provides a good starting point.

Samhain and Irish Myth

Many pagans prefer to use the term 'Samhain' to denote their festival rather than the Christian 'Halloween', consciously emphasising their links with pre-Christian paganism and the old native traditions. Accounts of ancient Samhain occur in early Irish literature and mythology and can serve to give an indication of the beliefs and ideas associated with the feast in ancient times. These have influenced the development of Halloween celebration in folk custom and in modern pagan observance.

Most of the surviving early Irish manuscript material is dated between the twelfth and fifteenth centuries, written down by Christian scribes and sometimes alluding to earlier manuscripts now lost. The stories recounted are set mainly in the pre-Christian period, though there are several tales depicting St Patrick's interaction with the existing pagan society. There exists no ancient written history of the Celts about their own society (the non-literate nature of which is often stressed by scholars) and so to study the nature of the feast of Samhain, we have to rely on references contained in the mythological literature.

Samhain is the time of supernatural occurrences and often provides a temporal context to events in the stories. Modern Celtic scholars have emphasised that many events of mythological importance are situated at this period in the calendar. Pronsias MacCana comments that Samhain constitutes 'a partial return to primordial chaos' and as such 'is the appropriate setting for myths which symbolise the dissolution of established order as a prelude to its recreation in a new period of time.'[3] From ancient Irish manuscripts we can obtain a flavour of the nature of Samhain and its associated beliefs, but should not regard the practices referred to in the mythology as factual depictions of ritual behaviour in ancient Celtic society.

In Irish myth Samhain functions as: a measure of seasonal time, a time for meeting and assembly and the payment of tithes and dues, a time of heightened supernatural activity and contact with the Otherworld when the fairy mounds are open and accessible, and a time when the death of kings and fire or arson are prominent. A brief look at a few examples will serve to illustrate these properties.

In ancient societies, time was ruled by the seasons and the tasks on the land. Even until relatively recently days were denominated by the Church feast day of the time. In ancient Ireland, Samhain was an important marker of temporal space as it designated the beginning of winter and a necessary change in lifestyle, and this function is apparent in several of the old stories. For example, Fionn MacCumhaill and the Fianna, a band of wandering warriors who travelled around Ireland living outdoors during the summer months were to be found quartered in the houses of nobles 'from Samhain to Beltane' and in return for winter lodging they would pledge allegiance to the lord of the house.

Samhain is important as a time of meeting and assembly, and a time when tithes were paid. The Book of Leinster tells of such an assembly where Conchobar, one of the high kings of Ireland, provided a huge feast at Samhain where all were obligated to attend: 'every one of the Ulstermen who would not come to Emain in All-Hallow eve lost his senses and on the morrow his barrow and his grave and his tombstone were placed.'[4] A sense of the supernatural danger of the time is implicit here. Fire is an important element in some of the stories and several king's dwellings and fairy mounds are set alight at this time, often by the other party, implying a certain amount of conflict between the two worlds.

Perhaps most importantly, Samhain was a time of contact and occasionally conflict with the Otherworld, and it is this aspect of the festival which has inflamed modern popular conceptions of Halloween. The closeness of the supernatural world and its inhabitants is the most conspicuous aspect of modern-day celebration and belief. This magical Otherworld is prominent in both Irish and Welsh myth and is an important element in contemporary pagan belief, and Samhain is a time when Otherworld activity and community are heightened.

The tale most frequently cited by scholars as indicative of the events which occur at Samhain is that of The Adventures of Nera which tells how the hero, with the advice of a dead man on the gallows who comes to life, goes into the fairy mound, takes a fairy wife, has a vision of the destruction which will take place the following Samhain against the court of Connaght and warns his king, whereupon the fairy mound is destroyed.[5]

Additionally, Samhain is cited as the time of divination when the Irish kings would encourage the Druids to augury, to foresee the events of the coming year. Halloween divination represents one of the most extensive areas of traditional lore associated with the festival.

The above is a brief indication of the nature of Samhain in Irish legend. As Ronald Hutton has noted, there is a strange absence of legend about the day in Welsh mythological texts, where *Calan Gaeaf* (1 November) and its eve are negligible when compared with the heightened supernatural occurrences of May Eve.[6] Once again this lack of evidence for the 1 November festival in Wales serves to remind of the inadequacies of visualising the Celts as a homogeneous culture with a definitive universal belief system. The Irish material gives an indication and an atmosphere of ancient Samhain, but does not provide a concrete system of religious beliefs settled around the festival, or imply a direct unbroken continuity of belief. Certain aspects however are prominent in the customs attached to Halloween in folk tradition when they are recorded centuries later, but prior to the eighteenth century (when the folk collectors begin recording quaint rural practices) many historical factors and influences serve to confuse the issue.

There have been many influences on the historical development of Halloween; as with many folk customs it has been subject to much political and social change. A consideration of influences in a rough chronological order will suffice to give an indication of the most significant elements.

The Feast of All Hallows

Halloween is frequently defined as a Christianisation of a pagan festival, and indeed on a basic level, the placing of the feast of All Saints on the first of November corresponds by inference with Pope Gregory's directive to St Augustine, recorded by Bede, that 'the idol temples ... should by no means be destroyed, but only the idols in them ... and they will ... be more ready to come to the places they are familiar with, but now recognizing and worshipping the true God.'[7] This form of conversion is held as having been applied to festivals also. However, the entire picture is not as simple as that. The origins of All Saints are confusing and the understanding of its history has been prey to erroneous concepts of cultural uniformity. Several dates are associated with a feast called All Saints in various parts of the Christian world and at various times in history. The name is conceivably a common enough dedication to have merited individual celebration in different parts of the Christian world, and it is not until the mid-ninth century that the feast becomes universally celebrated throughout the Western Church on 1 November.

The first documentation of such a feast occurs in Edessa in the Eastern dominions of the Church contained in a hymn composed by St Ephraim in AD 359. May 13 is the date cited therein for the commemoration of all the martyrs. Other dates occur in connection with the Eastern church: the East Syrians commemorated it on the first Friday after Easter by 411, implying a localised observance. The most prominent historical dedication to 'Our Lady and All the Martyrs' was made by Pope Boniface IV in 609 or 610 on the consecration of the Roman Pantheon building to the Church of Rome. This occurred on 13 May, and it has been supposed that there was an oriental influence on the choice of this day, and that this is the origin of the feast later celebrated on 1 November. It could be unrelated however, 13 May perhaps being merely an anniversary of a specific dedication to the Pantheon in Rome. It has also been suggested that this date was chosen to supersede the pagan Roman feast of Lemuria which placated the old gods and was celebrated around this time.[8]

Pope Gregory III (827–844) is credited with the creation of All Saints on the date of 1 November. A twelfth-century writer, John Beleth, states that he moved the feast from 13 May to 1 November because there were not enough provisions in the city on the earlier date to feed all the pilgrims who flocked to Rome. This date was gradually adopted by prominent churchmen in Europe and so came into widespread practice outside of the confines of Rome by 835. It seems, therefore, that on the surface that there is little evidence of a deliberate 'Christianisation' of Samhain, and it is perhaps a little unlikely that the Pope in the mid-ninth century would find it necessary to quell pagan practices possibly still taking place in distant Ireland more than two centuries after his predecessor Gregory III had sent his missive to Augustine.

However, the apparently localised nature of All Saints has led to further interesting debate. In early Irish monastic texts there are references to an All Saints' Day of some kind. The *Felire* (calendar) of Oengus, attributed to Oengus the Culdee around 804, mentions the multitudinous hosts which 'ennoble stormy All-Saints-Day', and this occurs as part of the entry for 1 November.[9] The text also refers, as does the *Martyrology of Tallacht* (which lacks the portion for 1 November), to the feast of All Saints of Europe on 20 April and All Saints of Africa on 23 December, again emphasising the hitherto localised nature of the event. Bede's (672–735) early *Martyrology* does not mention All Saints, but later copies dated at the beginning of the ninth century refer to a 1 November *festivas omnium Sanctorum*; this account predates Gregory IV. It seems therefore that there is evidence of a 1 November All Saints feast in Ireland and perhaps England also prior to that adopted by the Roman church, and this could be related to a desire to convert existing pagan beliefs surrounding this date.

Whitley Stokes, translator of the *Calendar of Oengus*, further complicates the issue by asserting that the grammatical structure of the poem places a *terminus ad quem* of the end of the tenth century, thus rendering its evidence with regard to dating the origins of All Saints invalid. The problems of dating Irish manuscripts are well-recognised, and Stokes does have a point, but the situation is further complicated by his translation which renders the word '*samain*' as 'All-Saints-Day'. '*Samain*' in this context could refer mainly to the date, summer's end, or perhaps even to an older pre-Christian feast day. There is a poetic implication that the Christian saints mentioned in the verse–'Lonan, Colman and Cronan with their fair sunny following'–are in fact ennobling a day which requires it, and are deliberately in contrast to 'stormy samain'. This perhaps highlights a need for the Christian hosts to brighten and ennoble a day that has possible negative associations, whether it be because of inclemency at the beginning of winter, or more romantically, to combat less sunny hosts which were traditionally abroad at this time!

It is difficult to draw any definite historical conclusions concerning the origins and dissemination of a 1 November All Saints feast one way or the other, but there remains the possibility as suggested by Hennig, that the universal date was eventually adopted in Rome from Ireland, and that there is no real connection with the dedication to the Roman Pantheon originally made on 13 May AD 609.

A study of Halloween traditions and practices can be confusing in that it requires reference to more than one particular date. *Samhain* refers to 1 November, Halloween to 31 October, and with the formal introduction of All Souls Day on 2 November in the eleventh century and its related customary practices, the definition of the festival's date must be broadened. Indeed, in Irish texts it is given a period of three days of observance and modern pagans sometimes celebrate on other days, sometimes relative to the moon. The calendar change of 1582, though not adopted in Britain until 1751, further complicated the issue by placing 'Old Halloween' on 11 November, Martinmas Day. Some people continued to live by the old calendar, and it is interesting to note that certain traditional customs relating to Martinmas are very similar to those of Halloween.

The Feast of All Souls

The feast of All Souls came into being at the beginning of the eleventh century when it was introduced as a formal holy day by St Odilo in 998. Its creation was directly influenced by the existence of the feast of All Saints which celebrated the martyrs who had died and were eternally blessed: All Souls remembered the lowlier dead who were lost in Purgatory and needed the prayers of the faithful to lessen their plight, for 'many pass out of this world without at once being admitted into the company of the blessed'.[10] While commemoration of the martyrs involved interaction with some kind of Otherworld beings in a loose sense, their relationship to the living faithful was somewhat distant, metaphysical and obscure: All Souls was easier to relate to on a much more personal level where individuals could remember their own personal dear departed and feel closer to them.

Most religions have a festival of the dead which fulfils this function, and this was lacking in an immediate sense in the Christian church. James Frazer argued in *The Golden Bough* that both All Saints and All Souls were a deliberate counteraction on the part of the medieval Church to a lingering festival of the dead celebrated by the Celts, and that they were fulfilling a need or desire for its Christianisation. He maintained that All Souls was a concession made by the Church which had hitherto been avoiding celebrating the dead as a concept that was too pagan, attempting to concentrate on the glorious Otherworld (i.e. Heaven) symbolised by the martyrs. As Frazer puts it, '[the] attempt to divert the devotion of the faithful from the souls of the dead to the saints proved a failure, and finally the Church reluctantly decided to sanction the popular superstition by frankly admitting a feast of All Souls into the calendar'.[11] His ideas have had much influence on beliefs about the origins and development of Samhain/Halloween, and folklore in general. He took the survivalist approach of folklore into the twentieth century where he is one of the most singular influences on popular conceptions about traditional custom and belief existing today, though most modern academic folklorists are adamant in their rejection of his premises. While All Souls fulfilled a necessary human function as a focus for the remembrance of the dead it does not have to be specifically Celtic, probably relating more to an emotional response to the plight of poor lost souls in Purgatory, but embodying the same essential basic human concerns.

Any funeral or festival of the dead, of whatever religious denomination, Christian or pagan, will embody certain observances or customs and therefore it would be erroneous to assume that the existence of folk practices surrounding All Souls' Day points to its pagan origins, though undoubtedly there would be similarities.

Traditions surrounding Halloween then incorporate the customs engendered by the folk religion of All Saints and All Souls, and the predominance of divination customs in Gaelic-speaking Ireland and Scotland may betoken the memories or ghosts of an older pre-Christian Samhain, though this cannot be presumed a certainty. (My Presbyterian grandmother maintained that ghosts and witches were abroad at Halloween because they needed a final fling prior to the intensive holiness of the following day when they would all be well and truly banished.) Certainly the souling customs attached to 2 November have an earthy and fundamental essence to them and the veneration of the dead embodied therein is in keeping with attitudes of contemporary pagans celebrating Samhain.

There were certain days in the medieval church calendar where customary largesse or begging was sanctioned and etiquette required the rich to feed or give handouts to the poor. All Souls was one of these. In return for charity, the recipient would be expected to pray for the souls of the rich. The feast came under heavy attack during the Reformation but elements of the custom survive in the souling songs and rhymes collected well into this century, some of which can still be heard in contemporary playgrounds. An interesting local custom on the outskirts of Sheffield is 'caking night' (from 'soul-cake') where the local people put on fancy dress and go to village pubs for games, meals and other social events on the first Saturday in November. Disguise is a common element in begging traditions, and this seems to be a modern manifestation of older souling customs. In Antrobus, Cheshire (where there is evidence of much souling activity in the past), the Souling play is performed around this time. It is essentially a version of the folk hero-combat play with its central motif of death and resurrection often associated with other dates in the calendar, being performed at midwinter and in spring. The Scottish folk play, Galoshins, though more commonly performed around midwinter, took place around Halloween time also. There is evidence of All Souls Day fires in Lancashire and Derbyshire in the eighteenth century, ostensibly to light the souls out of Purgatory, and these symbolically reflect the fires associated with Halloween and Samhain. At this time also there was a belief in supernatural activity as the ghosts of the departed were ostensibly closer to the earth and could return to pay visits. The visiting of cemeteries on 2 November was common all over Catholic Europe.

One important aspect of the Reformation was that it denied the existence of Purgatory, and so the associations of this time of year with the dead declined as did souling customs as customary largess was discouraged. After 1605 however, a new manifestation of the autumn fire festival came into existence as Parliament and the Church of England added a special State service to the calendar commemorating 'our deliverance and detestation of the Papists' on 5th November. The celebration of Guy Fawkes' Night became extremely popular throughout England to the extent where the authorities had to curb riotous and dangerous celebrations in the nineteenth century.

Some scholars, notably David Cressy,[12] insist that Bonfire Night is a product of politics, bears little relation to Halloween and is certainly not a manifestation of the earlier festival. It is, however, a beginning-of-winter festival which employs fire as its focus, and as such has a symbolic correlation with Halloween and ideas of Samhain. All pagans with whom I have conversed on the subject of Bonfire Night insist that it is a vestige of Samhain, symbolically if not actually, and view it as a seasonal fire festival.

Halloween in Tradition

Due to the relative lack of Halloween customs in southern Britain, Scottish practices will be looked at here. Peter and Iona Opie in their survey of children's folklore in the 1950s noted that Halloween was celebrated in the north and west of Britain, but Bonfire Night was predominant in the south-east.[13] These days of course children's celebration of Halloween is more widespread, with the custom of trick-or-treating having been adopted from America. The process has been aided by media representation: the hugely popular film *ET* (Spielberg, 1982) contained a scene depicting trick-or-treating and British children were quick to realise that there was a financial advantage to this practice. This in turn has been exploited by business organisations and various Halloween *accoutrements* are available on the market.

Many folklore collections from Scotland and Ireland are rich with folk traditions surrounding Halloween, and elements of these have influenced and are in accordance with modern pagan practices. Guising, the practice where children ring on local doorbells and sing a song in return for a gift (in much the same manner as souling), was common in Edinburgh in my childhood in the late 1970s. At school we used to 'dook for apples' and try and take a bite out of treacle scones on strings at Halloween. The most popular form of pastime historically seems to have been divination games and these are amusingly expounded in Burns' poem *Halloween* written in 1785.

Some merry, friendly, countra folks,
Together did convene,
To burn their nits, an' pou their stocks,
An' haud their Halloween
Fu' blythe that night.[14]

Nuts are burned and kail stalks pulled to divine information about future spouses. Two hazelnuts are named after a courting couple and thrown in the fire. If they burn calmly and quietly then it is a good match, but if they splutter and spark or, heaven forbid, 'start up the lum' (fly up the chimney) then the future does not look promising. The shape of the kail stalk pulled reflects the form and fortune of the inquirer's future spouse. The poem details a night of fun and games while leaving the impression that the outcome was apprehended. Another divination mentioned by Burns is that involving the eating of an apple at the looking glass whilst combing your hair–the wraith or spirit of your future spouse will appear in place of your own reflection, a terrifying prospect. Burns' Grannie in the poem warns against such practices:

'Nae doubt but ye may get a sight!
'Great cause ye hae to fear it;
'For monie a ane has gotten a fright,
'An' liv'd an' di'd deleeret,
'On sic a night.'

She sees such revelations as the work of the devil. A Scottish traveller and storyteller gave me a modern account of this: 'A' kent a lassie wa' done it once. She geed hersel' a hard fricht–Jack the Ripper appeared!' Such divinations, though amusing, contained a respect and sense of awe for the strange occult forces which were to be tapped to provide the information required.

Many traditional divinations of this kind involved some sort of vision or dream of the enquirer's future spouse or fortune, thus requiring some assumed supernatural connection. They are often related to rural tasks such as winnowing chaff in an empty barn at midnight or sowing nine furrows or pulling kail stalks. Apples and hazelnuts feature strongly in these practices, and would be available at this time of year, therefore functioning as both practical and symbolic. Turnips out of which lanterns were and are made were also available. (The pumpkin is a recent innovation, again imported from America.) The use of vegetable matter in a ritual-type act such as divination is ideally correspondent to contemporary pagan sacred practice with its emphasis on fruits of the earth combined with mysterious supernatural elements invoked to help the participant find an answer to a personal question. The apple is utilised in most modern Samhain ritual. Starhawk in *The Spiral Dance* makes it a central element in her ritual as the 'fruit of death–which is life' when it is cut open to reveal the five-pointed star or pentacle of rebirth.[15]

Scottish tradition has it that the fairies ride on Halloween and that it is a night when witches congregate. The ballad *Tam Lin* relates how its heroine Janet rescues her mortal lover from the fairies on Halloween as the host rides at midnight past the market cross, and Montgomerie's satirical poem *The Flyting Betwixt Montgomerie and Polwart* of 1621 gives an imaginative and grotesque account of the 'Halloween rade' attended by all sorts of dubious supernatural beings. Many of the people tried in Scotland for witchcraft cited Halloween as an important sabbat, and some spoke of association with the Queen of Elfhame at this time.

Mischief abounded on Halloween and its eve (30 October) when pranks would be played on unsuspecting neighbours and the fairies could be held responsible. Trickery remains an important aspect of Halloween, and was so long before the cry 'trick or treat' was first heard on the doorsteps of Britain. Mischief Night is celebrated on 4 November in the north of England, which is interesting in terms of the idea of the transference of customs to different dates, possibly suggesting an older Halloween influence. It is a popular way of having fun, relieving social tension and perhaps getting your own back on a grumpy neighbour or two. In the past, favourite pranks included stealing gates from their hinges, removing the neighbour's cow or throwing cabbages down the chimney. Nowadays tapping at windows and doors and running away (a fairly mild prank) is popular. One of my personal favourites in the line of modern pranks (for sheer grotesque imagination) involves the wrapping of a dog turd in a rag, setting it on fire, leaving it on someone's doorstep, ringing the bell and running away! The trickery custom was popular in the United States also, although it was increasingly disapproved of, particularly in city areas, and authorities attempted to organise Halloween celebration into community programmes, even seeking to introduce legislation to curb these anti-social activities. In present-day Detroit the custom has got somewhat out of hand where 31 October is called 'Devil's Night' or arson night where parts of the city are set on fire. Pranks in rural areas seem to have been tolerated more readily. A favourite prank in Iowa and some other parts was to move the outhouse that covered the latrine backwards three yards–to great dramatic effect, one would imagine!

With the loss of close-knit communities such traditional practices are becoming less acceptable and their perpetrators are more open to charges of vandalism and wilful destruction of property. Five boys were arrested in Manchester in 1992 for extortion whilst appealing for 'a penny for the Guy', and the unfamiliar practices of trick-or-treating have been criticised by many people, not least in local newspapers and national tabloids. In the U.S. trick-or-treating has an accompanying semiology which directs that children should not visit a house in the neighbourhood that does not have the lights on in the front room or a jack-o'-lantern prominently displayed. In Britain the choice of house is arbitrary and some people resent having their privacy violated by this renegade custom that does not have the sanction of English tradition behind it.

Halloween has been largely a secular pastime in society for quite some time now. As with many folklore practices, its celebration has been adopted mainly by children or it is used by adults as a time for recreation and dressing up. The Halloween parades of San Francisco and Greenwich Village in New York sport hundreds of bizarre and imaginative costumes, and individuals hold private parties on both sides of the Atlantic to celebrate. Here, as with traditional mischief, Halloween functions as a season of misrule, of carnival, where cross-dressing symbolises the inversion of social norms, and children can take control in the adult world.

Halloween and Contemporary Paganism[16]

In contemporary pagan celebration of Halloween, the festival takes on a strongly religious aspect again. Pagans emphasise the continuity of the tradition, relating the festival to a pre-Christian society more synchronised with the cycles of nature. The Christian interlude with its focus on All Saints is not considered to be relevant.

In a desire to explore how Samhain practices relate to folk tradition and history and the main features of its contemporary celebration, I commenced on fieldwork with individual pagans in Glastonbury and London, employing personal tape-recorded interviews or conversations and a questionnaire which was distributed at pagan gatherings. I wanted to see if there was anything like a universal ritual for Samhain, how elements and symbolism varied in the practices of different individuals, and how tradition and folklore were consciously employed to enhance or intensify ritual. Additionally, I have always been struck by the intensely personal nature of Samhain, and wished to collect some individual thoughts and experiences on the festival.

Approaches to the celebration of Samhain differ widely from relatively large-scale public celebrations incorporating aspects of ritual such as the Pagan Halloween gathering organised by the House of the Goddess, to private ritual or solo meditation, to a simple and convicted belief in the permeation of Samhain energies throughout everyday life. A rural community living in benders in Somerset, subject to the mercy of seasonal change on a basic level, did not celebrate Samhain formally with ritual but would refer to it daily in the weeks around the beginning of November, meditating upon its personal meaning. Date of celebration varies also. Some pagans celebrate on Samhain Eve (31 October) or its nearest weekend, whilst others favour dating by the moon, finding it a closer means of being in tune with natural time and more favourable than our complex and received Western solar calendar. The moon can be either new or beginning its last quarter, thus corresponding to the waning of the year. Others prefer to date Samhain's observance by signs in nature, such as a definite temperature change or the coming of the first white frosts of winter.

The most important focus of the festival for many pagans is the emphasis on death and rebirth and the vast importance of having a time specifically designated for letting go, being aware and acknowledging the more difficult aspects of life. It is 'the time of going into the dark', as one individual puts it. Samhain is the point in the year which embodies the concept of the mutual dependence of light and dark, and strongly acknowledges the presence of the supernatural world. The process of the earth's regeneration can be directly related to personal feeling and life experience. Loss and death are essential elements of life and cannot be denied: Samhain provides an opportunity for people to process these feelings, to experience 'the underworld journey' and through its experience obtain greater strength and knowledge of self. Several pagans told me that they recovered from the break-up of emotional relationships or bad experiences at this time, exorcising memories or 'ghosts' and psychologically discarding unwanted baggage from the previous year.

Samhain ritual incorporates this rejection of the burdensome past and the looking forward to regeneration, an aspect which can take several forms within the ritual. It may be verbal and simple such as each participant in turn stating out loud what they wish to cast off, or the repeated chanting of a pertinent phrase–'I free my bonds, I free my bonds'. Participants may physically reject particular burdens by ritually placing them in a cauldron or basket or bowl of clear or salt water. The personal psychological benefits of these actions and attitudes are self-evident.

In answer to the question, 'Why is it important to celebrate Samhain?' the majority of individuals emphasised the importance of remembering the ancestors, the ancient peoples of the land who lived in close accordance with nature. Some pagans formally invite the Dead to their ritual, others remember specific individuals and commune with them. Other important reasons for celebration include giving thanks for the renewal and regeneration of nature and being aware of the cycles of the earth. The belief in heightened supernatural activity at Samhain is universal among pagans and this was often expressed by the phrase 'the veils between the two worlds are at their thinnest'.

Many pagans employ divination frequently in the form of tarot or runes, and Halloween is believed to be an effective time for other-world enquiry, though the methods used are not those described by Burns, which are practised more as games these days. Scrying into a mirror or bowl of clear water is believed to be particularly effective at this time of year, and this is incorporated by some into their rituals.

The traditional drama of the souling plays has a modern counterpart in the number of ritual drama pieces that are performed at this time. These are often concerned with the psychological aspects of Samhain. For example the play *Pumpkin Fool* written and performed by five men in Glastonbury in 1993 concentrated on the issues of personal loss, ageing, death and rejection and the problems of male emotional expression. Each individual actor explored his own experiences of these, culminating in a cathartic self-acceptance. Other Samhain plays have utilised stories from myth to explore human confusion and fear of accepting darkness, again culminating in positive realisation and acceptance. Many pagans emphasise the importance of spontaneity in Samhain ritual and celebration and use myth creatively to explore its meaning.

Opposition to Halloween

In March 1986 the Inspector of the Inner London Education sent out a letter to schools warning about the concern expressed by parents over occultism in schools, advising caution on the part of teachers and specifically citing Halloween as one of the main areas of anxiety. Pamphlets began to appear suggesting Christian alternatives to education involving the exploration of Halloween.[17] It seemed that parents were worried that celebration of Halloween might move their children towards the practice of 'evil'. Along with modern Halloween itself, Britain had imported from America the controversy that surrounded it.

Halloween in America is a very popular festival. It is unusual in that its celebration is widespread, yet it is not an official public holiday; this unofficial status has made it even more highly regarded as a particularly 'American' festival. As such its existence in society is protected by its traditional status. As early as the 1950s, however, the matter of Halloween was being questioned by the Church and several Catholic education journals suggested a move to reclaim the feast of All Hallows for the Saints, suggesting concentration on its Christian aspects rather than its occult associations. This was a marked contrast to the publications of the 1930s directed towards a housewife readership which suggested ideas for the most perfect children's Halloween parties, to make them as spooky and exciting as possible (thus sealing one's reputation as the perfect wife, mother and hostess). The following excerpt is taken from Schauffler's book on Halloween first published in 1933:

> *So that witches may ever afterward know their own, every guest must be branded with the mark of Satan. Blindfolded, they are seated with great ceremony and the witches prepare to heat the branding iron. A pressing or curling iron is made to hiss and a piece of toast may be burnt to give an odour of burning. An electric pad, held near the face of the victim, gives a further illusion. After a moment or two of discussion as to whether the brand is hot enough, it is decided to brand the guest. With a piece of ice, next to which a red lipstick is held, brand the letter 's' on his forehead. Thus each guest emerges with a red S on his brow!'*[18]

If you tried to do this in Britain nowadays the police and welfare services would be round faster than you can say 'trick-or-treat'! Currently, fears for childhood safety have led to a curbing of Halloween customs in America with myths of Halloween sadism running rife in most cities, the myths initially preceding their own eventual enactment. Media hype has made razor-blade-infested apples and deadly candy a feature of the festival. Some hospital X-ray departments offer a free service of treat examination to ensure that they are free from pins and poison. Thus the darkness and chaos traditionally associated with Halloween is manifesting itself in a new and terrifying manner in post-industrial Western society.

Historically, Halloween exhibits a certain licentiousness in aspects of its celebration, such as trickery, costuming and wild unconventional behaviour. In America attempts were made to curb the chaos, trying to structure and order it, sanitising it into an organised celebration within the community where it could be more easily controlled. Spontaneous and destructive trickery was discouraged and formal 'haunted houses' became popular in America where Halloween spookiness could be contained.

The desire to order Halloween continues. Christian fundamentalists have waged a war declaring Halloween to be of no spiritual value, merely a celebration of evil which marks for children 'the beginnings of the slippery slope towards Satanism'. Pagan origins of Halloween are cited (often liberally sprinkled with references to druidic human sacrifice) and condemned in pamphlets. Videos are also available testifying to the dangers of Halloween and using interviews with 'ex-witches' to expose its evil practices. A handout imported from the U.S. poses the question: 'has it ever occurred to you that something might be wrong with Halloween?' and answers with five objections:

1. the roots of Halloween lie in paganism and the occult
2. it glorifies Satan
3. it treats the occult and evil as harmless
4. it is the appearance of evil
5. it is disobedience to God.[19]

The rise in numbers of practising pagans has fuelled the flames of scripturally-based Christians who cite the Bible, particularly Deuteronomy 18:9–14 against the practice of divination and the manipulation of supernatural forces.

While many of the arguments against Halloween are reasonable enough in their own biblical context, some of the more outrageous propaganda is particularly damaging. A particularly nasty American tract available in Britain called 'The Trick' exploits the myth of Halloween sadism and ritual abuse and links them with modern witchcraft depicting cartoon bubbles reading, 'Brothers and sisters, as you know Halloween will soon be here. This is a very important time to our holy and most glorious father Satan. This holy day was designed so that we can provide additional sacrifices for him'. Another pamphlet states that Halloween is Satan's birthday and that 'The Lord hates Halloween and its evil origins. Satanic human sacrifices are a slap in God's face'. In present-day Christian fundamentalism, Halloween seems to have become a focus for fears about the darkness and uncertainty of shifting paradigms in the modern world: passions and imaginations are running wild.

Halloween is a symbolic time embodying essential dualities such as light and dark, life and death and order and chaos. It is a temporal period where normal social rules are suspended and certain roles are reversed. Children dress up as the beings of which they are traditionally frightened. Halloween is a time when the chaos symbolised by physical darkness can be ordered by making it fun and putting nameless fears in a context in which they can be recognised and turned into play. Its function is most appreciated in the pagan community, where the ambiguous nature of Halloween is deliberately acknowledged and celebrated to great personal and recreational effect.

Notes

1 Traditional Scottish rhyme.
2 Graham Harvey 'The Roots of Pagan Ecology', *Religion Today* Vol. 9, no. 3 summer 1994:38–41, p38.
3 Pronsias MacCana *Celtic Mythology* Rev. ed. 1983 p128, Middlesex, Newnes Books.
4 Trans. Whitley Stokes 'Tidings of Conchobar mac Nessa' *Eriu* IV 1908, p27.
5 Trans. Kuno Meyer 'The Adventures of Nera' *Revue Celtique* X 1899, pp212–28. See also Helen Sewell Johnson 'November Eve Beliefs in Irish Life and Literature' *Journal of American Folklore* 81 1968, pp133–42.
6 For example *The Mabinogion* is strangely void of references to the festival. (Personal communication from Ronald Hutton.)
7 Ed. B Colgrave and R.A.B. Minors, *Bede's Ecclesiastical History of the English People* 1969, p107, Clarendon Press.
8 *New Catholic Encyclopaedia* Vol. 1 1967, p318, McGraw Hill Book Company.
9 Trans. Whitley Stokes 'The Calendar of Oengus' *Transactions of the Royal Irish Academy* 1 1880, pcixii.
10 Ed. H. Thurston and D. Attwater *Butler's Lives of the Saints* Vol. XI 1938, p19, Burns, Oates and Washbourne Ltd.
11 James Frazer *Adonis, Attis, Osiris* Vol II 1936, p83, Macmillan And Co.
12 David Cressy *Bonfires and Bells: National Memory and the Protestant Calendar in Elizabethan and Stuart England* 1989, University of California Press.
13 Peter and Iona Opie *The Lore and Language of Schoolchildren* 1959, p268, Clarendon Press.

14 Ed. James Kinsley *Burns Poems and Songs* 1969, p123, Oxford University Press. See also Mary Macleod Banks *British Calendar Customs: Scotland* 3 vols (Folk-Lore Society 1941) for an extensive collection of traditional Halloween practices.
15 Starhawk *The Spiral Dance: A Rebirth of the Ancient Religion of the Great Goddess* 1989, pp195–6, HarperSanFrancisco.
16 Details given in this section are based on evidence from fieldwork undertaken for my doctoral thesis collected from April 1993 to the present.
17 For example, Margaret Cooling *Halloween in the Classroom* 1989, Association of Christian Teachers.
18 Robert Haven Schauffler *Halloween* 2 ed. 1952, p85, Dodd, Mead and Co.
19 Russell K. Tardo *What's Wrong with Halloween?* (self-published)

Additional References

Ervin Beck, 'Children's Halloween Customs in Sheffield' *Lore and Language* 3.9 (1983) pp70–88.

Ervin Beck, 'Trickster on the Threshold: An Interpretation of Children's Autumn Traditions' *Folklore* 96 i (1985) pp24–28.

Bob Bushaway, *By Rite: Custom, Ceremony and Community in England 1700–1880*, Junction Books, 1982.

Ronald Hutton, *The Pagan Religions of the Ancient British Isles*, Blackwell, 1991.

Karen Sue Hybertson, *The Return of Chaos*, PhD thesis, Drew University, 1993.

David Porter, *Halloween Treat or Trick*, Monarch Publications, 1993.

Jack Santino (ed.), *Halloween and Other Festivals of Death and Life*, University of Tennessee Press, 1994.

Keith Thomas, *Religion and the Decline of Magic*, Penguin, 1973.

A.R. Wright and T.E. Lones, *British Calendar Customs: England* 3 vols, Folk-Lore Society, 1940.

Marion Bowman

CARDIAC CELTS:

Images of the Celts in Paganism

The Celtic mists are swirling once more, and in the twilight can be glimpsed an assortment of images of the Celts. Pagans, New Agers, Christians and society at large are reclaiming the Celts,[1] and while there have been various periods of fascination with Celts and Druids in the past, they have not had such spiritual significance for such large numbers of people as we are witnessing now. The role of the Celts in contemporary religiosity is both complex and compelling, but one thing is certain: 'Celtic matters are in fashion these days. At various levels of awareness, both physical and spiritual, a sense of Celticness or Celtic identity, real or imagined, is awakening'.[2]

The current quest for Celticity raises many questions. There are debates as to whether contemporary Celticism is the result of 'trickle down' to a popular level of the ideas of seventeenth- and eighteenth- century antiquarians, or a new phenomenon; whether it stems from romanticism or globalisation; PMT (Pre-Millennial Tension) or postmodernism. National identity and elective affinity, the relationship between centre and periphery, and the interaction between past and present are all part of this complicated phenomenon.

This chapter will explore the renewed interest in and honouring of the Celts, the different models of 'Celticity' and the various ways of being Celtic which are developing in contemporary paganism. The appeal of the Celts is enormous. There has been a growing consensus among pagans (and indeed many others) that late twentieth-century humanity is in a mess, that we have become spiritually out of tune with ourselves, with others, with the planet. It is also widely held that it was not always so, that in the past our ancestors understood the symbiotic relationship of planet and people, were in tune with nature, were aware of the sacred in everyday life, knew their place in the great scheme of things. This is not a new phenomenon.

Piggott points to:

> *a recurrent series of speculations which seem to arise in civilized communities as the result of a subconscious guilty recognition of the inadequacy of the contemporary social order, and involve the concept of simpler and more satisfactory systems, remote either in time (Golden Ages in the past), or in place (Noble Savages at or beyond the edges of contemporary geographical knowledge).*[3]

Increasingly people are looking back longingly to a Golden Age located in the untainted, sacralised life of the noble savage, and for many in Britain and beyond, that noble savage is undoubtedly a Celt. The Celts, traditionally the people on the fringes, instead of being despised, patronised or pitied for not being in the mainstream, are now seen as less tainted, as repositories of a spirituality, a sense of tradition, a oneness with nature that has elsewhere been lost:

> *It is the Celtic spirit which not only keeps company with the national folk-soul but, through it, with the folk-souls of other nations, so maintaining a web of unity which is at the very soul of our race.*[4]

Moreover, people from a variety of spiritual and secular backgrounds are not simply content to eulogise that Celtic Golden Age, they wish to recapture it. They wish to become noble savages. However, what people mean by Celtic, how people envisage that Celtic past, how the aspiring Celt seeks to acquire and express Celticity are areas of infinite variety, creativity and, occasionally, conflict.

Archaeologists, Celticists and historians may be unhappy about gaps in archaeological evidence, unreliability of sources, limits to what they feel can be safely inferred and the fact that the Celts in the British Isles and Europe were not and are not one homogenous group. However, many pagans, New Agers, Christians and others have come to perceive a self-aware, pan-Celtic culture and world-view, details of which are confidently enumerated.[5] The Druids often appear in this picture of the Celtic past as a wise priesthood, ecologically aware custodians of ancient wisdom. Furthermore, some–though by no means all–consider that this ancient wisdom was transmitted to Celtic Christianity in an essentially smooth and harmonious transition from the old religion to the new. (Gordon Strachan in his forthcoming book *Jesus the Druid* makes a particularly close connection between the two traditions.) Celtic Christianity tends to be characterised as more intuitive, more spiritual and more in touch with nature than its Roman counterpart. Details of this

Celtic past now emerging are often claimed to be the product of esoterically transmitted wisdom, new interpretations of cultural tradition, inspiration, channelling and past-life memories, overlaying and superseding more conventional data.

Academic Celticists, folklorists, archaeologists and historians would generally refute such images of the Celtic past on a variety of counts, based on what they would consider inadmissible evidence or shaky scholarship. The identification of Glastonbury as a Druidic Oxbridge is just one example of what is accepted as 'common knowledge' in some circles, though not recognised by more conventional scholars. Because of the spiritual aspect of current Celticism, however, we are dealing with belief, and therefore insiders and outsiders are operating different criteria of what counts as acceptable or credible data, and material is used in different ways. Here the religious studies usage of 'myth' as 'significant story' regardless of truth claims can be helpful.

The concept of 'authenticity' is also an area of potential disagreement between mainstream academics and pagans–indeed, between pagans of different orientations. There are differences in aims and outlooks between reconstructors, whose priority is to piece together as exact a picture of the Celtic past as possible, and revivalists, whose main concern is not so much to replicate as to reinvigorate. Many pagans consider that Celtic or quasi-Celtic beliefs and practices need to be rediscovered, reactivated and revitalised to provide a spiritual path for the present and the future. They would contend that the past need not be slavishly copied–even if that were possible. Elements of Celtic tradition are now being used to produce something which is not itself 'traditional', but which seems for participants to be appropriate for the present time and in the authentic Celtic spirit of the past.

As might be expected in the present Celticly-charged climate, people perceived as contemporary Celts can be regarded as special. In Glastonbury I met an American who, when I was in conversation with a fellow Scot, told us how thrilled he was to be in the presence of two Celts. Pamela Constantine, founder of the New Romantic Movement, has written 'It seems to me the Celts have a natural ability to reopen the "magic casements" and to help people reconnect with the lost dimensions of themselves.'[6] Celtic or quasi-Celtic ancestry is used to help establish credentials, like the co-organiser of a workshop at a Festival of the Celtic Spirit described as a 'Northumbrian Irish Celt exiled in London'. In Bath, Anne Hassett, the clairvoyant, has in recent years become Acuthla the psychic consultant 'in honour of her Celtic roots'. Rhiannon Evans, Welsh maker of jewellery and T-shirts based on Celtic designs and mythology, advertises 'Ancient Traditions from the British Celts of Today'. Whether for personal, spiritual or commercial purposes, the message seems to be 'If you've got Celticity, flaunt it'.

What is actually meant by Celtic, however, is rather fluid. 'Celtic', always an archaeologically, historically, linguistically tricky label is currently undergoing reinterpretation at a number of levels. At the great Celtic exhibition in Venice in 1991, the Celts were presented as the first Europeans. Within the British Isles, Celtic is increasingly broadly interpreted to embrace all Scots (not only Gaelic speaking Highlanders and Islanders), Irish, Welsh, Manx, Northumbrians, people from the West Country–more or less everyone who is not, as it were, mainstream southern English. Tim Sebastian, Chosen Chief of the Secular Order of Druids, is of the opinion that ultimately everyone in Britain is of Celtic descent. Embers Celtic Spirit, who run shops and a mail order catalogue, proclaim in their publicity:

> *Wherever you are in the British Isles you are surrounded by the Spirit of the Celts, the art, the history and the myths and legends of a civilization whose culture has lasted over 2500 years. The Romans and Vikings came and went, but the Celts remain within the names of towns, villages and areas of Britain. It is our heritage and roots.*

Nor is the phenomenon confined to the British Isles and Europe, as many Americans, Canadians, Australians and New Zealanders with any sort of Scottish, Irish, Welsh or generally British ancestry might think of themselves as Celts. An American of my acquaintance insisted that when he visited Scotland for the first time he suddenly realised that it was his spiritual home, and he felt sure he had lived there in some previous life. Commenting on the clamour for Celticity, Chapman observes:

> *Not only are there large groups of people thought to be Celts by others (as has happened before), but there are also large groups of people that think they are Celts themselves. This is a very modern phenomenon, but is nevertheless real: if people think they are Celts, who is to gainsay them?*[7]

Celticity is coming to be seen as a quality or a matter of choice rather than an issue of history, geography, language or ethnicity; it is 'a thing of spirit not of heritage'.[8] Caitlin Matthews has said of Celtic spiritual practitioners:

> *Celtic ethnicity is not necessarily a prerequisite, as might be imagined. We have entered a phase of maturity wherein spiritual lineage transcends blood lineage.*[9]

As one Glastonbury informant commented:

> *There's something there, a wonderful ambience, and we can localise it as no one is sure who the Celts really were. It doesn't matter about strict historicity–it sets up a wonderful warm glow of hope, helps you feel more integrated. What we need in the West is a Celtic renaissance.*

There are increasing numbers of people who might be described as 'Cardiac Celts': they feel in their hearts that they are Celts. For cardiac Celts, spiritual nationality is a matter of elective affinity.

However, as people both honour an idealised image of Celts and strive to become 'spiritual' Celts, issues of identity and expectation will inevitably arise. What happens when people considered 'real' Celts do not live up to outsiders' expectations? The spiritual, intuitive Celt, at one with nature and the fairyfolk may be a stereotype as unwelcome to many 'traditional' Celts as the comic Irishman, the mean Scot, or whatever. At the interface of cardiac and conventional Celt, there is a real danger that one will see a kindred spirit, the other a cultural transvestite.

At a time when there is greater geographic mobility than ever, we see the emergence of a new topophilia. This topophilia is dependent on a particular view of the past and a personal identification with that past. The development of a closer relationship with the earth, explicit in paganism, is fostering a renewed interest in and impulse for pilgrimage. For many pagans the desirable destinations are those perceived to have Celtic connections. Such pilgrimage becomes a way of expressing continuity with the Celtic past, however that is envisaged, and tuning into it. As many of the sites are in areas of great natural beauty, remote and unsullied, the contrast between late-twentieth-century urban lifestyle and that of the Celts is stark, reinforcing the idea and appeal of the Celt as noble savage. The effect of rekindled Celticity is strong enough to encourage many to settle in what are perceived to be more spiritual places, such as remoter parts of Wales or Scotland or the West Country.

Traditionally there have been many advantages to being culturally mainstream, being part of the dominant culture, at the centre making judgements about the periphery; implicit in the idea of 'Celtic fringe' is that the centre is elsewhere. But, being able to designate *oneself* a Celt allows some distancing from the mainstream, towards which there may be some disaffection whether social, political or spiritual. However, the relationship of centre and periphery can cause tension within pagan Celticism. The decision that 'we are all Celts now' does not necessarily emanate from the more traditional strongholds of Celticity–it might be seen as another decision taken at the centre without consultation. There are parallels with the situation in North America, Australia, New Zealand and elsewhere when people from the dominant culture approach their native peoples for spiritual wisdom, informing them that in the spirit of the New Age it is time to share spiritual knowledge. Some are happy about this, some are not. Frequently people 'sharing' such native ways, through books, workshops, and so on are not recognised figures within that community–indeed they might be completely outside it. One Scottish Druid sees cultural imperialism among some of the English Druids, complaining that they do not use Celtic language, dress or customs, while attempting to monopolise Celticity; he dismisses their activities as an 'English cover version of Celtic tradition'.

It is important to be aware that there are differences between images of Celts and Celticity within paganism. The Pan-Celtic view promotes homogeneity between Celts and assumes similarity of belief, practice and worldview among all Celts. From this standpoint, it is legitimate to consider myth or some other aspect of culture from one particular place or time to be applicable to or representative of the rest of the Celtic world. People with this outlook tend to think in terms of pan-European Celticism. Other Celtic pagans are more concerned with local traditions–Welsh, Irish, Cornish, or whatever–concentrating on the myths, monuments and traditions of their particular country or area. Outside conventional politics, then, paganism has its pro-Europeans, unionists, nationalists and regionalists.

There are pagan pluralists and pagan universalists. Pagan pluralists recognise different and distinct pagan traditions, and choose to honour one in particular, such as the Celtic, while respecting the choice of others and their integrity. Pagan universalists take the line that external differences are incidental and there is an underlying oneness in all religion. An English informant with 'Celtic blood' who attended a native American weekend workshop, for example, felt that what was being taught was 'all there in the Celtic past', that Native American spirituality is 'very close to the Celtic thing' and that 'When it comes to spirituality, it's all the same in the end'. One effect of this universalism is that Celts and native Americans, or Australians, or whoever, tend to be compared, if not conflated:[10] it almost becomes a point of pride or necessity to come up with Celtic equivalents of aspects of contemporary native tradition.

Celtic spirituality is being seen by some as the standard bearer of the Western Spiritual Tradition as opposed to Eastern philosophies. Celticism is regarded as the alternative or the antidote to Orientalism; the Celts are embraced as home-grown gurus. One Druid course specifically cautions 'Under no circumstances should incense of Eastern Manufacture be used for Keltic Druidic Rites, as it will be "charged" unsuitably.' Celtic spirituality, particularly Druidism, has a great attraction as a native wisdom tradition; Ecole Druidique des Gaules claims that 'the spirituality of the Celts is the only one which represents the collective Indo-European heritage common to all Europe.'[11] For those who are interested in the broader Western Esoteric Tradition, Celtic interacts with Egyptian, Christian, Qabalistic, Gnostic and other elements.

In these circumstances there is a lot of scope for varying models of Celticity, how to express and acquire Celticity, what the Celtic lifestyle actually comprises. The cub Celt turning to the *Pagan Index* would find a variety of Celtic avenues to explore. Many pagans are simply 'Free Range' Celts, who arrive at and express their Celticity in individual and fairly random ways. Observing the eightfold calendar of equinoxes, solstices and Samhain, Imbolc, Beltane and Lughnasadh, however, has become generally accepted as a Celtic activity.

Some take being Celtic more seriously than others. Clan Dalriada, for example, is a group of pagans living on the Scottish Isle of Arran who, as their literature states, 'have dedicated their lives to living and working the Celtic/Gaelic system of the late Bronze Age (the time we hold to have been the Golden Age of the Celts).' Cantiaci is a group devoted to reconstructing with technological accuracy the life of the Celtic tribe that lived around the Medway. The cerebral Celt might undertake some formal study: the Order of Bards, Ovates and Druids offers a correspondence course in Druidry; through the College of Druidism in Edinburgh one can train to be a Keltic Druid or Culdee Priest/Priestess. Clan Dalriada offers a correspondence course on Celtic Paganism, and for computerised Celts there is Dalriada BBS (Bulletin Board System), giving 'the opportunity to network with others both locally and internationally', and access to archive files on a variety of subjects from the Dalriada Celtic Heritage Society's database. Courses in Celtic Shamanism might have more appeal for percussive Celts.

If not wishing to study Celticity formally, the aspiring Celt can surround herself or himself with Celtic or quasi-Celtic literature. Books about the Celts and Celtic spirituality written from a variety of standpoints, including the specifically pagan, abound. Such books turn up in most Pagan, New Age and Alternative bookshops, as well as the Mind/Body/Spirit sections of national 'chain' bookshops. Particularly prolific in this respect, for example, are John and Caitlin Matthews, authors of numerous books on Arthurian and Celtic topics, both influential and illustrative of this type of specialist, insider literature. Caitlin is described as an 'initiator within the Celtic tradition', which captures the apparent need for Celtic roots coupled with the element of personal choice and inspiration which is a hallmark of contemporary religiosity. Writings from the late-nineteenth/early-twentieth-century Celtic revival are also in vogue in such contexts. Small presses up and down the country produce booklets on specialist Celtic subjects (e.g. Celtic totem animals, deities, tree alphabets) and Celtic topics of local interest. There are numerous magazines serving the Pagan community, some specifically focusing on Celtic and Druidic spirituality. Others are mixed in content, using Celtic themes or artwork, or containing Celtic articles, from time to time. *Dalriada Magazine* deals specifically with the Celtic Gaelic tradition and there are other regional specialist magazines. In addition, there are more general Celtic magazines, such as *Celtic Connections*–'dedicated to all aspects of Celtic culture, especially the arts and crafts', covering Wales, Scotland, Brittany, Ireland, Isle of Man and Catalonia.

Pagans tend to associate New Age with the marketing of spirituality, but there is undoubtedly a commodification angle to the current pagan Celtic scene.[12] At the general level, it is possible to buy a huge variety of Celtic or quasi-Celtic consumer goods: Celtic jewellery, Celtic coasters, Celtic watches, Celtic socks, Celtic clocks, Celtic mugs, Celtic T-shirts, Celtic ties, Celtic cards, and so on. Many people are attracted to such merchandise because they find it visually pleasing, and use it to express their affinity with things Celtic. Establishments such as Once and Future Celt ('Pagan Paraphernalia, Heathen Hoards, Celtic Crafts and Goddess Goods'), Wilde Celts ('Pan Celtic Art, inspired by the Golden Age of Celtic Creativity') and Mysteries of Albion, whose 'chosen work is to craft sacred tools' such as the Silver Branch, are examples of the more specialised spiritual market for goods and services, some of which have already been mentioned. There is an element of consumer choice in people's brand of Paganism, in their brand of Celticity (e.g. Welsh, Irish,

Scottish, Pan-European, universalist), and in the practical ways they choose to acquire and express Celticity (e.g. as Celtic shaman or Druid/Druidess in one of the increasingly numerous and varied orders). 'Mix and match' spirituality is *not* the sole preserve of New Age.

The Celts have undoubtedly made a comeback. The renewed interest in and honouring of the Celts among pagans is part of a broader social trend, in which the Celts have re-emerged as noble savages. However, pagans are more actively pursuing ways of converting eulogy to actuality than many other sectors of society. Among the most attractive, tantalising and infuriating aspects of the Celts is the sheer impossibility of arriving at any consensus about who they were/are, and how they were/are. Thus, inevitably, different models of 'Celticity', and various ways of being Celtic are developing in contemporary paganism. This may give rise to confusion, competing worldviews, consumerism and occasionally conflict, but it also demonstrates the vitality of both Celticism and contemporary paganism. Many pagans feel that they have seen the future–and it's Celtic.

Notes

1 The spiritual aspects of this are discussed briefly in my article 'Reinventing the Celts', *Religion* 23 (1993), pp147–56; Malcolm Chapman's *The Celts: The Construction of a Myth* (St Martin's Press, 1992) deals with the general phenomenon in depth.

2 Donald Meek, 'Celtic Christianity. What is it and when was it?' *Scottish Bulletin of Evangelical Theology*, 9:1 (Spring 1991), p13.

3 Stuart Piggott, *The Druids* (London, Thames and Hudson, 1968), p30.

4 Pamela Constantine, *The Solar Courier* (International Newsletter of the Sharkti Laureate), (Spring 1994), p2.

5 Examples of this are cited in my chapter 'Drawn to Glastonbury' in *Pilgrimage in Popular Culture*, I. Reader And T. Walter, eds. (Macmillan; Basingstoke, 1993), pp29–62.

6 Personal communication.

7 Chapman, p251.

8 Alban J. Gannon and Rosmar Feld, *Quest*, 91 (September 1992), p20.

9 Caitlin Matthews, 'A Celtic Quest' in *Exploring Journeys*, V. Barnett, R.B. Howarth and P. Williams, eds. (Shap Working Party on World Religions in Education, 1993), p7.

10 For further discussion of this phenomenon, see my article 'The Noble Savage and the Global Village', *Journal of Contemporary Religion*, p10 (1995).

11 Ecole Druidique des Gaules (EDG), Directory of Druid Orders, *The Druids' Voice,* 4 (Winter 1994), p38.
12 This aspect is discussed more fully in my article 'The Commodification of the Celt: New Age/Neo-Pagan Consumerism', *Folklore in Use*, 2 (1994), pp143–52.